WILD TRAILS TO FAR HORIZONS

WILD TRAILS TO FAR HORIZONS
'An ultra-distance runner'

Mike Cudahy

UNWIN

HYMAN

LONDON SYDNEY WELLINGTON

This book is for my children and for my friends

First published in Great Britain by the Trade Division of Unwin Hyman Limited 1989

Unwin Hyman Limited
15/17 Broadwick Street
London W1V 1FP

Allen & Unwin Australia Pty Ltd
8 Napier Street, North Sydney, NSW 2060, Australia

Allen & Unwin New Zealand Pty Ltd with Port Nicholson Press
Compusales Building, 75 Ghuznee Street, Wellington, New Zealand

---

British Library Cataloguing in Publication Data
Cudahy, Michael
    Wild trails to far horizons.
    1. Athletics. Marathon running
    I. Title
    796.4'26

    ISBN 0-04-440381-X

Typeset by Nene Phototypesetters Ltd, Northampton
Printed in Great Britain at the University Press, Cambridge

contents

acknowledgements

I would like to thank Ted Courtenay, Ted Dance, Geoff Bell, Chris Bolshaw, Rob Ferguson and the *Stockport Express* who donated photographs and I would particularly like to thank Inken who burnt the midnight word-processor in an effort to complete the manuscript for me. I am also grateful to John Beatty for the special efforts he has made to make the photographs so successful.

Grateful acknowledgement is made to Unwin Hyman Limited for permission to quote from *The Lord of the Rings* by J. R. R. Tolkein.

foreword by Jim Perrin

Jung wrote that: 'Every statement about the transcendental ought to be avoided because it is a laughable presumption on the part of the human mind, un-conscious of its limitations.' Most people would probably feel some measure of assent in that, yet there are times – as when reading Mike Cudahy's extraordinary book – when its scepticism can safely be suspended. Cudahy's whole text is a statement upon the transcendental which virtually avoids the use of that word and gives us instead a precise, richly-textured description of the states through which he moves to the surpassing experience. In a sense, it is clinical observation, but from inside looking out. The immediacy with which he conveys the physical actuality of British hill country – its forms, play of light, gradations of colour, even its feel underfoot is a tangible marvel of evocation and elevates his book to that select library which includes Borthwick's *Always a Little Further*, Praeger's *The Way We Went*, and the Monkhouse *On Foot* titles. But don't judge it simply on grounds of literary worth. There are two other remarkable dimensions here. Its presentation of the unpretentious, unheroic, unpublicised outdoor community from which these journeyings derive and amongst which they take place remove it from the isolated sagas of fraught individual achievement. This is communal activity, involving friends, lovers, family, within which Cudahy acts as excelling focus, always ready, when his day or time is done, to hand on the torch. This grateful interdependence is hearteningly humane. Beyond it and through Cudahy's consciousness as he engages in extreme feats of physical endurance and quest, we come to terms more clearly perhaps than in any other book written 'about' the outdoors with another dangerous and maligned word – mysticism. When Cudahy describes how 'a swathe of early sunshine falls on a thick bank of bluebells; raindrop-glistening lustrous blue against the fresh spring green' and gives him strength to carry on to his Pennine Way record, his language begins to take on the characteristic mystical concepts – of joy, of oneness, of the timeless moment: 'Never have I felt such sheer and simple joy . . . Moments such as these not only provide the answer to why one does things but why we are alive at all.' Read his book at whatever level you like – as social document, testament of friendship, sporting chronicle, topographical companion or transcendental quest. It sustains all these approaches, satisfies each of them, and takes you beyond exhaustion to an excitement and refreshment of soul which is perhaps the best response to our rare and beautiful hill country.

chapter one

DREAMS OF DISTANCE

National Hill Walking Conference, Buxton, 1985. A stage, a screen, a microphone and, out there in the darkness, a waiting audience. Waiting for me to communicate the incommunicable, my dreams of distance. I felt I should not have been there. I knew just where I should be. Out on the surrounding moors running gently through the soft October sunshine into the soft October mists. No need there to force unwilling words, to search the soul for reasons that others might understand, or might not. Nothing but the natural rhythm of my body moving at peace in the natural environment. How I wished I was out there now.

Yet I knew why I was in this new environment. I was there because I had seen lights shine in the eyes of those few people to whom I had attempted to communicate the experience of my long journeys. Long journeys beyond time and distance to new dimensions. Days and nights of running over wild paths to far horizons. Esoteric experiences, the joy of which, to my astonishment, I could share with others. At least, when I could find those elusive words. I was not there to justify what I did. How could I or why should I? I was not there to counter the half-dismissive, half-joking comment that my running records were 'obscene'. I was not even there because Alfred Wainwright had said 'bloody fool' when he had heard of my three-day Pennine Way. How could he think otherwise, his soul firmly anchored to a pair of stout boots? Against the odds of being able to do it I was about to attempt to share the intangible and unlikely product of an apparently mundane but extremely arduous activity with a group of people I did not know and could not even see. I was there to share my personal joy of running, my kind of running.

I hoped that those present would feel some of the magic and the joy that my running has brought to me. However, I had uncertain faith that my words alone could evoke the rich imagery needed to convey the altered sense of time and distance provoked by unceasing travel over vast changing landscapes. To help instil my words with a more powerful imagery I was to project a set of slides, the inspiration of my friend John Beatty. I triggered the mechanism, stared at the screen and paused as John's beautiful pictures, transcending the image and breathing the very essence of Nature, began dissolving poignantly above me. Bathed in the light of John's muse, I began:

Imagine a world where all the mountains are flat, where all the paths are paved, where all the grass is trimmed low. Imagine being lifted out of your bed and into your car and out of your car and into your office – and back again. Imagine a world where no effort was necessary – or even permitted. Imagine having no horizons to stretch your gaze, no difficulties to surmount, no aspirations to capture your imagination.

When I stand at the beginning of 100 miles of moor, mountain, valley and meadow I am standing on the threshold of a dream.

The sensory experiences I can describe and even provide a visual representation. I can describe the beauty which lies in the endless panorama which will move before me as the day passes into night and the night gives way to dawn, and the landscape continues its almost imperceptible change as I move across it and through it. But I cannot so easily explain how it is, that at the pinnacle of my physical preparation with all my senses tuned into endless movement and my mind totally occupied with the simplicity of running and walking, that I become more certainly myself and yet also part of the earth through which I am moving.

There are changes in mental and physical states which are somehow related to the act of continuous movement allied to minimal rest and sleep. For instance, time loses its exactitude, hours pass like moments, but a moment may expand and hang suspended outside any time constraint.

The longer I run the greater becomes my identity with the natural elements which surround me. I feel such times are as close as I will ever get to becoming an element in nature – a small speck but absorbed and absorbing. The edges of reality become blurred as weariness and joy enter into a vast swinging cycle and time, distance, dimension and intellectual processing all slide out of their usual relationship, and I move instead towards a simpler and more natural reality – a reality based in sensory and emotional experience.

Without doubt, one of the strongest sources of emotional energy, from which I draw enormous strength, is the support of close friends on my ventures. The bonding which takes place at such times is, for me, incredibly strong, and when I am spent, drained of my own resources, I will run for the love of my friends because they will give me everything and I can do no less for them.

What I find remarkable too are the troughs and peaks through which I move with a powerful rhythm from which there is no escape. From a trough of weariness and even depression I will climb to the heights of joy and optimism. Finally, as I approach my goal there is a tremendous release of joy and energy, which will spur me to quite astonishing feats of physical power.

Of course it is hard, the physical demands are enormous, the concentration and commitment needed leave no place to hide, no reserves to harbour – but in that giving of everything I find a release into peace and a great joy.

Do not make the mistake of thinking I rush through the hills with no feeling for them. As I am drawn out fine and stretched I find I become more impressionable to all kinds of things which impact on my senses and create images, which I will carry for all time. To give just two small instances: above Byrness on the Pennine Way after 230 miles [370 km] of almost continuous movement I entered the dusk of my third and final night. The murmur of the voices of my two friends and their warm presence cocooned me in a web of comfort. Against the dark, peaty ground the cotton grass floated and swayed in an ethereal glow and I found myself floating with it – detached and free of the ground and, perhaps, of reality. Another six hours on, with only 20 miles [32 km] of the soggy Cheviots between me and my long-cherished dream, the thick grey dawn entered into a conspiracy with a cruel east wind to imprison my mind and defeat my body. We retreated to a bothy and, with the trust of a child, I rested my head in the lap of a friend and, in perfect peace and tranquillity, I slept for just seven timeless minutes. When I awoke the wild spirit was rekindled and our last charge through the 'slutch' and rain was delirious and desperate, excruciatingly hard, impervious to pain and crowned with an indescribable joy.

I do not know what happens at such times, perhaps the artificiality of a conventional and sophisticated society is stripped away and the simple, ingenuous nature of a creature of the earth is laid bare. Our intellect places the scope of an amazing technology within our grasp and I will not gainsay that. But what calls to our nature is the beat of the bird's wing, the rise and fall of the seasons, the power of a mountain and the continuing rhythm and pulse of the earth as night follows day and my feet and heart and mind are drawn after.

While I was speaking floods of memories, both bitter and sweet, came welling up. When I reached the part played by my friends it was as if all their love, laughter and support was once more flowing round me and, quite astonishingly, I felt my eyes wet with tears. When I finished I was trembling, not violently but beyond my power to control. I cannot remember what the audience *did,* perhaps they applauded. It did not matter, for a few short minutes I had shared my dream with a group of sympathetic people and I knew it had been a moving experience for all of us.

I no longer believe it is futile to attempt to communicate my rather esoteric experiences. I can describe what I do but it is still not easy to put abstract images and emotions into words. I believe, however, that there does exist a common bond between all of us who love the natural environment and who have not yet lost that impulse enshrined by Tennyson 'to strive, to seek, to find, and not to yield'.

In attempting to discover the origins of my deep attachment to long distance hill running I find, perhaps inevitably, that it is not something 'grafted on' or discovered by accident but part of a long process of a running evolution. And so I spiral back to my childhood.

Why walk if you can run?

I was fortunate enough to be brought up in a house with a garden that bordered on a large natural park, an old estate. The park, of several square miles, had everything a child could desire: trees, ponds, a river, cliffs, grassy expanses, muddy tracks, wildlife and irascible parkkeepers to annoy. I climbed, ran, swam, caught newts and sticklebacks and generally made the place an extension of my home. My friend and I at 10 or 11 years of age even paced out a mile course and timed ourselves using an old alarm clock (I think we seriously threatened the 6.5 minute mile). I grew to love simply being active in such surroundings, and as I look back from a distance of nearly 40 years I can clearly see from where my roots first drew their nourishment.

I also began to realise that I could outrun most of the other children I grew up with and while this was pleasant, what was more deeply satisfying was the sense of having a natural gift. It was the only gift I believed I possessed but it really was a special gift. It gave me an edge in the competitive world of a schoolboy and it earned me respect and status. But above all it was good for its own sake. As I grew older I naturally channelled my ability into organised sport. A catalyst was provided when a friend at school having been nominated to represent the school in the under-16 championships at 440 yards tried to persuade me to take his place. We agreed that I should be timed round a track and if I bettered his 62 seconds I would race. I remember turning up in a pair of old cycling shoes – leather uppers and stiff rubber soles. I thought they really looked the part. I managed 60 seconds dead so I was in. My first race was at the old White City Stadium in Manchester. I got through the heats then ran in the final in a pair of borrowed spikes. I came second in 56 seconds, which rather surprised me.

My athletic career was not illustrious but great fun and I had the good fortune to join Stockport Harriers when there was a small but gifted group of junior athletes. The group split when we approached university and college age. I had not improved overmuch, partly because the club at that time was almost moribund. I got down to 51 seconds for the quarter mile and just under two minutes for the half when I was 17 but the following year, when I got very fit during the winter, we had no meetings.

It may seem odd that someone who was once a runner-up in the 'Youth Sprint Championship of Stockport'(!) should become a devotee of runs over 100 miles. You may think that inside the sprinter was a distance runner biding his time. It did not seem like that. Although I could get close to 4.5 minutes for the mile, races of a mile or more were anathema to me. What finally overcame these barriers was the combination of my love for the countryside and my inherent love of running (not to be confused with racing). The way it came about was this.

My club had a very long 'Harrier' tradition, that is cross-country running. Through all its vicissitudes a small band of devotees, who must have had mud rather than blood in their veins, would emerge with the onset of the autumn monsoons and engage in 'pack' runs through Woodbank Park and surrounding countryside for hours on end. Like an innocent to the slaughter I was brought to join them. Various strong influences made themselves felt now. One was my uncle, Wilf Brown, a lifelong Harrier and rambler. He was a bricklayer by trade, but at heart a runner and a keen walker. As our local scout leader he introduced me to rambling and camping, from the age of eight. He embodied all that was wholesome and good in Baden-Powell's philosophy. The banner-waving element occasionally evident in scouting he gently ignored. He loved his running, or rather, he lived his running. Wilf was a typical Harrier. During the summer he trained and competed on the track and during the winter returned to his real love, cross-country running. He was past his prime when he fostered my interest in cross-country but he was an inspiration for me. Not because of his ability but because of the simple joy he found in his running. As an impetuous, unthinking youth I loved Wilf but it took me till manhood to fully appreciate the worth of this gentle, wise man. I deeply regret I could not tell him of my Pennine Way record before his untimely death. But Wilf is and will forever remain a part of my running.

Another considerable influence at this time was my friend and contemporary Dave (Horsey) Clayton. Dave was a promising middle-distance and cross-country runner. He was also a dedicated athlete and much of his training 'habit' rubbed off on me. I remember he once threw his shoes at me when I was timing him because the watch showed he was several seconds slower than he had hoped. He was normally quite mild and chirpy and this show of temperament impressed me greatly. Dave tried to persuade me of the virtues of running distances greater than a mile, in order to 'strengthen the organism'. I enjoyed trotting round the countryside, but one Saturday afternoon I turned up at Woodbank to find him persuading me to join in a cross-country race. It was two whole laps, four miles (7 km). I demurred, but he said to just go round one lap and I could drop out if I wanted to. After racing for one lap I had had enough. The course finished with a hill at the end of the lap and this was hard, so acting on his suggestion I dropped out. Five minutes later I felt deeply ashamed. I could easily have gone on. I had quit for no other reason than I had felt a bit uncomfortable. I there and then made a vow that I would *never* quit any run while I could still put one foot in front of the other. This promise held good for many, many years and while I *have* quit record attempts I have never transgressed the spirit of that promise.

I actually began to enjoy cross-country running and, to a lesser extent, racing. What I liked best was the Harrier pack runs, when we would run for miles through the winter countryside chatting, joking, swishing up the leaves and

Stockport Harriers at Woodbank Park, winter 1963. Extreme left, Len Fitzsimmons; Wilf Brown, second from right; Mike Cudahy, extreme right.

squelching through the mud. On our way back there would be some unseen signal and the pack would begin to pick up speed, finally going full belt for the last couple of miles. I really enjoyed this and found I could run much better after I had been running steadily for eight miles (13 km) or so. I was to develop this attribute in years to come.

When I was about 17 another event occurred which served to shape my future running career. One of our senior cross-country runners, Ian Watson, lived on a farm on the slopes of Kinder, at 2,000 ft (610 m) the highest moor in Derbyshire. Ian was a gifted runner and with Kinder as a training ground he could get very fit. In the year he finished second in the famous Yorkshire Three Peaks race he was training hard and invited the club along to join him on one of his runs. I went along as, inevitably, did Wilf Brown. The memory of that day is still very much alive. I had a marvellous feeling of euphoria as I ran high above the valleys. It was almost like flying, up there between the earth and the sky. We ran much further than I was used to but I felt no fatigue, only elation. I remember Wilf turning to me and saying 'You're running a blinder Mike!' I knew I was, I could feel it in my heart. I had found my medium, my environment. On the track I enjoyed my speed but high up on the moors I had found and expressed my nature and it was gloriously and joyfully at one with the hills all around me.

I did not immediately start running in the hills, however. Instead, I continued to be active on many fronts. My excursions to the hills were mainly confined to fairly modest trips on the local moors, either alone or leading small scout groups. The solo trips represented excitement and adventure as well as a curiously refreshing spiritual experience. Of course I did not articulate this at the time, I was only aware of a sense of wonder and a sense of peace together with a kind of muted thrum of excitement that I was where I should be. With a very rudimentary knowledge of navigation and a compass whose needle would never stand still, my destinations were always in doubt. But I particularly well remember the first time I navigated my way straight across the Kinder Plateau after spending the night in the old shooting cabin in Ashop Clough. After what seemed like hours glued to my compass I suddenly burst out on to the sharp plateau edge looking down from a craggy outcrop into the beautiful green vale of Edale, the village nestling snug below me. Nowadays, the traverse of Kinder has become commonplace and my mental map is the only navigational aid needed, but that first time has never been forgotten.

Despite these early excursions I did not become a proficient navigator until I was introduced to the sport of orienteering by my mate Len Fitzsimmons. It was Len who was primarily responsible for my taking up the sport of fell running which is perhaps the strongest link in the chain which has led to my development as an ultra-distance hill runner. Len was one of the hardy souls who emerged every winter ready for the cross-country season. Despite his slight frame and gentle, self-effacing disposition, he was a redoubtable performer and a man of many talents and much initiative. While I was still a callow youth, Len was a county-class runner at both cross-country and steeple-chase. Always at the mercy of a chronic knee and deteriorating back condition, he would take himself off to the hills at home and abroad, usually solo, and demonstrate a tremendous ability to survive with the minimum amount of gear. In the years to come, Len was to enliven many a weary journey with spirited renderings of airs from Gilbert and Sullivan. On the hill his keen photographer's eye frequently drew my attention to subtleties of texture, light and shade I might otherwise have missed. It is now many years since Len and I raced, trained and tramped the moors and mountains, his knees and back severely limit his endeavours nowadays. Nevertheless, I regularly run past an inscription on a stone just below Shutlingsloe out beyond the Cat and Fiddle moors. Len pointed it out to me one training day about 20 years ago. It is from Burns and it says 'We clamb'd the hill the gither' – we did indeed.

Along with Ian Watson, Len had completed the 22-mile (36 km) Three Peaks race in Yorkshire. At the time this seemed a staggering achievement and a hell of a long cross-country race, way beyond my abilities, something to dream about. In his own quiet way, Len encouraged that dream. He set about preparing himself for the race and I began to join him on his longer weekend runs. As I continued to build endurance my dreams became ambitions and I decided I must attempt the Three Peaks as soon as I reached the minimum age of 21 years. In the event I had to wait till I was 22, but on the last Sunday in April 1963 I departed from the Hill Inn on my first Three Peaks race. Although I had prepared with long runs over Kinder, I had never done anything like this before. I was terrified! I thought I had an outside chance of finishing if nothing at all went wrong. After the first peak, Ingleborough, we got lost in the mist near Sulber Nick. Fortunately, I was with Len and another Stockport runner, Tony Broster. The field in those days was small, around 50 to 60, so there was no line of plodding figures to follow, nor were the paths the broad tracks they are now. Full of gloom and despondency I knew with this extra distance I would never be able to finish. Len eventually got us sorted out and galloped off leaving Tony and me to trot gloomily along. I do not know when I began to entertain thoughts that we might actually complete the course, probably when only Whernside stood between us and the finish. In the last few miles I experienced for the first time a phenomenon which has since become a familiar and joyful accompaniment at the end of any very tough challenge where high ambition has been commensurate with uncertainty of outcome. I began to feel stronger and fitter than I had done even at the start, and I wanted to prance off leaving Tony to manage as best he could. To my credit I controlled the urge and we linked arms and finished together.

Responding therefore to the very hard but stimulating challenge of long hill running I started doing the Three Peaks every year and in addition Len simultaneously introduced me to the new sport of orienteering and the Lake District Mountain Trial. This latter remains one of my favourite events. It is run over a different course every year and combines navigation with the fast traverse of difficult mountain terrain. The distance is not great, between 16 and 25 miles (26 and 40 km), but it demands around five to seven hours of hard continuous effort. I first entered in 1965, when the Lake District was wonderfully unfamiliar to me, and have run every year since. It really is a magnificent event, quite unique with a special atmosphere of fun, striving, continuing friendships and camaraderie as well as goodwill between runners and officials. Tales of fortunes and misfortunes over a beer later, the chance to make fresh acquaintances, to put one over on your mates or to help out a newcomer with a bit of navigation are all part of this scene. Here you can rub shoulders with some of the all-time great fell runners, Joss Naylor, Alan Heaton, Billy Bland or the one time greats like George Brass and Ted Dance, past winners, still competing an incredible 35 years after winning the event in the 1950s. All share common ground with the average fell runners/mountaineers who make up the bulk of the 250-strong field.

Len and I gladly took up fell running which satisfied our love of the hills and our need for competition, while posing the fascinating challenge of fast, often intuitive navigation. We tended to enter the longer races, partly to make the three-hour drive to the Lakes worthwhile, but mainly because the idea of long traverses of the beautiful hills was immensely appealing. I was also discovering that the further the races went, the more I could compensate for a lack of running ability with a kind of natural strength and endurance. These were the days of small fields, often only around 30 to 40 runners. One quickly got to know other runners and friendships were formed easily. On the long courses the runners were soon spread out over the miles of fell, and there was no sense of being part of a pounding mass of bodies. Today, with fields numbering several hundreds, a good deal of the attraction of fell racing has for me disappeared. However, one other race in which I still compete and which I associate with these early beginnings is the Karrimor Two-Day Mountain Marathon. This is a

Mike and Len Fitzsimmons with Thor training for the first Karrimor Two-Day Mountain Marathon, 1968.

race for teams of two and involves navigating round a mountainous course which is only disclosed at the start. Each pair has to be self-sufficient for two days, that is, they must carry tents, sleeping bags, food and spare clothing around with them. Len and I entered the first Mountain Marathon back in 1968 and I have entered every year since, only once failing to complete the course after an official inadvertently removed a control point we were looking for. This record is only bettered by my friend and current partner John Richardson who has completed every Mountain Marathon – or The Karrimor as it is now known.

There were only 34 teams doing one 50-mile (80 km) course in 1968. Today there are over 1,000 teams competing over five or six courses which range from the 50 mile/80 km 'Elite' course to the 30 mile/50 km 'C' and 'Score' events. The smaller number of 'Elite' competitors spread over the longer course reduces 'bunching' and trailing. This is further helped if the course offers diverse route choices and tricky navigation (not to mention mountain mist). However, both John and I feel that when we can no longer complete the 'Elite' course we should retire from the event completely. I already have misgivings about our invasion of erstwhile solitary mountain areas.

In 1968 Len and I had visions of a not too brisk stroll through the hills around Muker in Yorkshire. We were wearing heavy boots and our rucksacks bulged with picnic treats. Our one weight-saving gesture was that Len had jettisoned his torch batteries, scoffing at the idea we would be out in the dark. In a typically cunning move he had packed the empty torch with matches and other odds and ends. I certainly had the ethical edge on him as we descended a steep hillside of bog and heather in utter darkness, to say nothing of the edge I had whenever I got to a really awkward bit.

Transition to ultra-distance

Up to competing in the Karrimor the longest distance I ran or walked was 25 miles (40 km). I must have had the urge to cover longer distances, however, because in the summer prior to the first Mountain Marathon, Len told me of a route called the Derwent Watersheds. This had been evolved by the legendary Eustace Thomas of the famous Manchester-based Rucksack Club. It was, in effect, a huge circuit of the Bleaklow and Kinder Moors nearly 40 miles (65 km) in length. Along with route details, Len told me that Thomas and his party of 'grough-hounds' had completed the round in 11 hours 39 minutes. I resolved to have a go myself.

Without informing anyone I set off on a sultry summer day with my faithful dog. After 20 or 25 miles (32 or 40 km) of the unusually dry and dusty Watersheds I veered off the route and plunged into a rock pool competing with the dog for the deepest part! Having reduced my temperature, I decided to carry on into a cooler late afternoon. Eventually I tottered to the point on the circuit where I had started. I stood there looking down to the valley and my waiting van. I realised I had just completed my hardest ever run/walk. My dog just looked at me reproachfully. I told him we had done nearly three hours better than Eustace, he was not impressed.

My skirmish with the Derwent Watersheds and my competing in the Karrimor brought me into contact with yet another powerful influence in my transition to an ultra-distance runner. It was Eustace Thomas, former holder of the Lake District 24 hour Fell Record (65.5 miles (105 km), 25,500 ft (7,800 m)) and member of the Rucksack Club, who inaugurated the Watersheds route, and it was Ted Dance and Bob Astles of the Rucksack Club who won the first and second Mountain Marathons. There were quite a few competitors from the Rucksack Club in that first Mountain Marathon and redoubtable men they were too. Don Talbot, Neil Mather, George Rhodes, Stan Bradshaw and my own future partner John Richardson. Between them, these men had climbed in the Himalaya, run and orienteered for England, put up new climbing routes on rock, completed the Lake District 24 hour Fell Record and, above all, they had walked the most prodigious distances – including the first continuous traverse of all the 2,500 ft (750 m) summits in the Lakes, over 100 miles (160 km) and around 42,000 ft (12,600 m) of ascent.

I was on friendly terms with most of them from competing in the same fell races but I was only vaguely aware that they belonged to the same club. One fateful evening the phone rang. It was Ted Dance inviting me to join a Rucksack Club team which he had entered in the first ever High Peak Marathon, which was to be held round the Derwent Watersheds route. I was not a club member but Denis Weir had had to drop out of the team of four and as I was a local lad and known to Ted he thought I might do. I was exceedingly flattered and when I heard the names of the rest of the team (Don Talbot, John Richardson) I at once hurried out to get myself truly fit! Had some spirit from the future appeared to describe the years of torment to which I was committing myself, the lashing rain, the knee-deep mud, the sweat freezing on one's back, the mean winds whipping across the gritstone edges, the boggy holes which lay in wait, the numbed feet, the whole bone-aching weariness of it all, I might just have paused a moment to consider – but probably not. The catalogue of suffering, triumph, despair and humour associated with this deliberately perverse event requires a separate chronicle. Originally organised by Sheffield University Orienteering Club it was scheduled for February but the local press got wind of it and having no other headlines proceeded to fall upon the luckless students and their scheme. They produced lurid headlines; 'Peakland Killer Route Marathon', 'Carbon Copy Death Trek', and so on. Participants were informed that 'blizzards could strike without warning', and a Peak Park warden was reported as saying there was 'a point of no return on Bleaklow'. Strange to say, we never reached this point, but the short way off a moorland watershed is down not back. One was also reassured to hear from the deputy head warden that if anyone got into difficulties he would be on hand to 'pull them out'. Let me tell you, he was never around to pull me out of any of the black bogs into which I frequently sank. Having taken part in 12 events I now think the scaremongers were all absolutely right.

The Rucksack Club team duly won the first race, and indeed, we won six times in succession. Eventually anno Domini made an impact as did the emergence of ever keener opposition from what had now become the fast-growing sport of fell running. But the event still exacts a heavy toll.

The Watersheds race not only extacts its toll during the actual event, training for it during the winter months can inflict damage too. On one occasion the Rucksack Club team of Ted Dance, John Richardson, Don Talbot and myself deemed it expedient to have a run over the lonelfest section of the route during the night. Don Talbot was particularly anxious to do this, as he had had flu the week before and thought it as well to test his return to health before the race.

The night was of the particularly dark variety, and though raining but gently when we stepped from Ted's vehicle, it promised to become much heavier ere long. At this point Ted announced that having now done his bit for the team effort, he was returning home to bed. We were, in those days, too polite to tell him what we thought of that and stepped, with nothing approaching enthusiasm, onto the inky moor.

Don lasted out very well. In fact, he lasted out long enough to let us reach the lonely depth of the moor, the dreaded 'point of no return', I guess. Here he suggested a rest stop, so we all sat around on tussocks enjoying an al fresco if somewhat soggy Mars bar in the refreshing rain. It seemed to John and me that Don was taking this rest business rather seriously for, as we stood up to go, Don was observed to be prostrate on the tussocks, eyes closed and the rain bouncing off his unprotected face, which we now noted had turned a very pale shade of white.

It was obvious that, if Don were to be left in that attitude, he would be asleep for a very long time indeed. Grabbing an arm each we hauled him up and started to drag him in the direction of the Longdendale valley road, two miles to the north. Fortunately, being a tough old boot, he began to come round and saved us the problem of what to do on reaching the rather frothy River Etherow by ploughing through like a ship. At first no one would stop for us on the road until a van chanced to draw up to ask directions. Before the driver knew what was happening, Don was pointing out the way to Glossop from the passenger seat! After not too lengthy a consultation it was decided that Don should give the Watersheds a miss that year. But do you think we applauded Ted's undeniable wisdom in eschewing the soggy moors for a warm bed?

On another occasion, in early spring, I combined training for both the Watersheds and the Mountain Marathon in one run. The idea was that I would follow the route of the Derwent Watershed but carry lightweight camping gear and spend the night on the moor around the half-way point. Setting off in the afternoon, I enjoyed a most invigorating run in temperatures around freezing and many a snow shower driven in flurries by an icy wind. As evening drew nigh the showers increased, it was still at the invigorating stage, but I deemed it wise to make camp.

In those days you could either have sound but rather heavy equipment or ultra-lightweight but chancy gear. Naturally, I had opted for the latter, after all, who ever expects snow on the moors in March? My 'tent' was actually a flysheet, open at one end, but my *pièce de résistance* was my 'groundsheet'. It had been sold to my wife as a plastic tablecloth for 15 pence and I had gleefully commandeered it, it was amazingly light and thin!

I observed, during supper, that the snow was now falling in a thick, wet blanket and was deepening rapidly. Very little was finding its way past the open end of the tent, however, and I consoled myself it would keep the midges away. During the night I awoke with my hip feeling very cold. The blasted tablecloth had sneakily crept out under the sides of the flysheet and was catching snow, which it funnelled back in my direction. I was lying in a pool of wet snow. It was fortunate I was using a very thin and nearly useless sleeping-bag at the time, otherwise valuable gear might have been ruined. Craftily, I placed my map under my hip, took a firm grip on my dog – a large and hairy Alsatian – and passed the remainder of the night in, almost luxury.

Next morning, the snow was deep and even, but not crisp. My now warm feet revealed something previously hidden while they had been frozen. My shoes (in reality rubber-soled football boots) had sliced a thick lump of skin from my heel. As it was still snowing and I had obviously not reached the 'point of no return', I returned, but on an easier line. The snow eventually stopped and the sun cracked the clouds; soon everywhere sparkled. Just near my car I met a grizzled farmer rescuing his sheep. He asked me where I had spent the night. I told him (omitting the tablecloth – I thought he might not understand) and he stared at me awhile, then he said 'By heck! You must be a redoubtable character', actually, he was some distance away and he might just have said 'Bloody hell! You must be a right daft bugger' – I am really not too sure.

Apart from probably reducing my life expectancy, what the High Peak Marathon did for me was to bring me into such close and enjoyable company with the Rucksack Club men, that I willingly overcame my native reluctance to join clubs and became a member myself. And so the die was cast. Or very nearly, cruel fate made one evil attempt at nipping my ultra career in the bud, striking at me through another great love of mine – basketball. One dire Saturday in November 1973, just one week after competing in the High Peak Marathon I tried just a bit too hard in driving through for a lay-up shot and broke my leg. The break was a split of the tibial plateau, the weight-bearing surface of the knee joint. I was given to understand that this meant the end of serious sport participation, but, to be honest, I do not know exactly what was said because I knew that, as soon as the cast was off, I was going to run again.

A year later I had to have the cartilage removed, it had been smashed by the femur as it had crunched down on the tibial plateau. The muscle did not re-build and eventually I started special exercises, working up to leg flexion with a 35 lb (16 kg) lump of iron from a rail track strapped to my ankle. Slowly, with much blood, sweat and tears, the muscle was rebuilt, though I have permanently lost the first and last degrees of movement at the knee. I paid dearly for my commitment and love of basketball and, although pain became an inevitable accompaniment of my running, I learned yet another lesson about perseverance and dedication.

Although many people consider events such as the 40-mile High Peak Marathon, the Mountain Trial and Karrimor should be classed as 'ultra-endurance', none of these races occupied more than a dozen hours of continuous going. In 1976 all this changed. On the calendar of Club events that year was a walk called the Grassington–Langdale. I had heard of Grassington vaguely and, as I well knew that Langdale was in the Lake District, I assumed it was somewhere in the same area. I cheerfully agreed to go along. Just the week before the walk I discovered where Grassington was situated – and it was not in the Lake District, it was not even anywhere near it! It was 80 hilly miles (130 km) away. I thought there must be some mistake – I could not walk 80 miles as a continuous walk, could I? 'Nonsense!' said Ted Dance. 'You are a fit fell runner, Mountain Trial, High Peak Marathon and all that. There will be members along who never do that sort of thing, just ordinary walkers.' Well, actually acknowledging my physical limitations has never been something I am good at but I really thought this was a bit much. However, I drove into Grassington with another new member, my friend Geoff Bell, and was immediately initiated into typical Rucksack Club walk strategy. In this club a 9.00 a.m. start does not mean you meet at 9.00, it means that at that time precisely, you are enveloped (at least if you are actually there) in a cloud of dust as everyone endeavours to keep pace with and tabs on the leader who is often the only man who knows just where he is going. Geoff and I arrived at 9.05 to find the place deserted. 'Typical!' I said, 'these things always get going half an hour later than they are supposed to.' Just then someone leaned out of a car. 'You on the Grassington–Langdale walk?' 'Yes, when they arrive' I said. 'Arrive!' he replied, 'they left nearly 10 minutes ago, we are driving round to Mid Pasture to fix them some nosh.' 'But, but . . . where did they go?' 'Over there' he said waving his arm in the general direction of a large hill. 'John Richardson is leading the walk and he is going like the clappers!' 'But, but . . .' we stammered. 'Sorry, got to go' – and he was gone! 'Do you know where Mid Pasture is?' I asked Geoff. 'No' he muttered, 'I only know where Langdale is.' 'Same here', I answered, 'come on.'

We did eventually catch up with the Club walk and we did eventually get to Langdale. I arrived there tireder but wiser. Amongst other things, I had learnt what a delightfully comfortable bed a tarmac road can make when you have been walking all day and all night. I cannot say that the walk did much more than confirm my suspicion that I had no gift for ultra-endurance. However, the fact that I *had* actually completed the 80 miles (130 km) must have made a subjectively greater impression. This short-sighted view lined me up for a good dose of suffering the following year.

1977 was the Rucksack Club's jubilee year and Geoff Bell decided it would be a nice idea to link two of the Club's main centres of activity with a walk. Although he might well have chosen to link, say, the Snake Inn on one side of Kinder Scout with the Nag's Head on the other, he unfortunately decided he would walk from the Club hut in the Lake District to the village of Edale – the southern end of the Pennine Way – a distance of around 120 miles (195 km). We set off with great enthusiasm on a hot sunny day with the ground, for once, dry and firm. How miserable is the lot of the foot traveller. No sooner does he escape from the almost perpetual bog and mud than his tender feet are blistered and burnt by the unaccustomed heat. In my case I developed a singularly painful complaint, not exactly blisters, but a prickly tenderness on the pads of my feet.

This quickly reached the point where I began to examine my socks for the bits of broken glass I felt sure had found their way in. Perhaps paddling across Morecambe Bay in bare feet had not helped, but at 60 miles (100 km) I had had enough. Unfortunately, our support driver, by chance or design, failed to pick me up before the start of an excruciating road section and when I had done this bit, I decided to carry on for another few miles, then a few more, and then some more . . . Eventually I hobbled into Edale with my feet feeling like barbecued steaks but my complaint forever enshrined in the Club's glossary as 'Jubilee Foot'. The pain had been sufficient for me to be unable to remember whether the walk had been tiring or not – a very minor compensation.

Looking through my log-books I realise that 1977 was, perhaps more than any other year, the time of my truly becoming an ultra-distance performer. However, the transition was gradual. Less than two weeks after the Jubilee Walk I climbed Black Shadow, a rock climb graded 'Extreme', in the Llanberis Pass in the morning, then ran from the valley to Snowdon summit and back in 72 minutes in the afternoon. This combination of activities pleased me and it is with some regret that deeper involvement with hard running has restricted my development of other mountain skills. In the face of increasingly high standards it is commensurately more difficult to excel at more than one activity.

A few weeks after charging up Snowdon I attempted something rather longer. In 1932 Bob Graham, a Lake District landlord, improved Eustace Thomas's Fell Record. He traversed the tops of 42 major Lakeland peaks in under 24 hours, a distance of around 65 to 70 miles (105 to 115 km) and about 26,000 ft (7,800 m) of ascent and descent. Although this has been exceeded many times since, Graham's feat has become a 'standard' for other aspirant ultra fell runners. I knew sooner or later I would like to tackle the 'Bob Graham' round, and when Ted Dance invited me to join himself and two friends, I gladly agreed. I only had a fortnight to prepare specifically for the event, so I spent a couple of days in the Lakes, concentrating on steep ascents and descents. My training methods of those days appal me now, though I also applaud my nicely amateur and carefree approach – no doubt inherited from Ted, one of the world's great non-trainers. Just four days before the attempt I was charging round Kinder Scout with the aim of getting fitter, but the probable effect of getting tireder!

Our first attempt was washed out by heavy rain, but the following week I completed the Scottish Fourthousanders (1,200 m peaks) with John Richardson. The latter route is about 80 or 90 miles (130–145 km) in length and starts with the Ben Nevis group in the west and finishes over the Cairngorm 4,000 ft summits in the east. A truly magnificent walk, it was yet another walk pioneered by the legendary Eustace Thomas, who used his Rolls-Royce both as a support vehicle and as a means of covering some of the slightly tedious miles between the two groups of peaks. As neither John nor I possessed a Rolls we covered these miles on foot. We found them long, indeed, but not tedious.

Nine days after this, I again joined forces with Ted Dance to make another attempt on the Bob Graham round. In heat-wave conditions and with a certain residual tiredness from the Scottish Fourthousanders, I was forced to a very modest pace. Ted, by contrast, was in great form and I finally persuaded him to press ahead on the last sections. However, summoning a final flourish, I managed to finish within the allotted 24 hours.

Having now successfully completed a number of extended walks or walk/runs I began to take a keener interest in the Club's tradition of long walks. I had, of course, known about the 40-mile (65 km) Derwent Watersheds for some time, but now I learned of the 70-mile (115 km) Colne-Rowsley. This had for a long time been the Club's longest walk and a gruelling moorland test piece for its 'grough-hounds'. In 1953, however, one of these grough-hounds had hit upon the novel idea of linking England's two highest pubs, the Tan Hill Inn in Co. Durham and the Cat and Fiddle on the moors a few miles from Buxton in Derbyshire.

Extending the Club's longest walk by 50 hard miles (80 km) was an audacious concept. It was, however, undertaken by a group of audacious and determined men. The walk was, appropriately enough, first suggested by the then landlord of the Nag's Head, Edale, Fred Heardman, himself a Club member and keen walker. It was Ted Courtenay, however, who transformed the suggestion into an inspirational walk. Nor was Ted unaffected by the scope of the concept. After phoning his plans to fellow-walkers, he excitedly left the telephone booth with a set of directories clasped under his arm and his maps and schedules reclining on the shelf. The 120 miles (195 km) and nearly 20,000 ft (6,000 m) of ascent exacted retribution, of course. Ted completed his dream, along with stalwarts Vin Desmond and Frank Williamson. Both Neil Mather and even the Club's fleetest grough-hound, Phil Brockbank, were forced to retire, however. In typical fashion they were back the following year, this time with the young tiger, Ted Dance, for company. All were successful and the completion time of between 54 and 55 hours has become a 'standard' for the walk.

Phil Brockbank, apart from his walking talents was also noted for his keen wit and humour. He observed, mischievously, that the Tan–Cat refused to be

The start of the first Tan Hill to Cat and Fiddle, 1953. From left to right: Ted Courtenay, Vin Desmond, Neil Mather, Frank Williamson, Phil Brockbank.

downgraded in line with the usual Club tradition. According to Phil the degrading of classic walks was achieved by subjecting them to increasingly casual modes of attack. He claimed that the second stage of degradation was the traverse by an all-male party in winter, the first being completion by a lady in summer. He left open whether the third stage was a double traverse by a male party in summer or a single traverse by a lady in winter. But by the time a lady had achieved the double version in winter, the walk had reached the lowest classification and was best left to the attention of beginners.

The classifications, of course, refer to continuous effort – snatches of sleep are allowed but going to bed at night and continuing the next morning is definitely unethical. Despite a number of repetitions there have, to my knowledge, been only two winter traverses of the Tan–Cat (one of which I had the dubious pleasure of accompanying), no doubles and only one completion by a lady. The line is a particularly challenging one in foul winter conditions. Almost without exception it cleaves to the high ground, it does not eschew that which is trackless and its last 40 miles (65 km) traverse high, desolate and intimidating moorland: Blackstone Edge, Winter Hill, Black Hill, Bleaklow and Kinder Scout. My mate John Richardson was a veteran of this route and, furthermore, he had done the fastest ever traverse, supported but solo, in 37 hours.

I wondered, could I better this time?

chapter two

TAN HILL TO CAT AND FIDDLE

It is difficult to decide what constituted training for my proposed attempt on the Tan–Cat record. For ultra-distance hill running a general background of running fitness punctuated by long days out on the hills constitutes the general kind of preparation needed. My first attempts at the Tan–Cat produced two resounding disasters, but my preparation had been quite thorough. In fact, my estimation of my 'natural' ultra-endurance ability is so low and my desire to succeed so high that I am usually likely to be guilty of over- rather than under-preparation.

I emerged from the spring very fit having completed the Three Peaks race, the White Peak Marathon and a number of good solid 'mountain days' in Wales. The Welsh days were in part a preparation for a scheme I had hatched with Ted Dance and Geoff Bell to complete a double traverse of the 14 Welsh peaks over 3,000 ft (900 m). This was to be no record attempt, just a good hard day in the hills. What made it good was that the route would link a superb succession of summits in a satisfying logical line. We would see sunset and sunrise from some of the most beautiful hills in the country. What made it hard was that it entailed about 46 miles (75 km) of mountainous terrain and around 21,000 ft (6,300 m) of ascent by our line.

We started at lunchtime and, as I remember, Ted set off at a very smart pace which took us over the first two summits and onto Snowdon in one and a half hours. In just over two hours we were back in the valley enjoying a brew in our Club hut in the Llanberis Pass. From here the climb to Elidir Fawr is very long 2,700 ft (810 m) and Ted was obviously feeling in good form! Unfortunately, Ted is often the victim of his own enormous ability. His natural talent will carry him almost effortlessly and at great speed through a 'normal' hard day. Training is almost superfluous for him at this level. However, beyond the normal, even the greatest must needs be sustained by many, often boring hours of conditioning, a process which Ted assiduously avoids.

We jogged pleasantly over Y Garn and in the early evening we had Tryfan and the Glyders practically to ourselves. I love being on high ground in the evening, there is always such an air of peace about. The mornings can be special too, but then there is a more expectant air, a fragile stillness that is soon to dissolve into the bustle of a full day. The evening hills have the promise of a yet deeper peace.

At about 9.00 p.m. we reached our car in the Ogwen Valley. We ate a prepared meal, picked up supplies and torches and put on warmer clothes. Our ascent of the massive Penyrolewen was hampered by very full stomachs and it was dark by the summit. Quite magically, however, a full moon broke through sparse cloud and we had only occasional need of torches. Our pace had now slowed to 'very comfortable' which meant that as I had mentally prepared for a fast pace and donned appropriate clothes, I was rather chilly. The Carneddau are a big, rolling range of hills with a good deal of ground close to the 3,000 ft (900 m) mark. The very real sense of vastness is enhanced at night when the moonlit bulk of the mountains seems to occupy all space, one can imagine that under the sky's canopy there are nothing but endless mountain ridges over which one may journey for all eternity, would it were so.

On the col below the outlying summit of Yr Elen, Ted, abetted by Geoff, decided he would like a little snooze. I created such a fuss about already being frozen, they were forced to humour me, but I could see I might have some trouble getting them past the refuge hut at Foel-grach! Although our schedule was intended as a guide I had hoped to complete the whole journey inside 24 hours. However, we did not reach our terminus on Foel-fras until 2.30 a.m. which meant we had already taken 13 hours for the outward leg. It did not matter, the night was one to be savoured; a gossamer mist caressed the ground and overhead the stars glinted sharp around a moon bright enough to cast shadows. Unfortunately, by now Ted was too sleepy to enjoy this to the full. He made a bee-line for the Foel-grach refuge hut, where, to our surprise, we disturbed another walker. On finding a ready ear Ted immediately perked up while Geoff sneakily had a quick zizz. In the meantime Ted had invited this character to join us, which he did despite being hampered by a mass of clothes and hand-held carrier bags. He kept up amazingly well and I suspected he had little idea of where he was which consequently made him nervous of being left behind. At 6.00 a.m. we were dropping down to the Ogwen valley again. It was going to be a beautiful day. The valley was still sleeping in a pale grey dawn, but above us the crags had blushed pink and the sky was innocent and blue. At this priceless moment Ted decided he had had a surfeit of good things and would partake no more thereof. Morpheus beckoned him rather more imperatively than the golden hills. Geoff and I were thus left to complete the traverse alone.

Naturally, the tiredness entered our legs, but our spirits would not be denied. On Snowdon we survived a bombardment of stones from two little boys watched over by a fond father – that is until the normally imperturbable Geoff (having just headed a stone) drew daddy's attention to certain sub-sections of the Mountain Code. We brought our route to a fitting climax with a somewhat stiff-legged traverse of the narrow and airy Crib-Goch ridge. Ted was waiting for us at Pen-y-Pass and together we drove down to the hut for a wonderful shower and endless pots of tea. We had been out for 28 hours and in that time the hills had drawn our strength but nourished our spirits, we had shared the hills and we had shared friendship.

Less than a month after our memorable double Welsh 3,000s Geoff and I again teamed up to attempt a 'double Shap-Wasdale'. The route, from Shap on the eastern fringes of the Lake District to Wasdale at the very heart of the Lakes, is a traditional Rucksack Club walk of about 35 miles (56 km). Once more John Richardson was leading this classic and once more we were late (by 50 minutes).

A steady economical line brought us up to the Club, prostrate in midday heat, outside the Kirkstone Inn. Both Geoff and I had very fit 'hill legs' by now and found the hilly route to our liking. At the end of the day we dropped into Wasdale at a perfect moment – just as the setting sun was casting a marvellous and rare Alpenglow on Pikes Crag behind us. It was so beautiful we descended at least half the distance to Wasdale with our heads screwed round to gaze at the rocks behind us, not a recommended practice.

Now came the rather harder bit. While everyone else stretched around in a variety of luxurious attitudes and poured beer copiously down dry throats Geoff and I, pretending not to notice, didn't so much enjoy a meal as refuel our systems. With loins well girt and upper lips suitably stiffened we left at midnight on a balmy moonless night. Rarely do the hills fail to reward the patient traveller. As we meandered wearily past Stickle Tarn we were rendered immobile by a scene of immense beauty. At 2 a.m. on a still summer night, Nature was painting with a range of blacks and sombre blues. Before us stretched the waters of the Tarn, one would have said black had not the encircling arms of stony land clasping the Tarn been yet blacker. At the furthest and blackest extent of the Tarn and its rim was what had first drawn our gaze. Presage of a summer dawn was a band of the most delicate blue. We followed the pale blue ever up as it dissolved by imperceptible stages into always darker hues. At last with craning heads we stared into the immense void of the true night sky. We sat silent and motionless as the stones around us, then we got up and finished our walk. Pink Pikes Crag and cobalt eternity.

First Tan–Cat attempt

After all my solid preparation I might have been forgiven for feeling confident. Alas, I had yet much to learn! Geoff and I elected to start from the 'wrong' end, that is to go from the Cat and Fiddle to Tan Hill. For some reason this immediately felt wrong and my only other attempt to go this way also proved a disaster. Nothing seemed to go quite according to plan including Geoff and I getting separated. After waiting for some time I set off convinced he must be in front of me, I even picked up his stud marks! Despite my good pace I could not seem to overhaul him. I decided to press on alone to Todmorden, 50 miles (80 km) hence, and phone Geoff's home. As I was considering this I discerned very heavy breathing and turned round to discover a rather warm Geoff galloping up behind me. Being Geoff he was soon laughing about the incident as we enjoyed a large ice-cream and lemonade in Todmorden. We put the remains of the lemonade in a plastic bottle and jogged off. There was a subdued explosion from Geoff's sack and suddenly his nether regions were bathed in lemonade! We traversed the ensuing moors in gentle summer rain losing a little time, not much, just enough to ensure we would be tackling Jackson's Ridge in darkness.

Jackson's Ridge is Lancashire's answer to the Bermuda Triangle. It must be named after some long forgotten surveyor or insane navvy, for it is not a ridge at all, just an interminable ditch running along a parish boundary. It looks quite innocuous on the map and should give a direct line across the still private moor below Boulsworth Hill. At night it is a shifting malevolent place. The ditch disappears and attempts to find it using 'off-line' bearings lead to one becoming quite disoriented. Whole drainage systems displace themselves and the flat contours are blandly inscrutable. It is truly devious, in reasonable conditions it will drop its defences and allow untroubled passage. But return in mist or dark thus disarmed and it will trap you and spit you out hours later. You will be disillusioned, demoralised and you may be in Lancashire or Yorkshire for all you know or care.

I had reconnoitred Jackson's Ridge and had it well taped – with a slight doubt about a night crossing. But I was sure I could handle it, after all what moor can stand before the powerful magic of the Silva compass? We were soon to find out.

I am still unable to calculate in what way we managed to get off line. My suspicion is that the ground cunningly shifted or perhaps Jackson's ghost bewitched me for I remember abandoning my foolproof plan and trying something I had not rehearsed. We should have been going NE but when we did so the ground dropped away on our right so I corrected by moving back NW. Now the ground dropped away to our left so I swung back to the N – too late! We were now traversing awkward sloping ground but decided we must stay with this bearing. Wrong! We began to drop into and climb out of small valleys which split the hillside. As each valley was choked with wet head-high bracken we were soon soaked from head to foot. We tripped and fell down to each stream then fought our way up the impenetrable stuff on the other side. After some incalculable period of time we were brought to a halt by the unlikely prospect of a cluster of bright lights floating above the moor some distance away. We looked at each other – the bloody moor was haunted! Reason prevailed. Out came the map which revealed the only pub in the area, the Herders Arms high on a remote moorland road and well off our intended line.

Drawn as if by a magnet we approached the pub. Despite the midnight hour it was vibrating with noise, life and unthinkable pleasures of the flesh. Suppressing a sob we slunk past, bedraggled, outcast figures, out of blackness into blackness. Now we exchanged high bracken for a forest of tussocks. Tussocks are, perhaps, the walker's worst enemy. Now, I fell over one and banged my nose on another. It was the end, the final indignity – no, it was not!

At last, descending in now lashing rain into the haven of Cowling I skidded to a halt just in front of an electric fence and just in time to realise that Geoff was right behind me and closing fast, too fast. The fence was at a very unfortunate height and in splendid working order – unlike certain parts of me for some time after. Geoff's wife, Mary, was waiting to support us at Cowling. Before she could enquire of our needs Geoff was issuing home-bound instructions from the back seat of the car, and I was in such a hurry getting changed in the phone box I left several items of clothing behind! 'After all', I said to Geoff, 'if we quit now after 70 miles (115 km) we will still be fresh enough to have another go next weekend.' 'I'm sure you will' said Geoff, 'and, better still, next time *you* run and I'll support!'

I am at a loss to understand why some kind but strong friend had not the wit to tell me that a fairly rigorous 70 miles (115 km) one weekend is not ideal preparation for a further 120 miles (195 km) at record pace the following weekend. Perhaps I never asked.

Second Tan–Cat attempt

This time I started my attempt from Tan Hill and the most, in fact the only, enjoyable thing about the venture was the quart of Webster's fine beer I consumed the night before. I set off in humid conditions, which I detest. Soon it began to rain and did so for 10 hours non-stop. Despite a certain residual tiredness, which I found puzzling, I was making reasonable progress until Great Whernside, 30 miles (50 km) on. In the mist and surrounded by a maze of high stone walls I lost my bearings somewhat. When I reached the road a helpful motorist advised that Conistone, where Geoff was waiting, lay to my right. Three miles later I jogged into Kettlewell, reversed and jogged three and a quarter miles back to Conistone. This was a nasty psychological blow and, worse still, the road did something naughty to my right shin. Each succeeding bit of road or track wrought its own mischief and soon even soft, but rough, going began to send stabs of pain up the shin. I should have quit at the road before Jackson's Ridge, but I was determined to show the moor that I was equal to it. Although the light would soon fade, I deliberately refused to take a torch despite knowing that failure to keep to my scheduled speed across the moor would mean . . . well, do not think of the consequences, just get out and do it. It was the only satisfaction I got from the attempt, I just made the crossing in the last glim. Again, I should have quit at the support point, but stubborn pride would not let me. I reasoned that the slow night pace across the soft moors above Todmorden would allow my leg to recover. The pace was slow all right! The night was Stygian in its black impenetrability. Inexplicably, it did not seem to cure my shin.

Geoff was curled up, fast asleep in his cosy car, radio issuing soft music. If you ever do support, please at least attempt to give the impression it is hell for you too. Meanwhile, my demon was explaining to Geoff that it was necessary to test whether the air of Todmorden had miraculous shin-healing properties. Geoff nodded sagely and I limped off. In Todmorden the demon explained that one should never make a decision to quit in the small hours when low morale held sway and it was now 2.30 a.m. Geoff accepted this logic. But I knew that Todmorden was only 69 miles (114 km) on from Tan Hill and last week I had managed 70 miles (115 km) and the demon was thus not satisfied. I started on the five miles (8 km) to the White House. On the hard tracks by the Warland Reservoirs the pain made fresh investigations of my levels of tolerance. My limp reached very ungainly proportions, yet when I reached the car I said nothing but ate briefly and stared into the dirty grey dawn over the dirty grey moors. Geoff sat patiently waiting. At last I spat the words out 'Take me home, Geoff.' The demon started; 'But I'll get you next time !' he screeched petulantly. 'I'll try again next year, Geoff', I muttered.

I prepared very thoroughly, after receiving such a rebuff on the Tan–Cat. Along with other Club members, I did a walk of about 100 miles (160 km) in Wales, and the week after the Mountain Trial I decided to attempt the Colne–Rowsley. Logically, I should have tackled this route before taking on the Tan–Cat as it is similar in terrain but, at 70 miles (115 km), it is 50 miles (80 km) shorter. I knew John Richardson and Denis Weir had completed the route in a brisk 19 hours in semi-winter conditions – the fastest time, but not intended as a definitive record. In fact John now accompanied me for the first 30 miles (50 km), after which I continued alone. It was a lovely run, though tiring after the Mountain Trial. The moors were clean, empty and windswept. I can still recall the sound of the wind swishing through the rough moorland grass. I ran on into darkness picking my way along the gritstone edges above winking lights in the Derwent Valley, then finally descending to Rowsley where I arranged for Ted to pick me up. I was so weary on finishing that I donned all my spare clothes and curled up inside a horse-trough outside the rather posh portals of The Peacock – much to the chagrin of its clientele ('Oh, I say, do look at that old tramp asleep in the horse-trough!'). My time was a rather pedestrian 17 hours 20 minutes but the time was far less important than the sense of satisfaction I derived from the run as a whole.

The Colne–Rowsley rounded off my ultra exploits for 1978 and I then set to work on a more systematic programme of training than I had ever before attempted. I was careful this time to include road stretches in my training. The basis of my training was a long day each weekend – around four to six hours and several mid-week runs of eight to ten miles (13 to 16 km). Nor did I neglect to keep in touch with the long stuff. In March Geoff and I did a very tough 90-mile (144 km) Peakland circuit battling with the remnants of winter. At the end of May I put on a Club walk of 70 miles (115 km) in Wales. I found this relatively easy and relaxing and decided I must by now be ready to pit myself once more against the Tan–Cat.

Tan–Cat record 1979

We arrived at Tan Hill at 1.00 a.m. – regretfully far too late to sample the Websters. In any case I had to be up at 5.00, so perhaps it was as well. I set off alone at 5.30 with feelings of excitement and tension only just under control. I have always had a natural tendency towards slow, steady starts, but now I had to make conscious efforts not to run uphill. As I flowed over the first stretch of moor I became aware of tremendous concentration and a drive to succeed that was like a pure energy force. Tension is always greatest in the first stretches of an ultra attempt and because of this I generally prefer to be by myself. Alone, I can come to terms with myself and the course. In the first few miles I create a harmony in relation to the extreme demands I shall experience. I seek to establish a calm acceptance and a peaceful strength. If I cannot find these at the start, I will have nowhere to come back to when the going gets really tough.

I was to have plenty of company on this attempt, however. In order to give Geoff a break from driving I had enlisted Sue, a friend from the college where I lectured. Sue was a strong and committed walker who had taken to running, she could drive, rustle up a roadside brew in seconds and was as versatile as an egg! In short, a perfect member of a support crew. She was a good listener, too. When she joined me to stretch her legs after I had been running alone for several hours, I responded to the release of tension by talking non stop for miles.

The day continued pleasantly with Geoff and Sue alternating running and driving round to meet me at road crossings with drinks, etc. I cruised gently over the rolling Yorkshire hills, Great Shunner, Buckden Pike and Great Whernside. I made sure of getting Great Whernside right by having John Richardson as my guide. This hill is very much on his patch, so there were no six-mile (10 km) detours this time. By lunchtime I felt hungry and ate a large helping of fish and chips. As each section of moor and meadow passed behind me I began to feel increasingly confident. By the time I ran into Todmorden at 70 miles (115 km) I was nearly two hours ahead of my schedule. Instead of halting for a substantial meal, I decided to press on to the White House. This meant that I could concentrate on running the flat reservoir tracks on an empty stomach. Perhaps the ghosts of last year's anguished hobble still lurked here because for the first time I began to experience a real weariness, and I tasted fear in the simple arithmetic of 120 miles (195 km) minus 70 (115) still leaves 50 miles (80 km). I put my trust in my training and a good feed.

I had quite a long stop at the White House as I was preparing for a solo night section of some hours. Up to now I had run in shorts but the night was turning chilly and a damp moorland mist was licking over the hills. I put on warm tights and a jersey and picked up a small rucksack of spare gear. Finally I confirmed my estimated time of arrival at the dawn checkpoint with Geoff and Sue and with their words of encouragement in my ears I stepped across the road and onto the empty midnight moors.

In my heart I knew that the next few hours would almost certainly decide the record for me. First, my mind quickly probed my body. After a few dozen stiff and painful steps I noted with relief that my legs became loose and comfortable. My next concern was with route finding. To my consternation I observed the mist thickening. I was not going to have the clear, transparent summer night I had counted on. Now the map and compass provided the structure within which I used my memory 'feel' of the route to maintain me on course over the featureless terrain. I became utterly engrossed in this game which, at its best, is like establishing an extra sense, a direction sense based on information from many sources. So engrossed was I that I hardly realised how slowly I was moving. Of my two hours in hand all but 30 minutes had slipped away with the night.

It was with a feeling of great relief that I came out straight and true at the support car just as a steely dawn fingered its way into the eastern sky before me. I was touched to discover that Sue had sensed my approach and was already waiting with a warm drink. Despite my protestations they both insisted on driving to the next road crossing only 90 minutes running time away. With support like this I knew I must not allow myself to fail. I set off with fresh determination into a clear, grey dawn, the wild, lonely call of a curlew floating above the moors.

As I began to run the night pace out of my legs I detected a sense of urgency replacing the patience of the night section. I had opted for a slightly novel approach to Black Hill, one of the three major high moors which lay between me and my goal. Black Hill is usually approached from either the Pennine Way route over Black and White Moss or up the Wessenden valley from Marsden. My plan was to start on the Pennine Way path but outflank the horrible bogs of Black and White Moss by descending to the top section of the Wessenden. Working without a map I left the Pennine Way path and headed for the valley track. Suddenly, everything looked wrong; I had missed my 'attack' point. If I went down in the wrong place I could easily be committed to a hopeless deviation. At last I opted for the more southern of two alternatives on the basis that I was heading south overall. After 10 minutes of descent I dropped onto the path I had been seeking. I breathed a sigh of relief but cursed my fallible memory.

Soon I was crossing Black Hill. A vast area of rough tussocky grass capped by a black, oozing bog, Black Hill is a place with few definite features, just huge empty spaces. Feeling very strong under the waxing power of the early sun I began to trade accuracy for speed and slipped off route twice. Fortunately, I quickly recognised my errors and regained my line safely.

At Crowden I had a short food stop trying not to notice the bulk of Bleaklow looming before me. Sue joined me for this tough leg to the Snake Inn and helped to take my mind off the endless climb. Crossing the top of the moor at 8.00 a.m. in beautiful sunshine we were startled to see Ted Dance suddenly pop out from behind a grough with his camera poised. Ted's unexpected appearance gave me a great boost and I picked up from my steady plod and swept up to the Snake Inn in fine style. I had now completed 99 miles (158 km) and as the 100th took me straight up the side of Kinder Scout it was arguably the toughest. I felt I was crawling and became despondent until Ted authoritatively told me it was a perfectly reasonable pace after 100 miles (160 km). Ted's authority cannot be gainsaid and, sure enough, I emerged strong at the top of the climb.

However, I was now certainly into the area of fatigue. The steady uphill walking sections were not bad, but running on the flat called for a very definite act of will to get started. I kept plugging away, reaching out with my mind for the end of my journey. I had been sure of breaking John's record for some time but seemed to lack inspiration to summon any final flourish. At last, as I topped the high point on Comb's Moss above Chapel-en-le-Frith I could make out a tiny bump on the yet higher moors above Buxton; the Cat and Fiddle. The end of my pub crawl was in sight. For no good reason it suddenly entered my head that I must get to the pub before afternoon closing so that my friends could celebrate with a drink. This thought quickly assumed obsessive qualities and I increased my efforts, driving my tired legs through the wiry, clutching heather. As I approached the last hill I asked Ted, who was pacing me, to go a little faster; he did so. A few seconds later I suggested I could go faster still; again he increased speed. When I repeated the request for the third time he stepped aside and told me to take it on myself. I began to pump my legs hard, I reached my maximum walking speed and broke into a run. I crested the hill and reached the final undulating mile of track to the pub. I was expecting to pay for such a

*Mike and
Geoff above
the Snake Inn
on Kinder
Scout – the
Tan–Cat.*

ridiculous waste of energy at every rise, but instead my body was suffused with a vibrant and unassailable energy and I simply ran faster and faster, leaving my support behind me and my brain to wonder what the hell was happening! Two hundred yards of tarmac separated me from the Cat and Fiddle, I sprinted up, gave the gable end a resounding smack with my hand, then immediately turned to go back to my friends. As I looked for them the glorious energy which had flowed into my legs, flowed into my heart and mind. It entered my eyes and emerged as tears. I hugged my friends and the energy became still, changed now into a deep and peaceful joy. A joy that remained a guard against the ravages of fatigue for many days after.

I had taken over five hours off the record, finishing in 32 hours 20 minutes, which meant we were able to celebrate in appropriate style after all.

With Geoff and Sue outside the Cat and Fiddle. Mike's first successful Tan–Cat.

chapter three

BEYOND LIMITS

It is difficult to describe the euphoria I felt after running the Tan–Cat. Running has always been a very important part of my life. If I am honest, I suppose I should say it is not only part of my lifestyle, it *is* my lifestyle. I am reluctant to admit that, however, as I believe other things, family, friends, books, music, are just as important. In any case, what for me elevates running to such a position of importance is the intimate connection I have made between running and the hills. It is not necessary for me to run over the hills to enjoy them, nor do I have to have hills to derive satisfaction from running, but the whole is frequently greater than the sum of the parts.

For nearly a year I had cherished my dream of running smoothly and swiftly down that long stretch of the Pennine Moors. I had been out in rain, hail, snow and occasional heat. In the long, dark days of winter, when I might have been cosy before a fire, I had ploughed my lonely furrow. As spring had blossomed, so had those dreams of distance, long summer miles to hazy horizons. And along with the dreams was the desire to expunge the bitterness of pain and defeat, the physical and spiritual suffering which this tough sport had exacted as a first payment for my audacity. Well, I had paid my respects over the long months of training and now I had bought back my pride and won a degree of satisfaction and fulfilment, which I contentedly let lap about me. I had no immediate plans for any other epic runs, though there were a number of long walks I had in mind. I had established I could run a fair way at a continuous steady pace, but I did not particularly regard myself as an ultra-distance runner.

I ran contentedly through the rest of the summer and into autumn. Then one day as I ran along a muddy towpath I turned to my mate and said 'I think I'll have just one go at the Pennine Way record, but only one go because I don't really think I'm capable of it.' What a fateful decision, and what an abysmal lack of self-knowledge.

History of the Pennine Way Record

In 1969 when a friend told me that Ted Dance and Denis Weir had completed the Pennine Way in under five days I was staggered. Though I knew Ted and Denis from fell running, I wasn't a member of the Rucksack Club and knew nothing of its tradition of long continuous walks. (Ted still describes the achievement as 'only like doing five club walks one after another'.) The previous

*Ted Dance
(left) and Denis
Weir after their
definitive
Pennine Way
record in 1969.*

best time seems to have been some six and a half days by Arthur Puckrin. Denis
was obviously confident of bettering this as when Ted arrived home to enjoy a
long weekend he was told that Denis had arranged to start the Pennine Way
next morning. 'But', protested Ted, 'I've only got three days holiday'. 'That's all
right' replied Cath, 'Denis says that's enough!'

The idea of fast Pennine Way traverses began to catch on and in 1972 Alan
Heaton and Mick Meath of Clayton-le-Moors Harriers did just over four days.
Alan could undoubtedly have gone faster and had he been solo and fully
supported the three-day issue might have been settled there and then. However,
the big guns were assembling and in 1974 Joss Naylor stepped down from Mount
Olympus (well, the Wasdale Fells anyway) and made an attempt that seems to
have depended on gaining sufficient momentum to carry him through the three
day 'barrier' as it had now become. Joss covered 108 miles (175 km) in a
remarkable and, to my mind, ill-advised, 18 hours. Thereafter he proceeded to
become painfully stiff and shortly before Kinder, with his goal almost within
grasp, he was forced to stop and rest. He slashed the record but was still some
three and a half hours adrift of the three-day target. (At the time one pundit
proclaimed that this record would not be bettered in Joss's lifetime!)

In 1975 the modest and unassuming Pete Dawes of Kendal AC made an
attempt that excites my admiration more than most. He seems to have taken a
rather dim view of the prominence given to Joss's effort and made a heart-

warming bid to get back to the light-hearted amateurism of the Dance/Weir approach. Ace ultra-distance man Boyd Millen tells of turning up in Kirk Yetholm and wondering where all the support was gathered. Pete's wife informed him that she would cover the road crossings and he was the only runner for the first 90 miles (145 km). After accompanying Pete for the 30 mile (50 km) Cheviot stretch Boyd stood down for a rest but was so stricken with remorse as the diminutive and lonely figure disappeared into the Byrness forests that he accompanied him thereafter. Pete's plan was simple: go steady for 20 or so miles (32 km), pick up and go strongly for the next 40 to 50 (65 to 80 km) then hang on for the last 20 to 30 (32 to 50 km), have a few hours sleep then repeat the process – twice. Despite eating problems and associated stomach disorders (always a problem), Pete succeeded in smashing Joss's record (his declared priority) and coming close to three days (3 days 1 hour 48 minutes).

With three days now an enticing target, Brian Harney and Roger Baumeister attempted the record in 1977. Sadly, Roger had to retire at 140 miles (224 km) with a stress fracture, while Brian gave up at 90 miles (145 km), his feet like raw steaks. As ultra-distance fell runners both these men were of the highest calibre – Roger went on to complete a unique double traverse of the Bob Graham round, 140 miles (224 km) and around 54,000 ft (16,200 m) of climbing inside 48 hours. Two years later I heard that Brian, as he had vowed, was going to have another go at the elusive three-day barrier. Like most of the other attempts, Brian elected to go from north to south but unlike them, he intended only to take sleep when forced to. He set himself a very tough schedule for the first day and a half, hoping to hang on later. Brian raced through the first 113 miles (180 km) in 24 hours taking no sleep. He continued to press on and passed the half-way point in under 30 hours. At 163 miles (260 km) and starting his second night I believe he made a crucial error. His support team had a bed ready for him at Hawes, but feeling good he decided to keep going at least to Horton 15 miles (24 km) away. After reaching high ground he became very weak and his support got him into a sleeping bag where he slept for 45 minutes. After this Brian was still very slow to Horton and took another hour's sleep there. He had only a further 30 minutes sleep in the remaining 92 miles (148 km) but as he'd started at 9.00 a.m. he had to suffer Black Hill and Bleaklow in the dark, difficult conditions in which to recoup time. He came mighty close to the three days however, just 42 minutes short, taking over an hour off Pete Dawe's record. He professed himself well pleased and not particularly disappointed to have missed the 'barrier'. His statistics were very impressive, not to say daunting: 113 miles (180 km) on day one; 81 miles (130 km) day two and 74 (118) plus two (three) to finish off. He had two and a half hours sleep, which was included in his total stopping time (for eating, changing, etc.) of around six hours.

Having myself just experienced the reality of runs extending through day and night I was astounded. I did not feel my own effort was degraded. It had been a tough run over more continuously rough ground than the Pennine Way. And, just as important, it had been my best effort. I do not think you should feel ashamed of your best effort and I did not, but I was certainly impressed by Brian's performance!

The Training

When I announced that I would have just one crack at the Pennine Way record I meant just that. I had thought through the concept and what it entailed quite thoroughly and my decision was based on a sound rationale. I found the concept of a three day Pennine Way an intensely challenging one. I knew I would love to be able to meet this challenge and the possibility of being the first ever person to complete the route within three days was a powerful additional incentive. There was little doubt in my mind that such an achievement would represent for me the pinnacle in my life of running. As far as my running was concerned, I had never before felt any need to express any ultimate, but now an ultimate beckoned with an astonishingly imperative finger. At the same time, no matter how imperatively the finger might beckon, it was unlikely to be able to propel me along 270 miles (435 km) of hilly terrain. It was not that I ever doubted I should have the necessary strength of purpose. Unfortunately, sheer determination cannot replace ability.

Did I have the ability? I knew I had the motivation to undertake a long and rigorous training regime, but I had no conviction that I was actually capable of succeeding from any training base whatever. My feeling, on the whole, was that I had not the ability to achieve the record, but I owed it to myself to try. I set my limit at one attempt in order to not 'waste' more than one season in special effort and in order not to subjugate everything else to a hopeless dream for too long.

I must reflect here that it is little wonder that we have problems in communicating with others when we (by which I really mean I!) cannot communicate accurately with ourselves. I actually said to myself (and others) just *one* attempt at the Pennine Way record. What it transpired I really meant was, just one attempt which establishes to my satisfaction that I am never going to be capable of running the Pennine Way in under three days. This never happened and in that sense I stayed true (despite my seven unsuccessful attempts!) to my original promise. In that I was finally successful I suppose I might claim my judgement was vindicated, though of course you might well claim it was a triumph of bloody-mindedness over good sense. I shall not argue that point.

During the winter of 1979/80 I maintained a schedule which included some very demanding routes, mainly walking, but sufficiently strenuous to develop a deep endurance. The most ambitious of these walks was a winter Tan–Cat with John Richardson and Geoff Bell. The walk took place in severe winter conditions and occupied us for over 60 hours with little sleep. On a rather more lighthearted note, Geoff and I set out to improve on my Colne–Rowsley record. We only had one support point, at 30 miles (50 km), and after we had eaten and set off again I discovered I had left all maps and route cards with times and bearings in the support car. I assured Geoff I could find my way just using our one navigational aid, his compass, providing it did not get misty. This was the signal for an impenetrable mist to descend, and though I did my best, we were eventually forced to take a food break while I pondered our position. I was just about to suggest we go in a straight line in the general direction of our destination when we were surprised to hear the drone of a car in the middle of the desolate moor. Further investigation revealed we were about half a mile (0.8 km) from the main road and only about 200 yards (180 m) from our correct line.

Recovering from this mishap gave us heart and we set out to cross Bleaklow and the Derwent Edges to Moscar and the Snake road. Eventually, with my more intense training regime I began to do better than Geoff on the gentle but long, grinding ascents. However, on reaching the fields just before Rowsley, he suddenly flew past me at an amazing speed. Astonished, I raced after him and just succeeded in catching him As soon as I did, he collapsed like a punctured balloon, it had been a last defiant effort, but Rowsley was still one and a half miles (2.5 km) away. It was a weary but triumphant Geoff who tottered with me into Rowsley just four minutes outside our scheduled 16 hours. This time Ted was prompt in arriving and I was unable to initiate Geoff in the delights of The Peacock's horse-trough. Instead, we drove to The Monsal Head, where before a blazing fire we demonstrated the potent effects of real ale on the exhausted human body. Memory is hazy, but I think Geoff fell over and I fell asleep – or perhaps it was the other way round.

Having established a good solid mileage base during winter I now began to get down to serious training encouraged by a beautiful early spring. Throughout April I averaged between 120 and 140 miles (195 and 224 km) per week swinging from extreme fatigue to smooth effortless running – and back again. Hardly easing down I did my best marathon time, 2 hours 42 minutes, in the White Peak Marathon along the old mineral rail lines in Derbyshire. Early in May I started to extend the length of individual runs. In one period of nine days I ran and walked 250 miles (420 km), then, after only four days active rest, I entered the 60-mile (100 km) Fellsman Hike. After such high mileage this proved a tough event, particularly as it took place in very high temperatures. I got caught up in the competitive spirit and, despite the heat, found myself 'eye-balls out', as the saying goes. I was satisfied to finish in third place and felt I must be developing some endurance. In retrospect, I think this was when I peaked and should have started looking for a couple of easy weeks. After three days rest I did an 'easy' 35-mile (56 km) run on towpaths and was displeased to find I felt very fatigued. I followed this a couple of days later with a training weekend on the Pennine Way which, with the benefit of hindsight, gives an accurate estimate of my level of motivation and the extremes to which I allowed it to drive me in my efforts to attain even higher fitness levels.

I drove 200 miles (320 km) north to run the Roman Wall section of the Pennine Way. My old car was as subject to breakdowns as I was and I did not get to bed until nearly 1.00 a.m. However, I rose at 5.00 a.m. and during the day covered 58 miles (93 km). I started by feeling totally exhausted but began to pick up under the influence of the beautiful scenery. My slow pace meant I did not finish running until 9.00 p.m. and by the time I had eaten and changed I did not get to bed until 11.15. I was up, bleary-eyed, at 4.15 a.m. to drive further north to reconnoitre the next section. I covered 22 miles (35 km) in very hot conditions and returning to the car for lunch decided to run with as little spare gear as possible for the afternoon session. As I reached my turning point 14 miles (22 km) on it began to rain furiously. I cowered in a barn waiting for a break that never came. Eventually I set off back in vest and shorts, not only unprotected from the rain, but also too weary to manage more than a plod, which did little to keep me warm. When I reached my car I was in a wretched state; exhausted, cold and hungry. Relief at being able to sit in relative comfort and warmth obscured all other problems and I counted my hard won statistics, 108 miles (173 km) and nine and a half hours sleep in two days and two nights. I drove home, a box of food next to me, finally collapsing into bed at 2.00 a.m. I could not help reflecting that if I did achieve the record I could say I had earned it. I even began to wonder whether I deserved it. My conclusion was that this was a nonsensical and probably pernicious notion, which shows some sense.

After this tough weekend I scheduled an easy three weeks of gentle running. In retrospect I had, perhaps, ravaged my resources, both mental and physical. At any rate, I seemed unable to generate any feeling of concentrated calm. Instead, I simply became more and more nervous. Having experienced the crushing fatigue of training for the record I was anxious of what the real thing might mean. But this was not my major fear. What I was frightened of most of all was . . . failure.

The First Attempts

I stepped out of the car at Edale and cowered into the shelter afforded by the Nag's Head. It was 3.00 a.m., and still dark. A powerful west wind flung sheets of rain across the sleeping village. Ted Dance shook my hand and without the least sign of irony wished me good luck. Before me lay storm lashed and soggy moors, precursors of the 270 hilly miles (435 km) I hoped to cross step by step. Where was the fire in the belly? Where was the unquenchable spirit of 'to strive and not to yield'? Where was the bloody demon even, he of the insatiable ego? All gone. Only the black empty moors and me a small speck on them, searching to find a little hope. At 3.30 a.m. on the Kinder Plateau where a midsummer dawn should have greeted me, the furious grip of the storm wrack was clamped across the land, a grim hand permitting neither hope nor light. I had no torch but I could just see the luminous dot on my compass. I rallied a little. These were my moors and if I knew where north lay I could find my way. Stumbling up and down the groughs I manufactured my line across the moor acknowledging recognisable features as they loomed up: Crowden Brook, Kinder Gates, Kinder Downfall. Old friends, old memories they were, but now I was alien, they had no part to play in this mad ambition.

Thank God Ted was going to meet me on the Snake Road before I crossed Bleaklow, my morale needed some attention. As I approached the car I was appalled to see it swaying in the wind, morale sank even lower. Inside the car the roar of the wind and the harsh tattoo of the rain made me feel even more dismal. I was not, however, anxious to get out. Ted drove to Glossop to pick up Geoff so after Bleaklow I had someone to run with. Taking it in turns they made the way a little more cheerful for me. Disregarding the energy I was burning I bent into the storm clouds. I was almost up to my scheduled times but this was misleading. The wind and rain continued unabated and the effort needed to drag myself through the bogs sometimes against the wind was enormous. I was pouring three days worth of energy into these first few hours. Unless the storm abated, and quickly, I was doomed. Already, by Widdop Reservoir at 50 miles (80 km), I had used up all my spare clothing. These were pre-Gore-Tex days and under a heavy cagoule I was as wet as if I had had no waterproof at all. The end came quite suddenly, I guess I had been preparing for it unconsciously since leaving Edale, nevertheless it took an unexpected form. I had been aware of a dull ache in the Achilles tendon since just after Bleaklow. On the way over from Widdop to Cowling it flared into a crippling pain. I knew injuries to the Achilles were not to be treated lightly. I limped painfully, but perhaps with some relief, into Cowling to announce my retirement. As Geoff and I entered the village a stricken looking Ted greeted us with the news that he had had a collision in Geoff's car. What a wretched and bitter conclusion to those recent dreams. I was exhausted, injured, demoralised and now I was the unwitting cause of my good friends suffering for nothing on my behalf. For nothing? No, 60 miserable miles (100 km) less than nothing. Even the bloody demon kept his mouth shut. I knew I could not do it.

After such an abysmal failure as I had just suffered it was necessary to rebuild morale as well as recover from the injury. The tendon quickly improved. As regards the rather more sensitive injury to my morale I had to assess how much was due to my weakness and how much to circumstances. It was obvious that the weather would sooner or later have drawn a curtain across my attempt anyway. There might have been people around who could have withstood such conditions and maintained schedule, I was not one of them.

The injury remained a mystery but I guessed it might have been psychosamatically induced. I had been psyched up to the point of being psyched out! Instead of focusing on positive aspects my mind had been occupied with negative thoughts – fear of failure. I had thought less about success than how dreadful a failure would be. It has taken me a number of years to evolve appropriate strategies to cope with the formidable pressures of ultra record attempts. These pressures arise from my tremendous drive to succeed in an activity where there are no cop-outs, you either break the record or you do not and failure is always the more likely outcome.

At the time of my failure, however, such coping strategies were all in the future. My immediate response was, characteristically, to emulate Don Quixote and fling myself at my windmill – with much the same results. Unlike the Don, I had a plan. In fact I have had several plans in my battle with the Pennine Way, most of them nicely unorthodox, too. Alas, the Pennine Way had the big battalions and it would not play by the rules. It just hauled up the big guns; storm, tempest, floods or, for a change, searing heat, and contemptuously flicked me off the battleground.

After a month licking my wounds and devising a plan I was ready to tackle the Pennine Way again. My plan was to start, not in the morning, but quite late in the evening. This was not an attempt to catch the Pennine Way slumbering, I should add. My rationale was based on two principles; first, an evening start would ensure that I would have at least one night when I was fresh and better able to cope with the difficulties that darkness brings; second, it brought the second night much closer. This was important because I had scheduled a short sleep stop on the second night. On my first attempt, a 3.00 a.m. start had placed the second night a massive 44 hours and about 170 miles (272 km) away. I had not been able to handle this psychologically, but a 9.00 p.m. start meant that after a short night I would only have to run through one day before I grasped that little island of rest. A period of 26 hours and about 110 miles (176 km) was something I was better able to cope with.

The week before the second attempt my spirits had been rising as a spell of perfect weather set in. Perfect for me means cool and dry with periods of sunshine to lighten the spirit. If I can also have a sky full of those billowing fair weather cumulus clouds sweeping like galleons before a summer breeze then I am transported.

The good weather lasted an hour. By Kinder Gates a light rain began to fall. On Featherbed Moss I mistimed a jump across a black, oozing grough. As both legs sank to the knee I toppled slowly but inexorably backwards into the ditch. With a gentle sigh I extricated myself and continued my solo way across the deserted moors. The rain, equally gentle but also insistent, wept through the moorland night. As a sparse dawn light brought a rank mist rolling over the boggy wastes, I became aware of two disturbing events: one was that the mist seeping over the moors was warm and sticky, settling suffocatingly on the flesh; the other was that my feet, particularly the heels, were feeling sore.

And so, off into a day which constitutes one of the most unpleasant running experiences of my life. The mist transmitted the heat of the invisible sun like a warm, wet blanket. The sweat lay on my skin like an oily film. Encouraged by the warmth and the total lack of air movement swarms of flies rose from the ground and formed a buzzing cloud around my head. And as I ran it felt as if progressive layers of skin were being stripped from my feet. Soon, I imagined, I would be running on the flesh alone. My mind harked back to the sight of Brian Harney's feet when he had quit the Pennine Way. They were red and raw and their texture was like the bark of a tree. It does not matter how tough you think you are, when the pain gets bad enough, you quit.

In the meantime, I kept going. Still running solo but supported by Geoff I passed through Cowling with mixed feelings and headed for the limestone country around Malham. I was more or less on schedule despite frequent stops for foot treatment. I hoped the day might freshen, but it did not. Instead, a light rain settled on the hilltops and below all was dead and still. I began to try harder after Malham and made a little time up over Fountains Fell and Penyghent. However, as soon as I hit the stony track leading to Horton my shoes felt as if they were full of broken glass and in my heart I accepted that I had had it.

At Horton I confronted a dilemma. Len, my friend from the early days, had driven out with Ted to support me on the night section. I could not face telling them I wanted to quit. In any case, I thought that for the sake of our old friendship I owed it to Len to let him stretch his legs on the 15-mile (24 km) section via Dodd Fell to Hawes. We set off in gathering gloom. At first, I found I could just tolerate the pain and so pressed on. This was a mistake. Once the green lane gave way to bouldery track, I was like a cat on hot bricks. The darkness ensured that I was unable to pick a tolerable course and then it began to rain stair-rods.

That handful of miles over to Hawes remains one of the blackest memories in my battle for the Pennine Way record. The agony in my feet confirmed I was finished. In turn this meant that I had lost my concentration and commitment. We went astray several times and, in addition, despite the rain I had to slump down for a 10-minute sleep. From Horton at 92 miles (148 km) to Hawes at 107 miles (171 km) I had scheduled a generous four hours, it took me over six hours on the clock, but there are things time cannot measure – my spirit wandered in a dark eternity. Where was the gentle, effortless running over the sweep and roll of the curling fells? This experience was enough to break my spirit. And it nearly did, but not quite.

The Battle for the Pennine Way

A few years ago I was invited by Denis Weir to give an after-dinner talk on the occasion of the jubilee of the athletic club Horwich RMI. 'What sort of thing shall I talk about, Denis?', I asked. 'Oh just talk about all the amusing things that must have happened to you in the course of your eight attempts on the Pennine Way record'. I thought carefully. 'Denis, there weren't any amusing events!' Given my somewhat manic sense of humour this was a disturbing revelation. With the exception of some rather black humour, like a support runner almost dying of exposure in a May blizzard on the Cheviots, it was nevertheless true.

I am always embarrassed at having to admit to so many attempts at the Pennine Way. It sounds as if I just bashed away at it until it gave in or I got lucky. It was not like that from my perspective. Each attempt was planned with careful attention to detail. My physical preparation during the winter and spring was thorough and always arduous. As the miles slipped by, road, muddy tow-path, boggy moor, snow-crisp fell, so my thoughts would be ever turning to that twisting path down the long Pennine spine. And each time I failed was a time of deep grief for me. It was as if some living cherished entity had just died. Silly perhaps, but I would limp home with my broken dream, nurse it to me for a while then lay it to rest – stillborn again.

There seemed only one way to assuage the sense of loss. That was to plan again, train harder, try harder and pray that next time I would be granted a slot in the weather and that little slice of good fortune so far denied me. I wrestled with the objective and subjective data. Subjectively, I knew from my successful Tan–Cat that I could run better than I ever had on the Pennine Way. Objectively, I could point to the vicious combination of rain, wind and heat which had accompanied all my attempts. What I have now come to realise is that the time spent in training for, planning and attempting the record constituted the most thorough of apprenticeships in ultra fell running. Of course one had to survive it in order to benefit, and I nearly did not.

One thing the Pennine Way was unable to do to me however, was to destroy my faith in myself as a runner. I did eventually get round to accepting that I might well never achieve the record, but I would not accept this until I had adequate grounds. In 1981, for instance, I had a further two attempts at the record. The first took place at the end of May and I 'peaked' my training three weeks earlier. Running and resting a couple of days at a time I had clocked the equivalent of a marathon a day for 14 days, 360 miles (575 km) in a fortnight. It did not make a jot of difference. I practically swam as far as Hawes. Fortunately, I had fallen over a sunken notice board on Black Hill and this caused a sufficiently incapacitating injury for me to retire, if not gracefully, at least justifiably. My next attempt, however, was a very significant one and marked a turning point.

In addition to starting at evening time I now had an additional 'plan'. This was to take a long, 40 to 60 minutes, rest every six or seven hours. The idea was to break into the fatigue spiral by resting and stoking up on food and drink. The snag was that I had to run faster between those rest periods. The attempt took place at the end of August and I realised that with nearly nine hours darkness I would be under pressure to run faster during the daylight hours. Prior to Brian Harney, most runners had taken a break at night, but both my style of running and the keen record demanded running through most of the night. My poor luck

Mike, on the Pennine Way, standing in the River Aire near Malham trying to cool his feet.

continued, the night hours were of an impenetrable blackness making navigation very tricky. To compensate, however, the days were roastingly hot. The heat bouncing up from the ground began once more to play havoc with my feet, and the sticky heat made me feel as if I was running through treacle. Climbing up by Malham Cove I could hear and feel the blood pounding in my head. I wondered if I was acting sensibly, decided I was not and carried on.

I eventually reached my rest point at Hawes after 28½ hours, 108 miles (173 km) three hours down on schedule. My support insisted I had a proper rest and I was too weak to argue. After three hours I was roused and then John Richardson broke one of the cardinal rules of the game. Being now some five hours adrift of my schedule I was ready to quit, both to stop wasting my support's time and to put an end to my suffering. The decision to quit is by strong tradition the sole prerogative of the gladiator. In a kindly but firm voice John said that he and Ted had discussed my plight and noted that Hawes had become something of a sticking point for me. They therefore suggested I go as far as I could during that day and retire at night-time. They also stated that they were willing to support me even though they realised I would not complete the route.

The ensuing day was fiercely hot. I trundled on in a daze, my mind fixed on Dufton at 162 miles (260 km). I tried not to attend to the crowds of sunbathers along the Tees, licking melting ice-creams or sipping beer – not too difficult since I was nearly blinded by sweat.

It was as Don Talbot and I left the Tees behind and climbed towards High Cup Nick in the early evening that the miracle occurred. A deliciously cool breeze sprang up and almost immediately the layers of fatigue sloughed off. Like a snake slipping out of its old skin or a phoenix rising from the embers of my burnt feet I suddenly discovered myself running effortlessly – even up the inclines. It was ridiculous. I felt fresher and more full of energy than at any time during the previous 160 miles (256 km). Yet this energy was unfortunately unable to either regain my lost time or repair my damaged feet and, as agreed with John and Ted, I retired at Dufton. However, from that moment on I *knew*, rather than just hoped, that I could break the Pennine Way record.

This knowledge was confirmed in a despairing sort of way on my attempt the following summer. I was probably running better than at any time previously, slicing chunks off my scheduled leg times almost effortlessly it seemed. But the conditions were again too hot for my feet. I noted signs of deterioration almost with disbelief as early as 50 miles (80 km). By 70 miles (115 km) they had become extremely painful, but I was running so well I could not bear to think of retiring. I tried Vaseline, chiropodist's felt, moleskin, even stuck needles in to try to find blisters. But nothing worked. I endured the pain for a further 100 miles (160 km), then, when I could not endure the extra pressure of moving from walking to running, I gave up. With the record beckoning and my reserves quite untapped I had to quit. For the first time I shed tears, tears of despair, nothing was worth this frustration and heartbreak.

Now, also for the first time, I came to terms with not being able to achieve the Pennine Way record. I knew in my heart I was capable of covering the Pennine Way in under three days and this was a tiny consolation. But it now seemed unlikely my feet would last out long enough for me to actually do so. I made my peace with myself. There must be dreams we have and always cherish, which, despite our best efforts, we will never achieve. I could not see the point of even making another attempt. The pain and the grief, to say nothing of the vast calls on friendship, were such a heavy burden to be set against the chances of success. Such chances, always slim, were now apparently non-existent unless I could find a solution to my foot problems.

Still in the grip of despair I announced that I would not attempt the Pennine Way again. My friends smiled and shook their heads. I was adamant however, it was pointless. There now arose a somewhat paradoxical situation. My friends all thought I would go on attempting the Pennine Way, but I suspect they did not think I could succeed. Whereas I *knew* I could succeed, but believed I would make no more attempts. The resolution of this paradox came about as the result of three interesting factors: John Richardson stating an intention to have a go at the record himself; the discovery of Spenco Second-Skin as a foot treatment; and, later in the same year, a record Colne–Rowsley run.

Colne–Rowsley

Until Ted Courtenay evolved his Tan Hill to Cat and Fiddle walk in 1953, the Colne–Rowsley had been the Rucksack Club's longest walk at around 70 miles (115 km). Since its inception in 1926 it had gained a distinguished reputation as one of the Club's test pieces. The Club has a marvellous record of initiating long, arduous walks of great character. It has also been gifted with members possessing the literary ability to write entertaining accounts of them. I had steeped myself in the history of these walks and often, as I carried on the Club tradition of 'bog-trotting', I could sense the ghosts of those hardy men travelling at my shoulder, their indefatigable but wry humorous spirits sustaining my own. For instance, each time I pass by Marsden village, I recall Frank Kiernan's tale of arriving there in the early hours on his first Colne–Rowsley in 1936. After a large meal in Blake Lea Farm he sat dozing before the fire, praying his companion might have also succumbed to the weakness of the flesh. Alas, with a sigh his friend arose. They stumbled footsore and weary out onto Marsden's cobbled streets with Phil Brockbank's brisk words of advice echoing in Frank's ears 'It is essential to arrive at Marsden in such a condition that after a meal and a rest one feels perfectly fresh.' After sitting in a grough on Black Hill most of the night when their torches failed, they eventually completed the walk. They were exhausted, footsore, had been lost several times and chased over private moors by belligerent game-keepers. Nevertheless, Frank's sense of triumph over adversity comes rollicking down the years.

Like so many other walks evolved in the days of few cars but excellent rail links, the walk starts and finishes at a rail terminal. The one at Colne still survives, but Beeching's axe put paid to the other. It is also a matter of regret that the old cart tracks winding up onto the moors out of the Colne valley have been metalled, but if you are handy with a map, alternative footpaths may be found. Should you attempt this walk, and very few except Rucksackers do, you should aim to do it in one continuous go, or with just a brief pause to allow a couple of night hours to slip by. You should also choose a dry period. This is very much a moorland walk and after 50 miles (80 km) of oozing bog you may well be in no state to enjoy the last easy and picturesque miles. After leaving Colne you will have chance for second thoughts, because beyond the first set of moors (Black Hameldon) the necessity of crossing the Calder Valley will bring you into Todmorden. A great place is 'Yon Tod' and a brew and a bag of chips will set you up for the steady climb back up onto the moors. You should remember that unless you make the traditional detour into Marsden you will have little chance for further indulgence as the route commits itself to high lines from here onwards.

However, the moors are not so empty these days. For 20 miles (32 km) along Blackstone Edge, Windy Hill, Standedge, your route is shared by the more recent Pennine Way. The thought that the sometimes cheerful souls who greet you have 200 miles (320 km) further to travel than you may strengthen your resolve. If you are wise, you will turn aside down the old packhorse track to Marsden, for not only is it a homely village with welcoming pubs, it allows you to neatly avoid Black and White Moss. If you have a sadistic streak you may like to watch the antics of those with large packs trying to cross this vile piece of ground, but do not forget, it will be your turn soon . . .

The other great advantage in visiting Marsden is that you may then utilise the Wessenden valley to approach Black Hill. Furthermore, the summit of this soggy lump my be turned on its left (east) flank as you are now heading for Holme Moss and the lonely guts of the walk. Your route will take you past the transmitter mast near the summit of the Holmfirth road. Should you pass by on a windy, mist-shrouded day, or better still, at night, I defy you not to feel a tug of apprehension as the wind moans sadly through the mast's vaulting cables and invisible superstructure. Maybe it is only sound effects, but when all you see is dank mist wreathing to the murmurings and sighings all around and more particularly high above you, then, perhaps, like me you will hurry past.

Across the Holmfirth road, after a brief battle with the rather token resistance of a few minor bogs and peat hags you will win the relative ease of a winding path-cum-sheeptrod. Following an apparently erratic course this path strengthens its resolution and gains you access to the Swetland and Britland Edges with surprising efficiency. In fact, when I forgot my map and route card on the record attempt I made with Geoff, I discovered that there is only one overall bearing needed. Following this bearing using 'reck'o'th'ee' (reckon of the eye) will bring you just where you need to be. (I will not spoil your fun by disclosing this bearing!) Where you want to be is coming off the moors near the head of the Longdendale Valley road, Saltersbrook.

You are now, so to speak, at the backside of Bleaklow. Your task is to gain the Derwent Watershed line. To do this it is best to first visit the source of the River Etherow. This is not essential but it is a rather charming spot on an otherwise dreary section of moor. After imbibing of its waters (a very unsafe practice a dozen miles further on) a steady climb through foot-tripping heather will bring you to the broad moorland area whose only immediate feature is the faint track of the Watershed route, plus perhaps a few stakes. This is a good place to check your compass, and essential to do so in mist. In some ways this is the best part of the walk. It feels lonely and remote, and it is. The 'path', a fairly recent product of the High Peak Marathon, comes and goes and your reck'o'th'ee will be as much needed as your compass. Eventually, probably just as you are losing patience with the rough tussocky going, a boggy ascent leads you onto Outer Edge. At last a definite point which offers an unbeatable moorland prospect – at least on a good day.

The respite is brief. There follows rough going over to Margery Hill and as you make your way to Abbey Brook the path disappears entirely. You can take the easy option of descending to the Derwent valley and following the reservoir track. This is charming at first, but the flat going quickly becomes incredibly monotonous. I prefer to follow the trods to the west side of Margery Hill which keep the fine valley prospect in view and then enter the shallow valley of the Abbey Brook itself. The going is tricky but your mind is occupied in picking a line, hopping over tributaries or jumping across the stream.

At a sharp elbow in the valley the brook tires of the moor and goes rushing steeply down the hillside only to be swallowed by the Derwent Reservoir. Do not be tempted to follow the short but admittedly impressive clough carved by the brook but continue on your line. After just another couple of tough miles you will be rewarded by gaining Back Tor, one of the striking, elemental gritstone outcrops hereabouts. For me, Back Tor marks the true beginning of the Derwent Edges. From here on, you are very aware that your route lies along an escarpment edge. Notwithstanding a few obligatory bogs, there are now definite paths to carry you to your journey's end. However, before you gain the eastern edges proper you must follow the Derwent Edge to its end, swinging off to the east and crossing the Snake road below Moscar Edge. Since crossing the Longdendale road at Saltersbrook you will have covered 14 miles (23 km), it will seem longer.

But now you gain your reward, a dozen or more miles of superb gritstone edges redolent with a hundred years of climbing and walking history. Ignore Aunt Florrie and Uncle Jack out walking their dog. Forget the chrysalids harnessed to their hang-gliders. They are users of the moorland edges, and good luck to them. But after nearly 60 miles (100 km) of treading the peaty ground, breathing the air of the moors, enduring the mist, the night, the winds of the moors, you have stitched yourself into the fabric of the moors, you *are* the moors.

So tread firmly but go with awareness of the historic ground which you tread. Here is one of the cradles of northern climbing and walking. Mighty men have sported here, strode the edges, clasped the tough and rasping gritstone. Peer down Right and Left Unconquerable as you move onto Stanage; imagine Brown and Whillans, cloth caps and baggy pants, unsurpassed ability. The history makers are still here. As you move across onto Froggatt Edge, that lean figure emerging like a liquid spider from below a repulsive overhang could be Ron Fawcett, maybe completing another 100 Extremes within the span of a single day. Look into the eyes of the climbers sauntering back off the crags at the end of the day. There are those who will never belong, but in some you will get the flicker of recognition of a kindred spirit. Do not despise the Lycra-clad dandies, today's brilliant butterflies who may become tomorrow's Himalayan heroes. Should you be here in the dusk of early evening, with the awareness of the history of these places and with the weariness of the miles blurring the edges of reality you may well hear the calls and cries of long departed climbers. Hemp ropes, Norfolk jackets and the ethic that the leader never falls, for there were no runners in those days. I like to think that when everyone has left, the spirits of departed hill men return to the places they have loved and there sport again. Surely it cannot be that the spirits of those such as Stanley Jeffcoat, that affable giant and archetypal rucksacker who never came back from Flanders, do not return here to regain the peace of the moors, the sport of the crag and the love and laughter of long-ago friends? So tread firmly but with compassion and understanding, you may be treading on hallowed ground.

Although the Edges continue on, dwindling slowly as they follow the Derwent towards its rendezvous with the Trent, the route you follow leaves the Edges rather more swiftly than it gained them. An abrupt right turn beyond Baslow Edge brings you into Baslow itself. Nice houses, but not a place to linger, I think, unless you imitate Geoff and Eric. Towards the end of a hard 90-mile (145 km) moorland circuit and against my stern advice they gobbled down a large ice-cream apiece. Five minutes later Eric parted company with his in the local convenience (I must confess I had a little snigger). Leaving such doubtful pleasures behind, your way now leads across Chatsworth Park, ancient home of the Duke of Devonshire. It stands on your left, palatial or monstrous, impressive or ostentatious, depending on your view. It reminds me of the carcass of a dinosaur being picked over by hordes of day trippers. Perhaps I am unkind, but my eyes did so recently behold a greater glory. If you are tired, the open expanse of the estate will weary you, so follow close by the river. This is the river above whose gathering ground at Swains Greave you strode nearly 30 miles (50 km) ago. Then it was young and active, now it is broad and content, sliding past green banks and the well-tended meadowland. After a weir injects a little life into it you and the river leave Chatsworth, but before doing so look for the spring issuing from the stone wall on your right. In defiance of any drought these clear sparkling waters flood generous and cool into a small stone trough. Drink deeply, if these waters were good enough for the Duke's thoroughbreds, they will do wonders for you! Now Rowsley lies only a couple of miles away. When you get there visit the old (now dry) fountain outside The Peacock. If you are as weary as I was on my first Colne–Rowsley, settle down in the old trough, you will find it wonderfully comfortable. You could try The Peacock, of course, but you had better change your boots first! (It is a bit posh.)

A Record Run

As I mentioned earlier, I had done the Colne–Rowsley twice, one time at the end of summer by myself and the other time in semi-winter conditions with Geoff. Good do's they were, too. I thought it was a route that invited a fast traverse, nor too long, not too hilly, many sweeping vistas and an inviting finish. After our 16-hour traverse I said to Geoff and Ted 'I bet a good man, going well, in the right conditions, could get close to 12½ hours.' 'Pooh, pooh', they said (or words to that effect). Then, at the end of the dry summer of 1981, Denis Weir gave me a ring. Now Denis is a good man, very good. Formerly a top class fell runner, latterly a redoubtable performer at any distance from five (eight) to 100 miles (160 km), he had recently done nearly 130 miles (210 km) in 24 hours in a track race. And the conditions *were* good, in fact the moors were in part closed due to fire risk. Anyway as Denis chirpily explained, he had just done the Colne–Rowsley in 12 hours 35 minutes. I immediately felt vindicated, and perhaps just a little piqued. Well, 12½ hours was too fast for me, so I waved that ambition goodbye.

The following year I spent the two months after my despairing exit from the Pennine Way getting back into some steady fell walking and a little climbing. Then, for no good reason, at the end of July I felt I wanted to have a go at Denis's Colne–Rowsley record. I had a couple of weeks trying to get used to steady running again but my log-book reveals very lack-lustre performances. I decided to take a couple of days complete rest and trust to the superb condition I had been in for the Pennine Way attempt. For such a relatively short course as the Colne–Rowsley it is best to be in sharp condition, I was not, but somehow I really wanted to do this run, and do it well.

Sticking with his belief that 12½ hours was too fast to complete the Colne–Rowsley Geoff decided he would support me at road crossings rather than run with me. I left Colne railway station at 8.00 a.m. on a fine, sunny day with a cool wind holding temperatures safely in check. I entered immediately into a real cut and thrust battle with my schedule. Not being optimistic about bettering Denis's time my schedule gave only a 10-minute improvement on his record. I found I was coming into each support point a couple of minutes up but by the time I had had a drink I had lost them again. Although I only took a total of eight stops at an average of 3.5 minutes per stop, I could not seem to break through my schedule to gain some time in hand. Eventually, on the section over to Standedge I lost patience and throwing caution to the winds bought myself a 10-minute 'cushion.' Not only that, but when I had dug down I could feel there were reserves in hand.

This became the pattern of the day, whenever I ran as I felt I should, I maintained schedule. Whenever I wanted to gain a few precious minutes, I had to dip into those reserves. The reserves were there all right, but they had to be prised out of aching muscles and straining lungs. Then after Black and White Moss (mercifully dry) I found I had overestimated the severity of the rough leg over Black Hill to Holme Moss. Instead of 55 minutes it took just 43, another crop of minutes in the bag, and now I 'only' had to hang on for another 37 miles (60 km) and I would have the record. ('Hmm', I thought, 'that's more than half the distance still left!')

In my haste I lost the trods over the Britland Edges and went galumphing over the tussocks. Little time lost and feeling strong I homed in on Saltersbrook where Geoff was waiting to hand me over to Eric Mitchell for the rest of the journey. Eric had also brought a running friend, Pat Grundy. I did not particularly need company or a pacer but I did want someone to carry some water for me over this long, dry crux of the route. The watershed section over Outer Edge, Margery Hill, Back Tor and the Derwent Edges to Moscar is a rough and unbroken 14 miles (23 km). If I had miscalculated my schedule or if I had drained too many of my reserves then my ambitions would be in tatters by the time I had reached Moscar and the Snake road.

In fact, with the moors dry underfoot this was a lovely section to run. I soon finished the water, but it enabled me to reach the first good stream just above Cut-Throat Bridge. I sustained my effort across the Derwent Edges and down to the Snake road and cut five minutes off my scheduled time, but as I jogged woodenly up the road I felt shattered. I collapsed onto Eric's deck-chair and told him, very unhelpfully, that I did not know what I wanted. Wise and experienced, Eric thrust forward a bottle containing Complan, a composite 'complete' food in liquid form designed for invalids(!). 'Here', quoth Eric, 'double strength.' 'But, Eric, I can't manage that.' 'Gerrit down!', growled Eric. I gorrit down, all of it. It was great. I lurched athletically out of the deck-chair. 'See you at Fox House, Eric.' With a little smile Eric folded his deck-chair.

I was now in something of a dilemma. Not for the first time I found myself a victim of my ambition. With just 17 miles (27 km) remaining I had only to stick to my schedule to be a handsome 20 minutes inside the record. How nice to just cruise those last few miles, I thought. No good! An insistent voice was whispering 'Wimp, you're copping out' and 'You might be able to do 12 hours if you try.' I had been wondering when that bloody demon would stick his head up. In vain I pointed out that even my schedule times were optimistic. Nothing would satisfy him but I should continue to sweat blood. Tentatively, I tried an uphill jog, excruciating, but possible!

Chasing the minutes past the departing Stanage climbers; slowly up and stiff-legged down Carl Wark and Higger Tor, Stone Age hill forts; silly visions of woad-spattered figures defying the legions, did they too dodge among these boulders? A two-minute drink stop at Fox House and off with a lad called Alex, out for his trot along the Edges and interested in what I am doing. What he does not realise is my brain is scrambled and I have the greatest difficulty forming coherent sentences. My pride will not allow me to admit this, however, nor will it permit me to tell him he is running too bloody fast. Hey I have run 60 miles (100 km), slow down you bugger! No, just gasp nonchalantly along and try not to collapse at his feet. Thank God! He has disappeared over to Birchens and I can go at my own pace down to Baslow. Amazing! I have taken 10 minutes off the scheduled time for that leg – well done Alex!

Now only the flat meadows of Chatsworth Park before the run in to Rowsley. Pat is joining me for these last four miles (6 km) and I am glad because over the broad meadows one seems to be hardly moving. A chat will help the miles pass more quickly. The trouble is, Pat seems to think it appropriate to hold a conversation from five yards ahead of me. No sooner do I get to his shoulder than he is off again. Does the silly sod not realise the inherently difficult nature of carrying on an intelligent conversation across a five-yard gap when you are at the end of 70 miles (115 km) of eyeball-popping effort and your legs are like a pair of bent Woodbines? Obviously not. If only I can find the strength I will screw his wotsits off on the final run-in along the lane. Aha, got him! He thought he could stop when we reached the A6, he does not realise my penchant for The Peacock's horse-trough another 200 yards (180 m) on. What a finish! Zoom up in a lather of sweat and peer at my watch. Wow! Eleven hours, 44 minutes, 30 seconds, perhaps the demon got it right for once. 'Pat, there is something I need to say about accompanying a tired runner.' Pat grins 'It was Eric's idea. He said to keep just in front of you and never let you quite catch up.' Well, the crafty old bugger. But perhaps Eric got it right too. Now, where is Denis's phone number? I spent the drive home practising a modest nonchalance . . . 'Just had a spin down the old Colne–Rowsley. Lovely conditions, managed to pip your record, yes . . . a little under 12 hours, actually.' I picked up the telephone. Oh, sod it. 'Denis, I've had a great run. I don't know how, but I've done the Colne–Rowsley in under 12 hours!'

Pennine Way 1983: Final Tribulations

Some time after my frustrating defeats in 1982 John Richardson rather surprised me by announcing that as I had stated my intentions of retiring from this particular battle, he would have a go himself. At first I wondered whether he was serious, but John is not the sort of person who makes idle remarks. In many respects he shares the same attributes as Geoff, that is, a slow steady strength that seems to wax rather than wane with distance, a resistance to injury and enormous power uphill and over heavy ground. Naturally, I vowed my intention to assist John in every way possible. After all, few knew the route better than I and more than one aspirant has come to grief with faulty route-finding on night sections. Unfortunately, as I envisaged myself striving valiantly at John's side for mile after wearisome mile, the question of just how long I could run alongside occurred to me. In the twinkle of a demon's eye my concept of lengthy running support had changed to the concept of a two-man record attempt. My support I now envisaged as keeping John entertained with a stream of witticisms and possibly giving him a leg up over the stiles. In fact, had it been anyone other than John, with the possible exception of Geoff, I would never have entertained the thought of a two-man attempt. Two runners impose large extra burdens on the support crew. There is also the disparity in abilities. Quite a few attempts by pairs have under-achieved due to one member fading and the other being unwilling to press on and abandon his friend. However, John and I had shared many an epic walk and run in the most exiguous circumstances. I felt our close personal relationship would enhance our ability to meet the considerable psychological challenges of the undertaking. I also harboured the hope that my miserable luck with the weather would change with John as my talisman.

John was enamoured of the idea of 'running home', that is doing the Pennine Way north to south. We therefore drove to Coldstream on Thursday 27 May to enjoy the unaccustomed luxury of a bed and breakfast. It was a beautiful day, high fluffy clouds rolling round an otherwise blue sky, the most perfect of English spring days. As we strolled round the village on a mild and tranquil evening there was only one dark cloud anywhere. Invisible to everyone else, this cloud was floating gloomily above my head. In Albion nothing is more perfidious than the weather. The rest of the team chided me indulgently (and behind my back probably confided 'Poor sod, his nerve's gone!').

The next morning the sky was rather grey with a light drizzle that might stop . . . or might not. We set off on the undulating 10-mile (16 km) climb to Cheviot summit with Pat Grundy as our running support. The wind began to increase as we ascended and the drizzle made up its mind and became rain; heavy rain; then cold, heavy rain. Below the Schil we dived into the old railway cabin and crammed on all our spare gear. Stepping outside we observed with interest that the rain had stopped, it was now snowing; heavy and wet. Despite the wetness, the wind was sufficiently strong to plaster a layer of snow to our clothing.

At the corner of the border fence, in order to save Pat the worst excesses of the bogs around Cheviot summit, we advised him to follow the fence line while we visited the trig point. Going, at times, up to the thighs in icy water we 'collected' the summit and set off back to the fence and Pat. He had not gone far. Being unfamiliar with the route he had been concerned about getting off line without us. Consequently, when we caught him up he was rather chilly. Normally, we would all soon have warmed up, but despite going as hard as we could we were fighting a battle with possibly the worst conditions the British weather can impose, a wet blizzard, and we were losing the battle. At one stage I stepped into a bog which swallowed me up to the very vitals! Sinking into the ooze beneath the water I desperately grabbed a wobbly peat hag and dragged myself free of the sucking bog devils. For a time I was too shocked to continue the monologue of vile imprecations with which I had been warming myself. Of greater concern was the fact that Pat was having problems keeping up with us. Plucky man that he is, he kept on reassuring us he was OK and under the twin lash of schedule demands and the griping cold John and I pressed on.

Eventually the distance between us and Pat grew, so that for longer periods we lost sight of each other. The Cheviots are broad and featureless, Pat had never been over them before, he was cold, getting colder and slower. My mind flashed back to the runner who had died of exposure on Ingleborough during a Three Peaks race. After waiting for several minutes above the Roman Camps at Chew Green I told John he should press on while I went back to look for Pat. I did not have too far to go, he came slowly towards me still protesting he was OK, really! My hope now was that Dave Crutch, our support driver, had guessed our plight and had attempted to drive up the military road to below the Roman Camps. If he had he could look after Pat, but even if not, I told Pat he must follow the road back down to the valley and safety. Good old Dave had driven out. He had even walked half a mile from the road with flasks for us, but being unsure of our whereabouts and lashed by the storm had retired to the car again. Rather more far gone than I suspect he realised, Pat found Dave, who later unconsciously amused us with his account of the incident. Dave has a slight stammer and recalling the drama of the moment told us 'He got into the car and turned b'b'b'b'blue!!'

Tough and experienced, Pat made a swift recovery and was able to accompany us on further stretches. It was quite obvious, however, that unless the weather improved dramatically we might as well go home. Lower down, the snow ceased but the rain continued. In order to give it time to improve we decided not to run through the first night, but have a couple of hours sleep at Hadrian's Wall (70 miles/115 km). With John's usual, commendable efficiency he was stretched out in his sleeping bag, eyes peacefully closed within minutes. Unfortunately, this simply meant he had to endure my elbows, knees and feet as I performed my usual ritual of getting disorganised for sleep.

Next morning was better, but continuing wet. The support was having problems preparing nourishing food and we were getting by on large amounts of tea and biscuits. This was OK for me, but John has something of an aversion to tea administered ad lib. After a few hours the early morning quiet was disturbed by loud honkings as John was violently sick all over Wain Rigg. Ian Grant, accompanying us, was touchingly concerned at this performance. I had observed it many times before, notably during the High Peak Marathon races, and had a rather more callous response. Indeed, as I expected, John picked up very well after this episode.

The conditions continued to be abysmal. By now the ground was running with water, paths were like streams and the bogs were replete. At Alston (90 miles/145 km) we were informed that the forecast was for the bad weather to continue. We agreed it was senseless to carry on, but I suggested that we at least go over Cross Fell to obtain the scant satisfaction of completing 100 miles (160 km). This was not a soft undertaking. Water was pouring off the summit plateau in white frothing cascades and a biting wind out of the east mingled mist and rain. At Dufton there was no problem adhering to our decision to quit. For some reason, John has never expressed a further interest in running the Pennine Way.

I was reluctant to let the summer pass by without trying to cash in on the fitness so painfully acquired during the preceding winter and spring. I spent many happy and hard hours in the hills. It turned out to be a good summer after that unpropitious start and I became very hill-fit. Sense dictated that I should have a go at something with large amounts of up and down in it. I had long cherished an ambition to complete a continuous round of all the 2,500 ft (750 m) summits in the Lake District, something John, Geoff and Ted had achieved and which I had been promising to attempt with Don Talbot for years. Perhaps sense plays a relatively minor role in my life, for, instead of the Lakes 2,500 ft (750 m) summits, I flung myself back onto the Pennine Way.

The combined temptation of good conditions and what I imagined was my own level of preparation was too much. Furthermore, I had had a very generous offer of help from a friend and colleague, Inken Blunk. Already a lover of the hills, Inken had demonstrated a natural aptitude for endurance performance which I encouraged her to develop. I introduced her to tough club meets and after she had skipped her way through a few of these, I thought I noticed a few members blanching and muttering in their beards whenever she appeared. Inken had offered to do car support for me during the first night and most of the second day – the attempt was on.

Being holiday season, other support was a bit thin on the ground. However, for the first time, I had the help of my eldest son, Mark. When I first attempted the Pennine Way Mark was a spindly youth of 14, now, at 18, he was much more the part, a fine runner with natural endurance. As Mark could not drive, Eric had agreed to cover the first 50 miles (80 km) and Mark joined me on selected sections. At Hardraw my support would ring Ted to bring him out if the attempt was still on.

Conditions were very dry and I had problems with dust flurries in the stray winds. From the start I never went well. The heat and dust made conditions uncomfortable, but that was not the main problem. Perhaps there was something wrong with the body chemistry or perhaps my immediate preparation had been incorrect. The ground was so dry it was like running on concrete in places. Somehow, my legs would not seem to adapt and instead of settling into a comfortable rhythm they began to get stiffer and stiffer. We all have our strengths and weaknesses. While I never seem to lack for sheer strength, I have a tendency for stiffness and cramp. The further I went, the stiffer I got.

In contrast to the day, it was a balmy, sweet-scented night. Unfortunately, the slower pace did nothing to alleviate my stiffness and after any pause or walking section I found it difficult to start running again. The long section between Horton and Hawes was once more the place for unpleasant decision making. I deferred my decision until I began to descend Cam Fell. Here I observed that the stiffness had become so incapacitating I was barely able to overtake brisk walkers. I hobbled across the meadows to Hardraw and announced it was necessary to inform Ted he would not, after all, be required. Within an hour of stopping my knees became swollen and my legs locked solid. A deep depression entered my soul and a bitter sense of shame. The Pennine Way had at last given me a fair chance and I had completely failed, for the seventh time.

chapter four

THE WINNING OF THE PENNINE WAY

The wracking stiffness passed off within a couple of days, the bitterness burned on. I looked around for a scapegoat. What could I blame? I decided that it was either just one of those things, an off day perhaps; or I was not fit enough; or, though fit, had prepared wrongly. An 'off day' was possible but placed me in no position to remedy a future occurrence. I did not know what 'fit enough' was, but I was certainly hill fit. That left the last option. My log revealed plenty of good hill days, but the Pennine Way had been like concrete and I had done nothing on hard ground. That was it! With all my knowledge and experience I had prepared like a novice! The more I thought about it, the more disgusted I became with myself. It was not the hard ground that had stopped me, it was my failure to prepare for it.

After three days' rest I began to train with an anger and aggression I had never before experienced. I knew my body should be treated gently after just covering over 100 miles (160 km), but I had to expunge the feelings of humiliation and shame that followed my critique. For three weeks I lashed myself round my training routes, always pushing, always running at the 'hard limit'. After this time, inevitably, a great physical weariness began to engulf me. But by now, I had done penance for my sins. I had also reaffirmed my belief in myself, and I had made myself a promise that I would never quit my struggle for the Pennine Way until old age had blasted my vigour or arthritis had locked me into a wheelchair, and maybe not even then. At one and the same time I both avowed my implacable resolution never to quit trying, while I freely accepted I might still go to my grave with my dream unfulfilled.

I settled into a more sensible training pattern. I had begun to experience increasing stiffness in my knees. They had never been the same since I broke my leg playing basketball in 1973. Since then the thousands of miles in all kinds of weather conditions had encouraged the incursions of 'Old Arthur', as John, also a sufferer, terms arthritis. So I kept my road mileage to a maximum of 80 (130 km) per week but at weekends always had a long run or walk. I reserved one day, usually Saturday, for 'rest'. On this day I would take my younger children for a walk and my third son, Gerard, for a gentle run over the moors, introducing him to my favourite footpaths and haunts.

Despite my reservations about doing the Derwent Watersheds race every year,

*Following in
father's
footsteps. Mike
plus his
children on the
moors.*

49

the start of March again saw me alongside John, Geoff and Denis for my eleventh successive event. Now competing as 'veterans' we finished second overall and won the Veterans Prize, a magnificent sculpture by John of a scene from the event. My training was paying off, I had gone well and recovery was swift. Two weeks later I did the 'Haworth Hobble' with John. This is a 33-mile (53 km) event over the bleak Brontë moors around Haworth. The next day I ran the local 'Otter Half Marathon' in 1 hour 21 minutes, starting tired but getting better. My satisfaction was mitigated by my son Mark (aged 19) finishing over a minute ahead of me. After a small mental adjustment, however, I decided the moral victory was mine!

By the end of March I was ready to commence the 'long' hard stuff. In retrospect this was one of the most satisfying and enjoyable periods of training in my career. It started with an unexpected treat in the form of a snowy out-and-back circuit of the Welsh 3,000 ft (900 m) peaks. This was largely thanks to Inken who being brought up in Germany, barely knew the Welsh hills. I thought the 3,000s would be a fair introduction. I was not expecting the layers of both old and new snow plastering the higher ground. Wearing fell running shoes and carrying ice-axes we set off at first light on a fine frosty morning. The traverse of the snow-encrusted ridges connecting Snowdon with Crib-Goch provided an enormously entertaining challenge. Descending the steep 'Italian' (north) ridge of Crib-Goch I tied onto Inken with a rope – much to her disgust. Even without snow and ice, however, Crib-Goch is notoriously unforgiving to the misplaced step. I was ready to effect the classic technique of arresting someone falling off one side of a ridge by jumping off the opposite side. Thankfully the technique remained theoretical.

The glare of the sun on new snow over the Glyders was almost unbearable and I began to have thoughts about snow-blindness. I need not have worried, approaching the Ogwen valley over humpbacked Tryfan we could see streamers of cloud sailing across the previously immaculate blue. Over the Carneddau the light was failing, temperatures had risen and the snow was around our knees in places. I thought I began to detect the slightest flagging of Inken's pace at times, but I was not sure. On the return leg back over the Devil's Kitchen to our base in Llanberis it was not just Inken who was flagging! Some time around midnight we got back to the car. What a fabulous, tiring and wonderful day, and what a way to achieve your first traverse of the Welsh 3,000 ft (900 m) peaks.

I caught a cold after this which actually worked in my favour. Instead of going out on exhausting 50 mile (80 km) runs I had four relatively easy days of about 30 miles (50 km), just moving steadily. In the past I had driven myself as hard as possible and usually suffered some muscular problem or other. Now, the gentler approach provided a more stable base from which to stretch myself further. After a couple of days rest I commenced a pattern of two days covering around 45 to 50 miles (72 to 80 km) each, two days rest, then two days again of 45 to 50 miles. For once spring was kind, and my runs carried me into all parts of the White and Dark Peak in Derbyshire. As I ran I observed the return of the birds to the high moors and I saw the fresh new greens begin to swell from the lower valleys and dells and wash up and out onto the hills. I watched my native moors bend to new forms as the curving sun shaped and sculpted them on its journey across the sky. I rose to the pale spring mists and guided my sleepy first steps over the wet grass. A day of miles later the sun threw its glow above the quiet moors and I ran through dusk to home and rest.

These were truly days filled with love: of nature, of health and of life. As I ran I could feel the ebb and flow of my own life force. In the long, alone hours absorbing the immense but subtle power of burgeoning Nature I could sense the shared pulse. Again and again, as my body tired my spirit was sustained. When I finished this phase of my training I experienced a deep contentment. I was now physically and spiritually ready to undertake the most difficult part of my programme. A regime which I had attempted before but which I had never quite been able to accomplish.

I had long thought that it would be necessary to sustain consecutive days of around 60 miles (100 km) if I hoped to run the Pennine Way in under three days. For no particular reason it had become a symbol, signifying both sufficient fitness and adequate ability. To cover 60 miles (100 km) of hilly terrain in around 12 or 14 hours one must be 'fit', but, more importantly, the ability to repeat the run the next day requires that one has the resilience to absorb the miles without breaking down. My plan was to do two days of 60 miles (100 km), have a day's rest and then complete another two days of 60 miles (100 km). I intended to implement this along the Pennine Way, both to familiarise myself with every twist and turn and because specific training is best. Having rarely had success in involving my friends in joining my Pennine Way training I was delighted when Inken offered to drive a car so that instead of going out and back I could just keep going till my mileage was covered. Not only this, but she would meet me every 15 or 20 miles (24 or 32 km) so I could get a decent feed. Her 'reward' was that she would see large stretches of countryside that were totally new to her and could indeed mount an expedition of her own on my rest day.

It went perfectly. Well, to be honest, it was physically as knackering as I thought it would be! However, the first day was the hardest, after this I slotted into an economical if tiring rhythm. At the end of the fifth day when Inken and I had finished an out and back traverse of the Cheviots, I stood in a stream washing off and contemplating the best week's training I had ever had. I was tired, certainly, but I felt I could have gone on with that regime indefinitely. In that, I now believe, I was in error.

My training plan was not yet complete. I had the background now, but for a continuous 270 miles (435 km) traverse I felt I needed to complete an effort occupying a full 24 hours. Running all day is one thing, but running on into and through the night poses additional hardships. I had tried 100 mile (160 km) training circuits in the past and found motivation a problem. I needed something to 'go' at. I decided my Tan Hill–Cat and Fiddle record of 32 hours 20 minutes looked rather pedestrian now. A run of 120 miles (195 km) on hard but familiar moorland would do very well, I thought.

Now there was just one problem. I would need about three weeks recuperation after a hard 100 mile (160 km) run, so that fixed my proposed Tan–Cat for the weekend of 6/7 May at the latest. The problem was that I should then have had

*Mike setting off
from Tan Hill.*

only one week's rest since my 240 miles (385 km) in five days on the Pennine Way. Ordinarily, this was nowhere near adequate, but I remembered how relaxed I had felt at the end of training. I decided to go ahead with my plan.

The Tan–Cat strikes back

The Tan–Cat is a tough route. I had no right to treat it in so cavalier a fashion. But I was a different runner from he who had set out with such trepidation six years ago. I had now been over the 100 mile (160 km) mark at least a dozen times and twice over 150 miles (240 km). Perhaps it was the memory of those hard miles that gave me a very serious air as I set off from Tan Hill supported by John Beatty and Rob Ferguson.

Initially, I moved effortlessly and freely. Unfortunately, this is not usually a good sign. Perhaps, paradoxically, a sluggish start often indicates the gradual retrieval of those reserves of strength which only result from a good rest. Going over Great Whernside at only 30 miles (50 km) the tendons behind my knees began to feel stiff and sore. At Grassington with only 36 miles (58 km) completed I knew my legs were 'running on empty'. There was no fuel in them, they felt like wooden planks. All my running body/mind knew beyond doubt that my legs were finished, I had simply not had sufficient recovery time. But now a dilemma; I needed a long run before the Pennine Way, if I did not take this chance there would be no other. Yet the thought of another 80 miles (130 km) on these empty legs filled me with dismay. Eventually, I decided to 'come off' the pace a little, but keep going and treat it as an exercise in will-power. Well, it certainly became that. I could remember no other run when each stride seemed to call for a separate act of will.

Early breakfast in Todmorden. Rob Ferguson on support duty on the Tan–Cat.

The miles dragged by, each one occupying an eternity of time and space. Only John and Rob's wonderful cheer kept me clear of despair. I could now no longer run for myself, I had lost all contact with the route, but somehow I began to attach my spirit to theirs. I ran through them and for them. John ran 50 miles (80 km) with me and Rob 40 (64 km). Earlier, John Richardson had guided me over Great Whernside and his home ground around Cowling. Without these friends I would truly have been a lost soul travelling in desolation. This image was heightened rather horribly as we moved onto the moors beyond Todmorden. After a very dry spell the moors had ignited and we began to run through rolling banks of choking smoke. At first I held my breath, but the fires became too extensive and we staggered along, half-blind and half-suffocated, while flames licked around our feet. The fires died out by Black Hill and I could focus my full attention on finishing the route. There comes a time when your destination is only a couple of dozen miles away but if you are desperately tired this can be a terrible time. You can think of nothing other than finishing but there are hours still to go, and you are weak. So it was now.

At last, Combs Moss, my 'home' moor and the Cat and Fiddle in sight. A final indignity: I climbed painfully to the top of a shaky drystone wall, it was high and my legs were so painful and stiff I just could not get down the other side. 'John,' I croaked 'I'm stuck!' An amused but sympathetic smile lit his face, then he came back and gently lifted me down. At the last road crossing two of my sons, Gerard and Mark, were waiting to run in with me. After 24 hours of pain and effort it was, for me, an emotional moment. We ran the last few miles together, and as the Cat and Fiddle appeared around the corner I picked up my tired legs once more for that final flourish.

No tears of triumph this time, just total relief at finishing. A new record certainly, and at 29 hours 11 minutes over three hours better than the old one. John and Rob were delighted and for their sakes I tried to look pleased, but I was not, I had hoped for better. I kept my mouth shut, however, and made a mental note to renew the battle at some later date.

Thanks probably to my good condition the hammering I had just given myself resulted in no injuries, only an exquisite stiffness. However, once I had recovered the sleep loss I began to realise that the tremendous effort which my mind had wrung from my body was going to have to be paid for, and it was to be paid in a coin I was not used to expending. The week following the record I experienced a weariness which was not only physically crushing, but one which invaded my mind and, worst of all, my spirit. Perhaps for the first time ever, I felt spiritually weak and impoverished. I could find relief and comfort in nothing. Neither my music, books nor writing. I did not want the company of my friends and I could make no plans for the future. I waited with more despair than hope for the shadow to pass. Then, a week later, I ran round the park for the first time since the record. I felt like one emerging from a dark tunnel, the grass was soft and green, the sun was warm, somewhere a bird sang and at last my spirit stirred to the sound. I was going to run again. I was going to run through days and nights. I was going to run the Pennine Way, all of it.

The Pennine Way Record

The Nag's Head, Edale. Time: five minutes before 11.00 a.m. Weather: fine and sunny, a breeze and some cloud. Pulse: 90. Why must they play sentimental music as I wait for the radio time signal? Tears are for the finish, win or lose. I feel like an emotional time bomb. So many times have I stood at the bottom of this 270 mile (435 km) ladder, nerves twanging, stomach churning. So many hard miles, so many defeats, so much anguish. Please let me run well this time.

There goes the time signal. Touch the pub and go! Along the lane, down the steps, over the bridge, hell! Here's a family struggling across it. 'Excuse me, but I've only got three days to get to Kirk Yetholm.' No, keep quiet, you can afford five seconds. The meadows; run a bit, walk a bit. Now, at last, the symbolic 'Boundary of Open Country' sign. I turn to Inken who has elected to cover this first mile with me, give her a kiss, wave goodbye to her and Edale, and embrace the moors.

These early miles are awful. The animal instinct is screaming for me to hurry but the running brain, developed and honed by 30 years of running and racing, begins to exert an iron control. There will be no rash steps, no wasted effort. Each drop of energy will be carefully measured and skilfully applied. Now, start by monitoring the body. Don't want to feel terrific at first, best a bit sluggish, give the strength time to come through. Not bad, all systems feel OK. Careful, economical foot placement up rocky Grindsbrook. Ah! The plateau. How I love Kinder, its warm familiarity soothes my still jangling nerves. So clearly I remember my first ever run over these moors from Ian Watson's farm. Gosh! Twenty-six years ago. Leave reminiscing. Get back to pace judgement, strictly no uphill running – yet. Just inside the hour at Kinder Gates – good. Across Featherbed Moss, dry until the end where there are endless wet ditches. Steady, just step across, don't jump. Hell! I'm going to be late at the Snake road. I am too, all of five seconds. Calm down you fool!

Over Bleaklow I continued on alone. I wanted these early miles by myself so that I could deal with the turmoil I knew was inevitable at the start. I did not want anyone trying to 'take my mind off' this challenge of early nerves. It was my show, I had to impose control from the start. No one could get inside my mind and do it for me, nor would I have let them had it been possible. It was all my responsibility; the navigation, the night hours, when and what to eat, the speed of each step, the pain when it should come, for all these things I had to have full responsibility. But at the end, if this time there is to be an end, then the joy will be shared, I have the greatest need to share that. Keep the pain, share the joy. Someone close recently said that was wrong; is it? Perhaps it is not even possible.

After recent spring showers, Bleaklow was unexpectedly wearing a mantle of fresh greens. Almost incongruous it was, like a grouchy old curmudgeon in holiday attire. Hern Stones and Wain Stones slipped by like old friends and, soon, the magnificently cleaving Torside Clough opened beneath my feet. I could sense in my positive response to the moors, a spiritual well-being. Slowly I began to come to terms with my nerves.

At the road crossing I meet my support team. Inken and Mark saw me off at Edale and then picked up Ted Dance. Mark is to be my main running support all next day so for today Inken and Ted will share the running and driving between them. Now I've completed 14 miles (22 km) I feel ready to talk. Unfortunately for Inken, it's all about pace and schedule but I must get it out of my system. Gradually the conversation becomes more relaxed and interesting; so relaxed that I lose six minutes over Black Hill to Standedge. Never mind, here's Ted eager to stretch his legs and indulge in one of his favourite pastimes; contentious debate. On this occasion he exasperates me with a presentation of his case for runners attempting the Pennine Way relay record needing rules aimed at protecting them from their possible follies. I secretly wish someone would protect me from mine! However, Ted's company is never less than stimulating and I still regard him with affection as my friend and mentor.

Alternating two such good conversationalists as Ted and Inken helps these early jittery miles to slip by enjoyably, even, at times, almost unnoticed. The apprehension and anxiety provoked by an undertaking as serious as this does not dissipate immediately the running begins. With an event of this length, it may take up to 100 miles (160 km) before the body begins to reveal its secrets. Will the muscles renege on their careful preparation? Will the feet decide to opt out of the endeavour? Sitting at the back of my mind has been the ominous memory of that physically and spiritually barren week after my Tan–Cat record, that could well turn out to be the most Pyrrhic of victories. Have the three and a half weeks since then been sufficient to restore my usually buoyant energy? Too late to withdraw now. With all the battle plans drawn up and a whole group of friends primed to slot into special support roles over the next three days I am utterly committed. And to what am I committed? I am committed to covering the 270 miles (435 km) to Kirk Yetholm in three days or less. To that end I am dedicating all the strength and determination I possess. And if I should be heading for failure I shall only quit when that strength and determination has carried me as far as I can endure. When the strength begins to fail, the spirit will sustain me, if the spirit can endure no longer I will quit, but only this attempt. Until the fire in the belly is extinguished I shall not willingly hand on this particular torch to any other hand. Yes, it is as well I have friends to lighten the miles, the intensity of concentration can swing too easily into oppressive introspection.

With Ted, convoluted disputation. With Inken, the delight of revealing the many charming and often unexpectedly beautiful places along the Way. Bleak moorland predominates over the first 60 miles (100 km) of the route but every so often one dips into a softer valley or wooded dell. A scattering of late primroses or bluebells will catch the eye, their carefree charm enhanced by the stern, almost industrially grim, moors and by my own hard resolution. When I am through with this I will return and wander timelessly through these dells and sit and stare for ever across the stretching hills. But for now, share the unobtrusive beauty of my life-blood moors; the ever-surging spring of purest water that spills through the stone trough below sombre Stoodley Pike; neat cottages clinging in precarious Alpine fashion to the steep Calder Valley; massive stone footbridge over Colden Water in its miniature verdant clough; High Withens, austere embodiment of Brontë's genius, mute and gaunt, staring sightlessly over these 'Wuthering Heights'.

By now I had covered over 50 miles (80 km) in around 10 hours. Running into a spring twilight with Ted I started to mentally prepare for the coming night section. The moors were assuming the quiet of the night as, in the gathering gloom, Ted and I dropped off Ickornshaw Moor and into the village of Cowling. Here, I was very cheered and touched to discover that John Richardson and Dave Crutch had driven from home with most of their respective families to wish me luck. I experienced a great uplift of the spirit and much good natured badinage was exchanged. At this point Ted was to return home, while Inken and Mark retired for a rest. Although I had some support arranged for the whole route, it would not be present in force until Dufton at 160 miles (256 km). I had therefore elected to go through the first night alone, relying on John to drive round and meet me at two road points.

Taking up a small rucksack containing extra food and clothing I set off through the village, words of encouragement from my friends still sounding in my ears. How fortunate I am, a perfect May night. There are stars overhead, soft grass beneath my feet, the evocative scents of spring, hedgerow rustlings of small, wild things. I am a solitary traveller and my journey will be long but it has truly begun. My earlier nerves have changed to muted excitement and I am at peace under the night sky.

My scheduled night pace is little more than brisk walking. However, the slight stiffness after my stop at Cowling soon eased and I began to jog suitable stretches. John was due to meet me at Gargrave over three hours beyond Cowling. Gargrave formed an important point on my mental checklist. Reaching it would mean that I had lopped off the odd 70 miles (115 km) and could begin nibbling away at the remaining 200 miles (320 km). As I started the pleasant field pasture approach to Gargrave I realised I would arrive there 20 minutes ahead of my schedule. I guessed if John had gone home for a rest he may well have judged his margins rather finely. At the old bus shelter I was not too surprised to find no sign of him. I resisted the temptation to stretch out on the wooden bench to await his arrival. Instead, I visited the very conveniently placed convenience and scratched a cryptic message on the flagstones. I had no qualms about pressing on to Malham another seven miles away. The happy confidence I had in my support team translated in John's case, to complete trust.

On then towards the Aire valley, munching some marzipan. It is a pity I cannot see the wild flowers I know are here but the smells are fresh and the grass long and cool beneath my grateful feet. At 3.15 a.m. the wink of John's torch flickers through the light which precedes dawn and I flash mine in reply. It is rather too early to enjoy much breakfast but shortly before 4.00 a.m. Dave Crutch delivers Mark and we set off on what will be a long, long day. This day is the crux of the whole enterprise. Starting in Malham at 77 miles (123 km) it will end 85 miles (136 km) later in Dufton at about 1.30 a.m. Far enough now to experience real fatigue but too soon to even begin to think of finishing. I try to draw some comfort from that phrase of Churchill's, 'This is not the end, it is not even the beginning of the end. But it *is* the end of the beginning.' Strangely, it provides no comfort whatever! Furthermore I feel rather apprehensive about the next three sections over to Horton. I've had some very bad times on them in the past and early morning is my time of lowest running ebb.

Concentrating very hard and feeling anxious, I manage to carve a few minutes from my schedule over Fountains Fell. Approaching Penyghent therefore, I feel most aggrieved when John and Dave ask what they should get ready for me. I tell them rudely that having just screwed myself to gain those few minutes I'm not prepared to hang around waiting for them to get organised. After this little outburst I pressed on, feeling a touch embarrassed. I realised however, that John knew me too well to take much notice of my tantrum.

Penyghent is hard and steep but it is my experience that the uphill does no real damage. Frequently, the change of pace acts as a rest and can be a welcome break from running. For once I ran into Horton with my feet in fair shape and, perhaps because of this, in good heart. I was now ready for that substantial breakfast which John provided so efficiently I was away again with a two-minute saving (surprise, surprise!). The next leg is a long one; 16 miles (26 km) across the side of Dodd Fell and through Hawes to Hardraw. I'm pleased to have Mark for company again and at 7.30 a.m. 30 minutes up on my schedule, we set off on the three-hour leg.

Near Kidhow Gate and 22¼ hours after leaving Edale we pass the 100 mile (160 km) point. I mention this to Mark and am relieved he doesn't say 'Good show, only 170 (275 km) to go!' My own mind touches briefly on this daunting statistic but I quickly switch to a positive thought; I am going well and will be able to leave Hardraw at 108 miles (172 km) precisely on the 24 hour mark. This proved correct but as I came into Hardraw my feet began to feel sore. In the past this would have been very disturbing but over the previous 12 months I had experimented with the use of Spenco Second Skin. I had found that when applied to burning feet it immediately cooled and soothed them. I taped a strip of jelly-like material across the pad of flesh just behind the toes. It soon went squelchy as I ran, but, as expected, seemed to eliminate totally any heat producing friction. It is difficult to describe what a sense of confidence the discovery of this material had given me. If only I had come across it sooner!

With blobs of Spenco squashing up between my toes I started to ascend one of the 'big lumps' on the Pennine Way. Great Shunner Fell climbs gently but does so for several miles. Rising to a height of 2,340 ft (702 m), it took me to my highest point so far. Assisting the effects of the Spenco a less welcome ally appeared on the scene; misty drizzle. The summit of Great Shunner is a lonely place in these conditions and I hurried down to the little hamlet of Thwaite. Real Yorkshire Dales country this, my own, more featureless moors, are now well behind me. The path over to Keld clings to the side of Kisdon Fell and affords the most magnificent views down into Swaledale. I have come to appreciate this area as one of the most beautiful along the Way.

By now a very familiar spot is approaching, none other than Tan Hill, the highest pub in England. Although the Pennine Way route to Tan Hill is five miles longer than the Rucksack Club's Tan Hill–Cat and Fiddle route, I have covered the distance an hour and a half quicker than when I set my record three weeks ago. This is an indication of the generally easier going along the Pennine Way but I also encourage myself by accepting that it must also mean I am going quite well. The ground over to Tan Hill becomes increasingly wet. The drizzle is changing to heavy rain and as I duck into John's car outside the pub, a real downpour ensues. I feel very reluctant to leave this haven but after 10 minutes John decides it is not going to stop anyway and kicks me out, alone. However, he does add that I'm going well. These words of encouragement from my close friend are sufficient for me to tackle boggy Sleightholme in arc optimistic mood. The heavy downpour eases and, back again with Mark, I start to hope for better conditions. Some 20 minutes later we are getting steadily wetter and belatedly retreat inside our cagoules. As the rain falls, so also do my spirits, only our arrival at the attractive old farm of High Birk Hat affords a quickening of interest. This is the half-way point, 135 miles (216 km) and, at 30½ hours, right on schedule.

The half-way mark on any very long event can be a blade which cuts both ways. A thirsty man will interpret a half-full glass as half-empty and a very tired runner may view the prospect of repeating all his previous miles very negatively indeed. I find it much better to tell myself that I'm now heading for home; Churchill's 'beginning of the end' in fact. Apart from this being a sensible strategy to adopt, it is also a notion based on my experience of changes which take place in the processing of time and the perception of distance on a long run. At the beginning of an ultra run I am frequently so alert and nervous each minute passes like an hour. After a day and night of travelling however, the hours start to pass like minutes. My mental faculties seem to adjust to the slow swinging rhythm of the run itself. Hence my perception of a long run is that the second half is much shorter than the first.

While this phenomenon continues to be reinforced, it did not, at the time, prevent me from feeling increasingly despondent. The rain had a nasty, insistent quality and I had begun to feel very tired indeed. Concern with the weather and my own, apparently, deteriorating form gnawed away at my self-confidence. A few miles outside Middleton-in-Teesdale a car shot past on the road ahead, screeched to a halt and rapidly reversed in my direction. It was Geoff Bell and Don Talbot coming out to help. It was a tonic to see such old friends and campaigners but somehow I could not match their good spirits, my response was lack-lustre. I departed alone for Middleton, still grousing to myself. When I actually reached the appointed place I indulged in a really good moan; they had parked the car off route. I had to go all of 100 yards to reach it. Isn't this journey long enough?

At this juncture I spotted Will McLewin of Dark Peak Fell Runners. Will had most generously offered to support me through the coming night and into the next morning. In doing so he filled an otherwise large hole in my running support. John and Mark retired here after supporting me for over 80 miles (130 km), nearly 50 (80) of which Mark had covered with me. Don and Geoff were nursing old injuries so had it not been for Will I would have had to continue the second night alone. It therefore behoved me to put on a less cantankerous face. I had never met Will before. He was thus the only member of my support team I did not know well but one glance at the determined jaw and the holes in his running tights convinced me I was in the hands of a real professional.

All through this long day I have been encouraging myself to get to Middleton on time. Getting to Middleton on time means I can negotiate the slippery boulders of the Falcon Clints in daylight. This in turn should ensure I will reach Dufton on schedule. Being on schedule at Dufton will mean I can have a short sleep. Dufton is where all my friends will be gathered, waiting and resting. From Dufton, with batteries re-charged, we can look forward with real hope to covering the last 108 miles (172 km) in 30 hours. And now there are just 20 miles (32 km) separating me from Dufton; just 20 miles (32 km) to rest and friendship.

The apparently easy miles along the Tees are in reality quite demanding. As they are predominantly flat, much prolonged running is required. By now, Will and I are chatting like old friends. There is still a strong camaraderie among fell runners. Will is a fell runner-mountaineer of the old school; highly individualistic, even idiosyncratic, determined and resolute. Despite the floating mist and steady drizzle we are able to admire the impressive river scenery. As I cast an eye over the brown froth of High and Low Force I can't help wishing it was less impressive; Maize Beck will be difficult to cross in the dark. On aching legs the alternating sections of wooden footways and wet boulders around High Force are awkward. If your feet and mind get out of synchronisation here you could snap your leg like the proverbial carrot!

At Langdon Beck we have a last support point before the 12 miles (19 km) to Dufton. Make this one quick; the shades of night are sliding through on the mist. I must get over the Falcon Clints while I can see where to put my feet. Hard away now across the pastures, deliberately taking the effort to where it hurts. A slight lifting of the cloud grants me at least half-light and I ask Will to go behind me so I can see far enough ahead to plan a line. As I totter along using hands and feet over the greasy rocks, I spot Will hopping nimbly over the boulders which are half-submerged along the river side. A slight miscalculation and Will hops nimbly into the river! He says some naughty words and hops nimbly out again. The slimy rocks seem never-ending; but apart from almost going headfirst into a massive block while being entertained by Will, I escape unscathed. By comparison, the rocky scramble beside the thundering cataract of Cauldron Spout is relaxed and enjoyable.

At the top of Cauldron Spout, a pleasant surprise; Geoff, after driving part of the way, has run down the private road with a flask and food. We sit munching chocolate while I carry out minor foot repairs. Now that the Clints are behind me and the rain has stopped I begin to feel my spirits rise; a little cautious optimism takes root. With a cheerful farewell Geoff gallops off to drive to Dufton where he will prepare for our arrival in some two and a half hours time. Will and I now step into a very black night. We step into other things as well. The moor over to Maize Beck is still very boggy and pocked with slimy holes. Will demonstrates an amazing aptitude for divining the deepest and slimiest of such holes. Putting his earlier boulder hopping performance to shame, he leaps with extraordinary vigour into holes I can't even see. By the simple ruse of staying several lengths behind Will I am able to steer a rather drier if less interesting course. I am nonetheless careful to remain in sufficiently close contact to profit from this opportunity to refine certain aspects of my vocabulary.

Maize Beck is only ankle deep, no need therefore to use the flood route. Across the other side is, I remember, generally good going. Only five miles (8 km) now separates me from my long anticipated arrival in Dufton. No sooner have we crossed the beck than a bank of mist rolls over us and we are alone, almost disembodied in two smoking pools of torchlight. There is nothing visible save the patch of ground beneath our feet. I am navigating by memory without even a compass. My knowledge of the topography of this area is good. High Cup is arguably my most favoured place along the Pennine Way; it has such a wonderful atmosphere of lofty spaciousness. Its rugged symmetry has a wild but architectural grandeur. Always, as I run along the craggy rim above steep walls sweeping gloriously down to the scooped valley, I experience an indefinable sense of excitement and mystery. Despite the mist I knew I was now heading for the rocky lip above the headwall of the valley. Intent on avoiding the least chance of falling over the unseen edge, I aimed off to one side. After some time, the feeling that the ground was not 'right' began to intrude on my consciousness. I expected that moving to my left would take me to the edge, rocky and unmistakable; all I found was a grassy slope. I tried again; same result. A feeling of shocked dismay swept over me and I began to curse my over-confidence and haste. Will produced a compass; at least we were heading in the correct direction. My mind now started to race with all manner of possibilities and their consequences. We must be coming down a wrong valley, parallel to High Cup. How far from and to what side of Dufton would we emerge? If I did not stop at Dufton could I regain time lost? Would everyone start looking for us if we failed to arrive on schedule?

After an indefinable period in this confused state my befuddled brain began to examine the coincidence of our being on a track remarkably similar to that leading from High Cup to Dufton. A more critical faculty rejected the coincidence, then my whole mind leapt at the sudden realisation that this *was* the track to Dufton. Though I did not realise until much later, I had merely examined a slope at the point where the rocks ended. Waves of relief washed away my despair but were immediately followed by a harsh self-criticism of my over-reliance on memory. It had, in fact, guided me correctly, but I should have reinforced it with the compass. Still, thoughts of the record, recently as insubstantial as the mist which had blighted them, took firm hold of my mind once more.

By now, the 45 minutes I had gained on my schedule had slipped away with the mist. The dark and murky nights are doubly treacherous; if you hurry on, trusting to instinct, knowledge and memory you will almost certainly make an error eventually, then, your very speed will be your ruination. If you opt for absolutely precise navigation, you will hardly realise until daylight returns just how slow your pace has become; it may then be too late. I had gambled and I just broke even, but my nerves were frayed; I needed a rest.

I still cannot properly account for what happened at Dufton. Since leaving Edale I had fixed Dufton in my mind as the most important sub-goal along the Way. I believed that if I could reach Dufton on schedule I would have time to sleep a little, eat a lot and regain strength enough to battle through the remaining miles. Not only that, I had arranged my support plan so that everyone would be at Dufton, ready to join forces on the final assault. This was not just good logistics, I had also been very conscious of the tremendous drawing power which would be generated by the thought of all my good friends gathered together, waiting to run with me over those last climactic miles.

But now in Dufton I feel so tired I can hardly eat. My mind seems to be moving through treacle and whichever way I sit, joints, muscles and feet produce pain. The plan is for Geoff to feed Will and me, allow us one and a half hours sleep, then get us up and off again. Everyone else, John, Mark, Inken and Don should, at 1.30 a.m., be sleeping, gathering their strength. I cannot understand therefore, what Inken's doing up and about. I ask her very bluntly and she seems a bit upset because she got up to help Geoff and because she was concerned. I didn't mean it like that, I simply cannot understand anything outside my plan and I cannot express myself clearly. No matter; I'm bundled into a tent, onto a mattress. I mutter something about my head and a kindly hand slips a pillow under me and gently pats me on the head, more eloquent than words this little gesture, reaching through the fogs around my brain, Inken again; thanks.

It might have been better not to have attempted this sleep. I cannot find rest for my legs and my knees are sources of shooting pain. I can remember no dream as such, but through the desolation which begins to sweep my mind as my conscious defences fall, there stalks a spectre whose name is haste. There is no rest in this; asleep, the spectre's lash drives abstract images of haste through my brain; half-awake, I hear the depressing, deadly tattoo of heavy rain on the tent. Locked into this grotesque state of consciousness I spiral into a black void. For an incalculable and horrible period of time I experience an almost complete negation of mind and spirit, is this to be the sole and bitter fruit of my high endeavour? I no longer care for I can no longer think.

Some time later Geoff appears in the tent doorway. He has a cup of tea ready, but the rain is still hammering its message of despair. I wait for him to say 'Hard luck Mike, you've done well but you can't go over Cross Fell in this weather.' To my surprise he just hands over the tea with a few cheery words. I don't understand this; it's quite obvious I can't go on, so why the charade? My own mind seems paralysed and numb and, quite mechanically, I begin to effect foot repairs. I'm not really interested, I know I've had it. I refuse all food, I'm not hungry and I don't need to eat if I'm quitting. I find myself outside, outside in the cold dawn rain. This is stupid and uncomfortable. Still I will not say the fatal words of quitting to Geoff, I leave it to him, he's experienced enough to know the score. Then I spot Will. Will looks almost as tired as I feel. The slow thought dawns that Will is ready to go over Cross Fell with me because that is what I came here to do and he came to help me do it. OK, so I'm not going to quit in camp, I haven't got the guts to turn to Geoff and Will and say what is in my heart. I'll make a token gesture out there on the hill, protect my pride a little, go through the motions. I set off walking slowly, no need to go faster, no call for haste now. I feel craven and defeated and what is worse I haven't even the strength to acknowledge it. The only flicker of spirit remaining is that manifest in the dull awareness of being in the midst of friends, friends who have endured alongside me over the miles, indeed, over the years, that I might accomplish this dream. For their sake, if not mine, I must go on until I can *truly* endure no longer. Such an end will be full of bitterness but I will have avoided the shame of not at least trying to crawl out of this pit.

Slowly then along the grey wet road, dragging down to defeat. The bulk of the fells is lost in darkness and mist. It is 4.00 a.m., was there ever such a grey and weeping dawn? At odds with the uniform drabness, a peculiar light attracts my attention. A tiny patch of what for a moment appeared to be blue sky, opened then closed to my view. I frankly disbelieve it, but then it shows again. I am very puzzled, this is quite anomalous to the scene in which I am acting. I dismiss the possibility and carry on. Automatically, my mind explores my body. Again, with disbelief, I register that my legs are no more than morning tired, no aches or strains, and my feet are fine, almost comfortable. I decide to suspend both disbelief and acts of faith for a time and start a conversation with Will. We both gain vigour as we stretch our legs into the miles once more. Then, around a bend in the track, a small miracle. Oblivious to my disbelief, a swathe of early sunshine falls full on a thick bank of bluebells; raindrop-glistening lustrous blue against the fresh spring green. The impact on my parched and weary spirit is almost tangible. It is all so innocent and generous, so heartbreakingly beautiful.

In the scant moments it took to absorb the scene my spirit was restored. I was emerging from the pit and carrion despair would not take hold of me again. One strange thing, I have passed that spot several times since, in spring too, but I have never again seen my bluebells on that bank. Furthermore, I would have thought that at 4.30 a.m. on the west side of the hill we would have been hidden from the sun in the east. Ah well, 'There are more things in heaven and earth Horatio, than are dreamt of in your philosophy.' Must either Nature or our spirits be circumscribed always by laws of matter?

The climb up Knock Fell to reach the high ground leading to Cross Fell was long and hard. I felt to be going very slowly but was content to take my cue from Will. He also seemed to be finding it tough so I reasoned the pace was adequate for the time being. The hard effort gradually restored us to full wakefulness and just as well. Above 2,000 ft (610 m) a thick wet mist was sweeping along on a biting easterly. Next, we traversed the two Dun Fells where I realised that in my despairing mood at Dufton I had left my map and route cards behind. However, I was full of confidence once more and with the compass a little west of north I brought us across the boggy gathering ground of the Tees watershed and at last onto the mighty summit plateau of Cross Fell itself. This flat and featureless plateau is often ravaged by fierce storms. At 2,930 ft (895 m) it is the highest point on the Pennine Way. It is also truly remote, being miles from any real sanctuary. In bad weather it can be an awesome place with a desolate, almost primeval atmosphere. Perhaps because of this, it is magnificent. It does not compromise. As mountains go, it is not even beautiful but it commands respect. I do not doubt it is the most committing place on the Pennine Way. While it has nearly always been kind to me, I fear it as much as love it.

Navigating again from my mental map, I aim for the top left-hand corner of the plateau. Sure enough, the trig point looms out of the mist and at last we can descend to softer climes. A fairly good descent, just a little astray from the path, but, with an eye to ethics, avoiding Wainwright's suggested shortcut which saves a mile on the official footpath. Our slight deviation produces a few green Sphagnum bogs for us to avoid or stumble into, but soon we are near the refuge of Gregg's Hut, damp, but a possible lifesaver in a storm.

As I looked back, grim Cross Fell was encircled by a string of old snowfields which it seemed to be wearing like a gigantic necklace. We turned our steps towards the South Tyne valley, Garrigill and breakfast. Truly, Cross Fell is magnificent but it is not trustworthy. I was not sorry to be leaving it. As we dropped lower on the interminable stony track leading directly to Garrigill, the mist disappeared entirely. The views were enormous. My tiny patch of blue now stretched across the horizons and in the rain-cleansed air we could see the brown hills rolling to impossible distances. Brown may seem monotonous but under the low sun every imaginable hue and shade was represented; curving, rolling, sweeping; a heaving brown sea in its vastness and, above, billowing cloud ships and the sweet blues of an early summer sky.

We rolled gently down the track, not speaking much, absorbing the peace, solitude and beauty around us. A wonderful healing was taking place, my life forces were being restored as I ran. I switched on to automatic pilot, letting my mind become empty of thought but open to the power around me. I was in a state somewhere between sleeping and waking, sensate but without cognition. After some time my mind re-surfaced, stretched itself and began to re-engage with reality. My crisis at Dufton which had almost paralysed mind and body had resulted in the loss of 45 minutes on my schedule. Better get moving! I increased pace, kicked a large stone with a tender toe and gave vent to a loud curse; 'normal service has been resumed'.

Garrigill is a charming little village on the banks of the South Tyne. Geoff had everything ready for me including a perfectly-angled deck-chair. Then, as an unexpected bonus, he switched on 'Nimrod' from The Enigma Variations. I had such a feeling of comfort, well-being and total relaxation there was considerable danger I would never leave the deck-chair. In Dufton I had experienced a black despair, but for my friends it would have engulfed me. In traversing Cross Fell I had crossed not only a topographical watershed but a truly significant psychological watershed. On the most important run of my life I had survived a terrible crisis and now I had reached further than I had ever reached before. At Garrigill, 180 miles (288 km) along the Way, I believed at last that I was going to reach my journey's end and achieve a record, not 'eventually' but now!

It could be that my unbounded optimism was not entirely appropriate. Whereas my support were beginning to feel a cautious optimism based on a review of the objective factors involved, I had no such concern with mere cautious possibility. I had emerged from a journey through dark and horrible caverns. I had given all, more than I thought I possessed. In return I seemed to have become imbued with an unassailable strength of body and spirit. For a while a powerful inspiration would enable me to transcend the limitations which restrict merely physical endeavour. I did not question the source or scope of this inspiration. Nor yet did I concern myself with the remaining brute statistics of this journey. Perhaps I should have done, they were not without interest.

At Garrigill, in order to finish within three days, I had to cover 90 miles (145 km) in 26 hours. At the time I felt nothing but confidence. The weather was superb and I was enjoying an almost unique sense of well-being. Of course, one long spell of bad weather, a bad route-finding error, an inability to survive the third night without sleep, all, or any of these things could easily blast my hopes, but I hardly considered them. Had I known what the Cheviots had in store for me I might not have been so blithe.

Perhaps in a euphoric state I looked no further ahead than sufficed to guide my footsteps along the river footpath beside the sparkling South Tyne. This is a delightful stretch of the Pennine Way and in the new summer sunshine my eyes drank in the verdant and glittering greens. It had been a long, dark night and even the beautiful moorland browns below Cross Fell had carried a sombre echo of it. Down here, soft sweet Nature bestowed gentler charms. There was joy in being here, joy in being alive, and there was joy too in my running.

Moving with a slow but easy rhythm, just beyond Alston there was a happy moment for me as the support car from Dufton drove by. I allowed my pace to surge a little and waved enthusiastically. I was slightly surprised to see anxious faces peering at me. Surely everyone could sense that the time for anxiety and fear was past?

Accompanying me from Garrigill to Slaggyford was the last hard toil for Will. He had joined me at 141 miles (226 km) and, with only that one short break in the night, had covered 48 miles (77 km) through the difficult hours. Now he insisted on sprinting ahead to open every gate so I could pass through without pausing. As these few miles were littered with gates he was engaged in some very arduous interval training indeed. At Slaggyford he at last stood down. I tried to thank him but just couldn't find the words. 'Never mind all that,' he said 'just go on and take the record.'

Now at last I was joined by my old friend and Karrimor partner, John Richardson. John and I have shared so many hard and humorous miles together, it was like slipping into a pair of comfortable old shoes. John had the ability, like no one else, to lift from my shoulders some of the burden of the heavy miles. His experience, his wisdom and his concern meant that I could safely transfer to him some of my weight of responsibility. He told me that I was going well enough and that he would only start to prod me along if it looked necessary. It was as well he took this stance because although I was indeed going strongly, I had perhaps become dangerously euphoric. I had begun to think that now nothing *could* go wrong.

And for a long time nothing did go wrong. I established a superb rhythm of

*Coming into
Alston with
Will McLewin
on the Pennine
Way.*

running and walking, each blending into the other without conscious thought as I followed the ebb and flow of the Way across moor and meadow. The day became very warm and as I am a lover of cold, dry conditions, I began to suffer a little. However, at 2.00 p.m. I received a great boost as the 200-mile (370 km) mark was passed. I had been going just two days and three hours. In fact I was an hour and a half down on my schedule but this was not critical. Over this last day I had allowed for both increasing weakness and a two-hour sleep. Not only did I reject thoughts of weakness, I believed I could, if necessary, dispense with the need to sleep.

Going north, 200 miles (320 km) marks the start of the Roman Wall. This is a fine stretch, endless vistas to the north and beneath one's feet history, both sensed and real. Hadrian's Wall once acted as a barrier to marauding Scots, now it serves much the same function for Wayfarers. Describing a vicious switchback of ups and downs, it precludes any rhythm but presents every chance of a stiff-legged trip to bring the whole affair to a fractured close. After 10 miles (16 km) of it I was pleased to slot through Rapishaw Gap and wave the Wall goodbye. Somewhat wobbly of leg I headed with John for the welcome shade of the Wark Forests. By now John was encouraging me to jog the gentle uphill stretches. I would have like to have walked but he either believed I could manage it or needed to do it. I trusted his judgement and reached yet deeper into the well of my reserves. Would they be sufficient? I had never before run so far or drawn so much from myself. But never before had I felt such glory spreading within me.

At Ladyhill a familiar enemy assailed me. Jubilee Foot with all its burning pain began to hamper my stride. I had been wearing a comfortable but sloppy pair of road shoes. Now I discarded them, stripped my feet of all dressings and applied layers of Vaseline. This done, I crammed my feet into my usual rough terrain shoes. I walked rather circumspectly out of the support point, with 53 miles (85 km) still to go, sore feet could easily slow me to failure. After just a few but painful moments, the burning eased and the shoes expanded. I fitted a pair of soft insoles to ensure my feet were well locked in place and there they stayed until the finish.

Relieved, I began to chat to Inken back on running support. At first she eyed me anxiously. She had caught a glimpse of my feet back at the stop and I don't think she had been too impressed. As ever my mouth was the barometer of my spirits and under the influence of my incessant, if perforce, inane chatter she began to relax and we talked pleasantly on into the mild still evening. Like Will, however, she was alert to any gates which might be opened in advance to facilitate my progress. At one such spot I observed her ahead of me wrestling with one of those dilapidated constructions held together with wire and string. This one had obviously relinquished its role as gate years ago and settled for a less demanding existence as a barrier. I called out to Inken not to bother but she ignored me and with a display of ferocity quite remarkable in one so slight and gentle, proceeded to utterly demolish the recalcitrant obstacle. I jogged through the gap and over the debris regarding Inken with a new respect. I fear her recent acquaintance with the genus 'fell runner' has marred her previous rather more

*'Embracing'
the mug of tea
above
Bellingham,
225 miles
(360 km) from
the start of the
Pennine Way.*

ladylike qualities. I had to endure some quite unnecessary remarks when I made a smart diversion to visit the loo in Bellingham.

As I approached the support point above the town, Don placed a mug of tea enticingly on a gatepost and I 'sprinted' forward to embrace it. I was in great spirits now. Often the evening hours are my best times and over the easy moorland which followed I ran almost effortlessly. I thought I was mentally very sharp too until I realised I was correcting a route error I had not made; perhaps too sharp!

At last I started on the final leg before Byrness. Byrness, the last major support point before I began the 30-mile (50 km) traverse which would take me through my third night over the Cheviots to journey's end at Kirk Yetholm. The early summer night had an atmosphere of immense stillness and calm. Don and Geoff led away and I followed the gentle murmur of their voices as they chatted with the easy comfort of old friends. The sky held the pale northern light but a soft dusk was cloaking the peaty ground. We ran through a bank of fluffy white cotton grass which floated ethereally in the darkness and I, suspended in time and space, floated with it.

The much despised pine forests above Byrness were, for me, perfumed avenues of easy progress. I knew the track through them ran for miles so I felt no impatience, I simply soaked up that wonderful sense of quiet peace. And as I jogged and walked, I prepared myself for the final test.

The plan was simple. John, Inken and Mark were all very strong and keen to accompany me the whole way to Kirk Yetholm. Don and Geoff would attempt to drive to Chew Green where the Way passes close to the road used for military purposes. This road is apt to be closed at times but we had hopes it would provide a chance for a final food stop and even, maybe, an opportunity for me to snatch a half-hour's sleep. Right now though I had to consume as much food as I could manage and change into warmer clothes. I thought I was very much in control of myself and the situation and could not understand why John kept peering through the car window asking if I had finished my plate of stew. I thought this hardly the best of manners, most unlike John. After all, I'd only just sat down hadn't I? No! I hadn't. Apparently I had been ladling stew into my mouth in slow motion for 20 minutes. My mind and body were working well but only at half-speed. My original plan had allowed for a sleep stop at Byrness but with night hours and the boggy Cheviots ahead John reckoned that with now less than 12 hours of the three days remaining, I should keep moving.

We set off just after midnight and, despite my tiredness, I could sense a muted thrum of excitement within me. The steep climb out of the valley passed comfortably and soon we were on uneven but level ground, heading for Chew Green. I began to experience some difficulty on stretches of going which were rougher or more stony. My torch threw shadows across the irregularities, and as I moved, so did the shadows. My speed of information processing continued to be slow and from time to time I stepped over shadows that were not bumps and stumbled over bumps that were not shadows. Down in the next valley we could hear the sounds of gunfire, the army playing at soldiers. There were amusing references to Geoff and Don being mistaken for the enemy but more seriously we were concerned about the car being prevented access to Chew Green.

My progress must have been even slower than I realised because John and Mark could not resist forging ahead, ostensibly to look for the car. I was grateful to Inken for staying with me. I felt fine physically and also in spirit but, staring into the torchlight, I found it difficult not to become disorientated and lose touch with reality. After a brief re-grouping John and Inken moved ahead leaving Mark to look after his dad! I observed that a cutting easterly had sprung up and asked Mark if he was cold. 'Not at all,' he replied. A few minutes later as the wind increased I made the same query and got the same response. After the third repetition I realised that hints were useless and ordered the callow youth to help me don a windproof. Only just in time, the wind was now penetrating to the bone. Then we saw returning torches, Geoff and Don had run the gauntlet, the car was close by.

In view of my tiredness I had been counting on having a short sleep in the car. Despite my fuddled thinking I quickly realised this was not a good idea. The car was small, and with Geoff and Don there would be six people plus a mass of gear to accommodate. I would not ask my friends to stand around in the cold wind while I snoozed inside. I climbed into the car, the heater going full blast and proceeded with the laborious task of getting more food down. I can vaguely remember a convoluted discussion about what clothes I should wear in view of the deteriorating conditions, then off we set on the last lap and into the final crisis.

It was 2.00 a.m. and the weather was most definitely on the change. A strong and bitter wind blew into our faces from somewhere north of east. There was no light in the sky and a pall of cloud held back the dawn. Although I did not feel physically weak I could not control my brain which was making efforts to close down in sleep. I continually stumbled over tussocks as sleep snatched my legs away. Those tussocks looked so inviting; if only I could curl up among them.

I realised my progress was becoming ever slower and despite exerting my will I could not force my brain to a normal level of consciousness. After about five miles of this, as we were approaching a refuge hut near the border fence, John asked me if I wanted to take a sleep. Hell! What a conundrum to wrestle with. Time lost sleeping versus time lost stumbling compounded by the unknown factors of would I be able to sleep (or wake up) and would it help anyway? I realised the importance of coming to the correct decision, and quickly. Although the mental effort actually aroused my brain a little, I elected to try a five-minute sleep. Inside the wooden refuge all was amazingly quiet and peaceful. The wind was a murmur and it seemed positively warm in comparison with the hostile elements outside. Reviewing the various muscular alternatives available, I quickly chose Inken's as by far the softest lap on offer and with my head thus pillowed stretched full-length on the hard bench. I allowed myself a moment to switch off all systems and then, with the trust of a child, I slipped into a wonderfully deep, calm and refreshing sleep.

'Come on Mike, you've had seven minutes!' I felt my heart give a bound of excitement. Swinging my feet to the floor I shot through the door like a startled hare. John was already steaming up the hill. I stuck my head inches from his rapidly retreating backside and followed his lead. This was the only time in the entire run that anyone set a pace for me and it was perfect. I knew John was going as hard as he possibly could and I knew he was right. There could be no further weakness now. I was finely poised between success and failure. A merely ordinary finish at a speed commensurate with having travelled 255 miles (408 km) would not be enough. I had to produce something special. That wonderful sleep had opened up the chance to do just that.

So nearly it was not enough. As we ploughed onwards the ground became wetter and the bogs deeper. Eventually we were too tired to steer round the swamps but charged desperately through them. The route over the Cheviots trends steadily uphill to Cheviot summit itself. Time was slipping by and still the summit seemed no nearer. From leaving Byrness with the three-day record apparently safely in my grasp, I began to see my dream sinking into the mire around me. By now my throat was inflamed, I could not swallow properly and when I tried it felt like tearing open glued paper. Sucking boiled sweets helped and I chewed these as if my life depended on it. I longed for a drink but did not want to cause upset to my loyal support by pointing out they had neglected to bring any water. I thus deprived myself of the liquid they had carried from Byrness as a matter of course.

At last, the bog-encircled summit of Cheviot itself. I examined my watch and was suddenly filled with a joyous astonishment. If I could cover the last 10 miles (16 km) in two hours I would finish a full two hours under three days. We swung away from Cheviot re-tracing our swampy footsteps in the direction of the Schil.

John and Mark were jogging ahead and this meant my supply of sweets kept disappearing. Eventually, I raised myself on a peat hag and screeched for Mark to come back to me. Like the dutiful son he is, he did. I then delivered a very stern rebuke indeed. Did he think that I was Superman that I should be able to keep sprinting after him in order to re-lubricate my poor throat!?! I thought I achieved a splendid note of righteous indignation; dignified and firm but reasonable and so on. However, while Mark seemed suitably impressed, I noticed Richardson smirking in the background. I made a mental note to give him a hard time on the run-in – if I could!

Cheviot summit now behind us and the wind no longer in our faces, I begin to pick up pace. I shout to John that if I can reach the summit of the Schil by 8.00 a.m. I will throw everything into an effort to finish by 9.00 a.m.; that two hour sub-three-day target. Gradually the bog gives way to better going and after painfully picking my way down the steep slopes of Auchope Cairn I get onto a gentle descent and start to stretch my legs. After over 260 miles (420 km) of carefully hoarding my reserves I joyfully abandon caution to the wind and let my energy flow as it will. Layers of clothing go flying off for the support to snatch up. Schil summit is looming some 500 ft (150 m) above us but a reckless charge carries me nearly half-way up before I consent to walk. I can tell from his breathing that John is having to hang on ever so slightly here and Inken has started walking quite early. I've no intention of blowing away all my energy here however and a brisk walk claims the top by 8.00 a.m. Again on the steep downhill it is my turn to suffer on legs which have strength but no elasticity. Yet I will not be denied. There seems to be an upsurge and swell of power and energy within me. The pure joy of running into my dream has flooded my entire being and there is no place for weariness and fatigue. After all the years, all the countless miles, the crushing disappointments, the pain of body and the lonely aches of the spirit, I am finally running into my dream – I am truly now running the record. It is glorious. There is no fatigue, no pain. There is a pulsating excitement, a joy in movement and a thrilling urgency to reach the finish. Yet, if I could, I would live these moments forever.

In my haste and excitement I lead us down the wrong hill! The only penalty is more rough going, the added frustration merely fuelling the fires within me. We reach the road rather early and I have to restrain myself from sprinting down it, my breathing informs me there are still limitations in the amount of oxygen I can consume.

The last hill on the Pennine Way is half a mile of road at a gradient of one in six. I attacked this with the resolve to yield not one step of walking. I had the satisfaction of seeing Don peering down in some amazement then Geoff, with camera, having to back-pedal furiously to keep us in shot. Like wild Border raiders the group of us swept through now lashing rain up to the Border Inn. I grabbed the gable end and tried to focus on my watch. Before I could do so John's voice rapped out 'Two days, twenty-one hours, fifty-four minutes, thirty seconds.' After only 30 years of steady training I had become the first person to run the Pennine Way in under three days.

*Yards from the
finish of the
Pennine Way in
Kirk Yetholm.
Left to right:
Mark, Mike,
John, Don.*

My memories of what followed are quite clear in some aspects and hopelessly vague in others. Immediately I heard the time announced I turned and jogged back up the road to meet Inken who, after 60 miles (100 km) of hard running and countless hours on support, day and night, had been unable to stay with our finishing speed. I gave her a kiss and then, at a rather more sedate pace, returned to the portals of the Border Inn. I remember by this time I was fairly saturated. The proprietor of the establishment had opened the door as he thought we should sign the Pennine Way book he kept. Without being particularly presumptuous I thought he might at least offer the use of his garage so that we could change out of the rain. No chance! After I'd signed the book and entered the time, he politely but firmly closed the door in our faces. What a miserable bugger, I thought. I was on such a high I could not feel the cold but felt very aggrieved on behalf of my friends. I need not have worried, they're as tough as they come and soon we were all changed and snug in the cars. First stop a transport café where my mouth would not stop working. I think I must have been almost delirious; I chattered incessantly while my friends looked on with indulgent amusement. It was several hours before I began to calm down and as I did so, sleep at last claimed me.

There are (thankfully) no medals for breaking these kinds of records, but when I arrived home I found something which I would not change for any olympic gold. It was a brown envelope and it was stuck on our front door. It was from my four youngest children and on it was written: 'Welcome home, Dad. And well done. Gerard, Liam, Sara, Michael.' I have it yet, and always will.

chapter five

LIFE AFTER THE PENNINE WAY

It had taken me five years of specific training and eight attempts before I was able to break the Pennine Way record. As gratifying as my achievement had been I felt much valuable time had been lost and other ventures had passed me by. Life is short and our fleeting dreams run faster than our failing strength. I had no plans for a prolonged period of recuperation. I was as keen to run as ever. I felt I could now enjoy my running without the burden of unfulfilled ambition to carry with me. Unfortunately, my joints decided to play a part in past and future dreams. Painful knees reminded me that the price of victory was a mortgage with a lifelong term and a high rate of interest.

That the Pennine Way had not destroyed my tendency to over-ambition was demonstrated three weeks later. I thought I would just 'tootle' round as much of the Bob Graham as possible (meaning all of it!). Starting at Threlkeld I set off in the evening to climb Blencathra, Great Calva and Skiddaw. The only reason I can find for relegating the prestigious Bob Graham to a relatively minor jaunt was that after the Pennine Way it appeared very much shorter and easier. I did however take the sensible precaution of packing an extremely thin and most unwaterproof cagoule. Should I experience a stiff-necked obstinacy to continue in the face of bad weather, this garment would not enable me to do so.

As I started up Halls Fell ridge in oppressive conditions, writhing tongues of mist licked down from unseen heights. The summit-springing ridge carried me to a rain-splattered, wind-blown top. However, with the wind on my back the rapid deterioration in the weather system was easily ignored. A fleet-footed ascent of Calva and Skiddaw followed by a raid on the 'chippie' in Keswick would, I blithely imagined, see me safely onto the Derwent Fells, easy ground for the dark. This attempt to bolster my morale was blasted as I turned headfirst into the weather on Great Calva.

Thrusting against a wet gale I desperately sought lower ground where I hastily unpacked a small torch and the thin cagoule. The latter exceeded all my expectations, I was soaked through in no time. Without, for once, the slightest hesitation I bolted back to my car at Threlkeld. Later, as I drove back with the huge wind bending the summer trees and squalls of rain being flung across the windscreen, I reflected that the weather had done me a favour. I had gone just far enough to establish that my legs (and probably my head) had not recovered to do even half a Bob Graham.

Gradually, I did recover my hill legs and at the end of July led a club walk round most of the summits above 2,500 ft (760 m) in North Wales. Unlike my ill-fated tilt at the Bob Graham, the major problem on this walk was tremendous heat. I remember we were refused pots of tea at a café on the Aber Glaslyn Bridge. As the Afon Glaslyn thundered past we were sternly told that we should realise there was a water shortage and lemonade was all we could have. Our subsequent ascent of Moel Hebog was accompanied by much popping, spluttering and minor explosions; no tea, just very large bottles of fizzy lemonade.

The North Wales 2,500s was a walk of great character, undertaken in the best of company. Although the route is a demanding one, there was nothing at stake other than that we should enjoy the hills and enjoy the camaraderie; not too difficult a task. After 22,000 ft (6,705 m) of ascent on this Welsh walk I felt my legs were sufficiently prepared for my next and final adventure for 1984. I hoped to simultaneously support and accompany Inken on a Bob Graham attempt. To an unfortunate minority of fell runners, the Bob Graham represents little more than the ultimate test of prowess in running the fells. There are those who lose sight of the fact that it is a superb route in any circumstances. The round sweeps over much of the best ground in the Lake District. It covers all the 3,000 ft (915 m) summits and nearly every other major peak.

The route stands on its own merit, the challenge to complete within 24 hours simply adds that extra spice of competition with oneself. With customary thoroughness, Inken reconnoitered the round by sections, building fitness, knowledge and that indefinable sense of being part of, or 'belonging to' the route. After coming through the final test piece of the Welsh walk so well, I thought she had a good chance of completing the round and a fair chance of completing within 24 hours, a target with about a 30 per cent success rate. After her sterling support of my Pennine Way record, I was determined to render Inken every assistance on her attempt. To this end I had to examine my conscience that I really was prepared to subjugate any personal ambition for hers, there must be no appearance by that bloody demon on this occasion!

Looking back on the round I think it epitomised much of what characterises ultra-distance fell running and the Bob Graham in particular. Initially, we were blessed with good weather and we had the joy of being in high places with so many of the Lakeland hills stretching ahead in the sun, beckoning us onwards. There are many runners attempting the round nowadays yet there never seems to be any shortage of friends to accompany them at all hours of the day and night. We too picked up that wonderful golden thread running ever through these endeavours; companionship, laughter and the strong sustaining love of friends. Completion of the round is a deeply satisfying experience. What I find even more remarkable, however, is the willingness of friends to assist in the endeavour, to lighten the burden of the miles with good cheer, to suffer fatigue and hardship so that faltering steps may yet carry the runner within reach of his dream.

By Dunmail Raise it was time to prepare ourselves for our night section over the Helvellyn range. It was also time for me to assume sole responsibility for navigating Inken safely through the night. With the exception of my eldest son, Mark, all our other friends had to return home. With farewells and good wishes exchanged on both sides we departed on our very different ways, they, on the hectic journey down the motorways, we, onto the high and by now empty fells.

We left Dunmail with time in hand on our schedule but as the night deepened, so it brought an opaque, soaking mist. As the mist continued to thicken I was forced to navigate ever more carefully. In turn, this meant that we were unable to jog over the easier stretches of ground. Beyond Helvellyn, there are paths which are perfectly satisfactory as lines along the grassy Dodds, but which frequently cut under the summits themselves. I agonised over the possibility of bypassing a summit. There are mountains in the Himalaya where respect for a summit-dwelling Deity does not permit the actual top to be violated; such an ethic would scarcely be entertained as an excuse for shortcutting a Bob Graham round!

Despite several minor miscalculations we 'collected' all the required tops. However, as we stood at last on Clough Head, I realised all our time in hand was gone. The weather too, was continuing its unhelpful ways. Associated with the mist were very heavy banks of cloud which smothered any chance of an early dawn. We lost more time on the rough descent with my temper mounting in direct proportion to the number of drainage ditches into which I fell.

At 3.45 a.m. in the village of Threlkeld, it was essential that Mark, waiting in my car, should have everything ready for immediate consumption. He was in fact so well organised that we were fed, watered and away with a two-minute saving. Mark shouldered the rucksack and led off up Blencathra, Halls Fell Ridge springing unseen into the still dark sky. The ridge, rocky and greasy, vaulted endlessly upwards. Speed was both impracticable and inadvisable, and the dawn stubbornly refused to come to our assistance.

It was 5.30 a.m. before we finally had the benefit of true light. I guided us down early to the track in the valley. My own legs were shaken and tired after the steep descent from Blencathra but with a good track to follow and only Calva and Skiddaw remaining I felt a surge of optimism. It was with a sense of shock therefore that I heard Inken say 'It's no good. I've lost it!' There was a note of despair in her voice and her face was drawn and pale. I had never seen her like this before and I felt a deep dismay. I tried to re-assure her but just when I felt I should have been of most help, I found she was not responding as would every other fell runner I had ever known. She interpreted my encouragement as an attempt to force from her the kind of effort of which she was no longer capable. Her feeling was that the round had been a wonderful experience so far and the kind of effort I was now demanding would destroy her appreciation of it. She felt she was no longer capable of finishing within 24 hours and that fact was far less important to her than that she should be allowed to finish the circuit in her own way. These were ethical points whose validity I could not very well deny. They did, however, place me in something of a dilemma. I knew she was right but I also knew that steady application might still achieve full success whereas anything less would certainly not. Totally exasperated, like Dr Doolittle, I thought 'Why can't a woman be more like a man?'! My best efforts at encouragement, being perversely interpreted, I was unfeeling enough to utter harsh words. Eventually, I noticed that despite avowals to the contrary, she was still trying harder and going faster.

Struggling to keep my disputative nature and hot temper in check, I focused my attention on both finding the very best lines across the hills and covering the ground at the optimum pace. The country Back O'Skiddaw is rough and a sore trial to weary legs. I now realised however, that Inken was going as well as she possibly could. I would have liked to have offered words of encouragement. How galling! With all my knowledge, experience and silver-tongued eloquence to place at Inken's disposal, I was condemned to impotent silence.

After crossing the fence below Skiddaw summit we reached the top with a suddenness that took me unawares. Surprisingly, we still had an hour and a quarter to cover the remaining five and a half miles (9 km) to Keswick, most of it downhill. I pointed out to my protégée that she now had both aspects of the round within her grasp and left it to her. Several miles of often steep downhill is not an easy way to finish a tough 70 miles (117 km) of mountainous terrain. Our progress was not fast but it had about it a steady determination. I could now address myself to the final problem. I was not absolutely sure of the last half mile of the route through Fitz Park to the official finish at the Moot Hall in Keswick. One wrong turn now and it would be I, not Inken who had blown the chance to finish inside 24 hours. My mind flashed back to my own Bob Graham. Entering the boundaries of Keswick, I had been just about to toddle off down the road to Carlisle, when Boyd Millen laconically called from his recumbent position on a bench 'Oy, Mike, over here!'

This time it was Mark who quested ahead and, despite a slightly erratic course across the park, found an improbable route through a car-park. We popped out of a narrow ginnel and saw the Moot Hall 50 yards away. 'Can you do 50 yards in seven and a half minutes?' I asked rhetorically. We did rather better. Inken became only the twelfth woman to achieve the Bob Graham as, with just seven minutes in hand, we arrived back at the spot from which we had started 42 summits ago. Unlike Inken, I don't think I had ever come to terms with leading her to a complete but out of time Bob Graham. My chief emotion on finishing was one of tremendous relief and thankfulness.

The rather nice ethical points raised towards the end of the Bob Graham provided scope for many a subsequent discussion. I think both our points of view are valid in theory. In practice it is essential that the individual sets his or her own levels of striving.

The Bob Graham had taken place in the middle of August and marked a satisfying conclusion to my long-distance running that year. To some extent it had marked an act of faith with myself that life would not end with the Pennine Way. Though I continued to train I began to feel as if I had asked as much as I could expect from my body for one year. After the Marsden-Edale race at the beginning of December I did not run again until Christmas. The tradition of running with friends over Christmas and alone on Boxing Day, which is my birthday, is a long and a strong one. I have never probed the significance of these runs, I just accept that they restore, heal and bless. Echoes of a happy childhood perhaps.

As the year drew to a close I ruminated on just how good a year it had been. I could not hold all the outstanding events in my memory and began to jot them down in my log-book. This is my list:

1984: Summary of a Good Year:

7/ Jan.	Double Marsden Edale (Walk)	45
14/15 Jan	Lakes Passes (Walk)	45
3rd March	Derwent W'sheds Race (11th Consecutive) 2nd overall, won vets trophy.	40
17th March } 18th }	Haworth Hobble with John. Otley V. Marathon 1.21 45/400	33 13
6th April	Welsh Threes Circuit in snow - with Helen.	25
10-13th April	4 x 30 mls round home	120
16-20th April	4 x 50 mls in 5 days round home, lovely weather.	200
24-28th April	4 x 60 as above - on the P.W. More lovely weather	240
6/7th May	Tan/Cat record (29 hrs 11m) Very hard work!	120
31st May - 3rd June	Pennine Way record (2.21.54) At last!	270
7/8th July	Saunders M.M. Tough hot day. heatwave!	40
21/22nd July	N. Wales 2,500's Wonderful club walk.	60
5/6 Aug	Bob Graham round with Helen (Just made it!)	70
1st Sept.	Bullock Smything race. 2nd, equalled previous record. (Shos 38m)	56
9th Sept	My 20th consec. Mntn Trial - pity I was knackered!	25
5th Oct 6th Oct.	The Cairngorm 4,000's in snow - real mountains! The Mamores ridge in clearing mist	
27/28th Oct.	The Karrimor - at home. My 17th ('Ow',9th with John	55
2nd Dec	Marsden-Edale race (full circle!) 3.08. 19/270	22

MILES 1,500

(Calculated training miles = 2,000)

chapter six

A LONG WAY FOR A PADDLE

Preparation for the Coast to Coast Record

It had been my ambition for several years to attempt the Coast to Coast record as soon as I had successfully completed the Pennine Way. The route was devised by Alfred Wainwright who, despite his marvellous and indispensable *Pennine Way Companion* seems to have been disenchanted with the Pennine Way itself. Wainwright set about planning his own line for a long-distance walk taking as his main theme the linking of points on the north-west and north-east coasts of England. Obviously not a lover of the Pennine Bog (who is?), Wainwright sought to steer a somewhat drier line while still including high, and often remote, areas.

The route is an easy one to conceptualise. It starts in the west by traversing the Lake District, its central section crosses Yorkshire Dales country and the final section takes one across the North York Moors to finish at the quaint and romantic Robin Hood's Bay. Wainwright gives the mileage as 190 (306 km) and the three sections are roughly equal in length.

When I reconnoitered the Coast to Coast in the spring of 1985 I found both pleasure and disappointment. I found places of great charm and beauty and the start and finish both offer wonderful cliff-top scenery. In particular, the traverse along the cliffs above Whitley Bay is inspirational. My other impression however was that this was a walk of good sections linked far too often by stretches of road and hard track.

The two miles of road into Bellingham is easily the longest continuous stretch of road on the Pennine Way, whereas the Coast to Coast has a number of road sections of several miles. For me, roads destroy the character of a walk. Disparate and illogical as the Pennine Way might appear to be, it has a sense of unity. 'Wild trails' do not belong to roads and each time one is used, the trail is lost. One of the delightful aspects of any continuous traverse of a long-distance route is the sense of completeness and cohesion that it brings. The slow exploration of a route is also rewarding of course but unfolding it continuously is an experience I find uniquely satisfying.

After training on the Coast to Coast I had some misgivings about the amount of road. Apart from the eight-mile (13 km) section beyond Richmond however, these were slight. Wainwright's later edition of his companion book to the walk stated that poor behaviour by walkers had resulted in permissive footpaths round

Orton being withdrawn. He stated that it was now necessary to follow some seven miles (11 km) of road through the village due to lack of rights of way. This is happily not correct. A little beyond Beacon Hill, a system of bridle ways and field paths (all on rights of way) skirt Orton and give an attractive approach to Sunbiggin Tarn. These paths are clearly marked on the Ordnance Survey maps and I was determined to use them as being more in keeping with the general ethos of the walk.

Part of my training plan was to again include extra long runs with something at stake to help me 'peak' my preparation. My success on the Pennine Way had not imparted any sense of invincibility. Indeed, although my training for the event had passed off with no real problems, I had never felt particularly good. A wet spring had not helped, but even allowing for this, I felt I had to prove to myself that I had not burned out in my struggle for the Pennine Way.

I set myself two subsidiary targets prior to attempting the Coast to Coast record; one was a hundred-mile (160 km) event, scheduled for the end of May and organised by the Long Distance Walkers' Association (LDWA). The route of the LDWA Dalesman Hundred followed an attractive course in Yorkshire Dales country. It contained a good proportion of hills, some remote country and scenery both beautiful and varied. I thought the odd road section annoying but not too intrusive. I subsequently discovered that many LDWA members complained that the course was too tough. It appears that the chief concern of many is simply to complete 100 miles (160 km). To these, the nature of the course seems to be unimportant excepting that it must not hamper that ambition. I feel that those who do hold this view are mistaken. Miles which do not feed the senses and nourish the spirit are just empty statistics. Distance is, in a sense, meaningless. It is the journey through time and nature that matters. This may be physically as hard as you wish to make it. It should always be spiritually satisfying.

When I had finished reconnaissance and training for the Coast to Coast it was the end of April. I decided I had time to fit in one other long event before the Dalesman Hundred at the end of May. I had no time to learn a new route so I turned to an old adversary to provide a challenge. The Tan–Cat would certainly not respect my new status. Its 120 moorland miles (193 km), still heavy with spring rains, would be as testing as ever.

It may be difficult to understand how I could entertain self-doubts after 'proving' myself on the Pennine Way. I did so partly because it is in the nature of an athlete never to accept that he is at his peak of fitness and strength, but apart from this, I did not know what last year might have cost me in terms of a real depletion in the energy reserves needed for me to continue to participate in my sport. Although I had enjoyed most of my training during spring, I had found the wet conditions very trying at times. My knees, in particular, were becoming increasingly stiff and sore. Continuous hours running through mud and rain can dull one's appreciation of even the best scenery. The necessity of always having to bulk my training in spring forces me out in conditions I would often prefer to avoid. I had noted a reluctance to face some of these miles. If I had indeed developed any mental or physical chinks in my armour, the Tan–Cat would surely discover them – and it would show little mercy!

Comfortingly, I had as ever a top class support team. My two eldest sons, Mark and Sean, were to act as runner and cook/driver respectively, while Inken would share the driving and accompany me on the night section. One other important aspect which gave me confidence was my mental preparation. On the drive up to Tan Hill I felt relaxed but alert. My mind seemed to slip away onto some remoter plane so that although I was aware of everything happening around me, I was also detached from it. I could sense the 'motor' was ready to go but mentally I enjoyed a feeling of peace and calm.

The run itself turned out to be almost a reverse of last year's effort. I ran only moderately well to begin with and the big sweeping hills in the north; Great Shunner, Buckden Pike, Great Whernside did not give me an easy passage. Coming off the last into Grassington at 36 miles (58 km) I felt distinctly tired. It was here that last year my legs had 'gone' and I feared the same kind of thing was about to happen. I need not have worried. I came in feeling tired and left feeling strong. The parts had bedded in after their two week lay-off and I was now ready to start running economically and purposefully.

The rest of the run was both tough and enjoyable. I felt I was being stretched but my rest had restored my reserves of strength. And strength was certainly needed. There was a scythe of a wind whistling out of the east. I ran dressed for a winter's day and my poor support looked frozen. Once again I probed the night-time evils of Jackson's Ridge. It was that treacherous hour before first light when body and brain are at a low ebb and anxiety for the dawn may lead to uncertainty and poor judgement. This time Jackson allowed me to pass almost unchallenged, just one grough system of finely reticulated drainage channels wandered across our path, unmarked on map or memory.

By Todmorden at 5.40 a.m. and now 70 miles (115 km) beyond Tan Hill, I was into the uncertain light of a pinched and bitter morning. 'Yon Tod' provided a brief but cheering respite from the searching wind and I gulped a hasty breakfast. The attractions of the bleak little town grew in my mind's eye as I ascended once more to the even bleaker moors. Here, the wind, with little to oppose its progress from origins in what appeared to be Spitzbergen, screamed over the walls of the huge Warland reservoirs. Despite this arctic blast, my head felt muzzy and my senses seemed out of focus. I departed from the White House over Blackstone Edge feeling anxious.

Under the stimulus of this anxiety I ran the next leg very quickly and, what was better, strongly and smoothly. From here on I slipped into a lovely running–walking rhythm, I even found strength for little extravagances such as having a boost up Rollick Stones ridge on Bleaklow. I suppose such surges represent a delight in gaining a temporary freedom from the carefully regulated shackles of a strict schedule.

From Bleaklow Head the route takes the line currently used by the Marsden to Edale Fell race. The Marsden–Edale is also one of the most venerable of the Rucksack Club's winter walks and long familiarity enabled me to follow the most economical lines to Edale. With only 12 miles (19 km) remaining, the sun belatedly remembered its spring duties. More out of bravado than warmth, I changed into shorts, enjoying a sense of liberation, fresh air on bare legs. After the windswept northern Pennines, the long cold night and the bitter desolation of the moorland morning, it was so good to be treading my home ground; a pale sun on my face and the wind on my back.

The top of Long Hill is but a mile from my Buxton home. Foregathered to see me safely to my destination were my three eldest sons, Mark, Sean and Gerard. My fifth and youngest son, Michael, was also there. At seven, he was too young to run with us but being in my mid-forties, I was too old to be doing this kind of thing much longer. Before I am reduced to reminiscing in front of those fires which warm from without when those that burn from within are extinguished, I want my children to have a memory of me as a strong and active man.

Dotage is still some way off thankfully, at least surrounded by my fleet sons I was inspired to dismiss any weariness. Together we made short work of my scenic Goyt valley extension of the original route and once again joined that exhilarating charge for the Cat and Fiddle. I can't outsprint the lads any more but I could at least make them blow a bit as the now familiar adrenalin surge picked me up and carried me powerfully to spot height 1,690 ft (508 m), home of the second highest pub in England.

My time was 26 hours 36 minutes, over two and a half hours faster than my painful record of last year, nearly six hours faster than the record I had been so proud of six years previously. The latter had represented a major achievement for me, an anxious yet exciting journey into physical and mental unknowns. Now the run had become a test piece, an opportunity to prove and hone my fitness. And yet I had lost no respect for the route and the challenge it imposed. It was like an old and very tough friend, always ready to give you a metaphorical box on the ears should you attempt to take too many liberties.

My new time made me reconsider something I had thought theoretically possible for years. In the mid-1970s, George Rhodes, a club member and former international cross-country runner, had set off with Denis Weir to attempt a 24 hour Tan–Cat. Their attempt foundered when their support failed to materialise with torches for the night. I'd heard however that they were on target at the time. It is not too difficult to be on target half-way through a run and it was intriguing that neither had seen fit to try again. When I inspected the breakdown of my schedule times I reached the conclusion that, for me, a 24-hour completion would require 'speed training', perfect underfoot conditions, good weather, a short summer night, a dash of inspiration and a slice of good luck; a fascinating combination of variables which *may*, some day, tempt me to rattle these old bones just one more time.

The LDWA Dalesman Hundred

I'm not sure I was ready to tackle the Dalesman Hundred. One really should have extra reserves for an event of this length and be looking forward to it with fresh anticipation. I felt rather too relaxed and a little jaded as I set off alongside John Richardson *en route* for Ingleborough and Penyghent, two of the famous Yorkshire Three Peaks. We were in a group designated 'runners' while in the group of 'walkers', set off four hours previously, was Inken on her first attempt at 100 miles (160 km). There was good company around us too, Brian Harney, whose record I had broken on the Pennine Way, was there, as also was Pete Simpson, whose record I hoped to break later on the Coast to Coast. I did not feel to be running very well and constantly re-assured myself that this run was simply a build-up to that record attempt. It is difficult however for an old war horse not to respond to the bray of the battle trumpet – and these guys around us certainly meant business! Either they were over-estimating their abilities or I had, up to now, over-estimated mine.

My schedule was a fairly trustworthy one however and produced a final time of 22 hours. Having covered the route in training, I thought this was a slightly over-ambitious estimate. The leading group were already well ahead of my leg times. I decided to let them get on with it and concentrated on keeping a tight rein on John who was in danger of being dragged along with them.

The light rain at the start had assumed stair-rod proportions on Ingleborough and by Penyghent I thought we were in a monsoon. Having endured this kind of weather throughout spring, I became totally disenchanted. I felt tired from my Tan–Cat, I was not up with the leaders and altogether, I just wanted an excuse to quit. To make things worse, John was suffering from painful ankle tendons and was unlikely to be able to keep me company for much longer. The only excuse I had to quit was severe lack of enjoyment! Good enough really, but as my demon readily pointed out, I still needed this one as preparation for the Coast to Coast. I splashed onwards.

The ground was astonishingly waterlogged. The valley paths, in particular the Dalesway, were sticky mud ribbons along which I slid, skidded and cursed. After about only 25 miles (40 km), I began to pass walkers, often well-clad figures in stout brogues, some with the traditional blackthorn stick. In comparison I felt like a drowned and ill-equipped rat. A bad-tempered rat who muttered rude things about their great feet, nearly 400 pairs of them, which had churned this mud up to a quagmire.

By now, John had dropped behind. I pottered on alone thinking jaundiced thoughts about the British climate, the futility of ultra-hill running and my own recalcitrant stubbornness. Following the Pennine Way across Dodd Fell and down to Hawes brought me to Hardraw, a major support point. Here, the demon belatedly emerged and flared his nostrils as he caught sight of Brain Harney and an impressive group of other hard men. They looked rather cold, wet and tired. This was exactly how I felt, in fact I'd been ready to have a good feed and change into drier clothes; until now. I grabbed a cup of tea and a bun and, with a cheery wave, galloped straight out again. It really is amazing what a stimulating effect the misery and suffering of rival runners can have on me. I suspect something quite nasty is lurking under my pleasant exterior (probably the demon).

Light was fading and I hurried to make use of what had not been trapped by the sullen grey clouds. After a few miles I came across a stricken figure who yet had the guise and gait of a classy performer. It was Pete Simpson and he was suffering from 'hunger bonk' (hypoglycemia – low blood sugar). As he had just applied the usual remedy of a chocolate bar, or several, I assured him he would soon recover. In fact as darkness fell, he re-joined me and together we dropped back to the road.

The next support point was one I had been looking forward to. It was almost at 50 miles (80 km) and in my terms meant I was ready to head for home. In the support tent was one of those characters who represent a, thankfully, rare infestation on this type of event. An erstwhile leader, he had obviously started to run out of steam here. The rules of the LDWA Hundred allow the organisers to require walkers to form groups of four or more during the night; those first in are given 'waiting time' until sufficient numbers arrive to form a safe group. When dawn comes the group may split and those with 'waiting time' carry this advantage with them. As this particular night was merely damp with a little mist, the grouping rule was not being applied. However, this character complained that he did not know his way over the next set of hills and he should therefore be granted 'waiting time' until he could attach himself to someone who did!

I resented both his dependence on us to do his navigating and on his gaining a half-hour rest without penalty. By the time Pete and I arrived he was sipping his umpteenth cup of tea and grooming his feathers. As the three of us set off up Wild Boar Fell I made some pointed and rude remarks in this man's direction, they slid neatly off his back of course. I was not sure what rules were being applied but I had every intention of leaving him in the lurch at the first opportunity.

Such opportunity was sadly not forthcoming. Pete was far too much of a gentleman to divine my intentions and I had no axe to grind with Pete. Soon I had to concentrate all my intention on good navigation as a thick swathe of mist rolled across the fells and obscured all but a few feet of ground ahead. After successfully visiting the control point on Wild Boar summit we headed across Scarth Fell for remote Grisedale. Once we dropped below the mist route finding was relatively easy and I'd lost my chance to slip away I thought. However, at the next control both Pete and the other man seemed slow to get organised. Seizing my chance I poured my scalding tea into a plastic bottle and crept surreptitiously out of the shelter. No one followed and after a few fairy footsteps I went scampering off down the road. I kept up the pressure for a mile or so then eased off. I felt pleased to be rid of the pest but sorry for Pete.

After crossing the moor below Aye Gill Pike I began the three-mile (5 km) road section to Dent. I was now running almost effortlessly and passing scores of mainly silent, shuffling figures, like some ghostly, vanquished army. I had also passed another runner who thought he was the leader but as a matter of caution, I disbelieved him. Approaching Dent I heard a cheerful hail; it was Inken. I had not expected to see her so soon but she had spent an unscheduled hour on a scenic tour of Swarth Fell. She was in remarkably good spirits, however, so I guessed she was not too perturbed, as I would have been.

Together we ran into the church hall at Dent where I quickly swallowed a jar of peaches I'd sent on here. At 3.00 a.m. I did not fancy the cooked breakfast on offer but got moving quickly again. I'd heard there was only one person ahead of me. He was 15 minutes up but with 37 miles (60 km) left to catch him I fancied my chances. After only a few miles I passed a small group and ascertained that the former leader was one of their number. He was lightly clad and carrying only a 'bum-bag' which could not possibly have held all the equipment demanded by the rules. I was not concerned, I could see by his gait and the look in his eyes that he was a spent force. As I ascended high on the shoulder of Whernside *en route* for Ribblehead, a long, cruel shower came splattering in on the chill dawn wind. I guessed it would demoralise my rival sufficiently for him to give up the ghost at the next checkpoint, which I believe it did. I was more concerned about the men of proven character like Brian Harney, Pete Simpson, Roger Baumeister and so on, they were behind me now but they would not fade so easily nor would a little rain deter them. I also thought about those 'walkers' who were still ahead. What if one of them was a dark horse who had joined the 10.00 a.m. start to disguise his intentions? I decided I would only be really sure of my position when I had passed all the early starters too and was first in the field.

Acting on this decision I set out to press home whatever advantage I had. At Nethergill I came upon my old friend Denis Weir out for an 'easy' day with the walking fraternity. After sharing a mile or so with him I set off with much lighter tread. Following the very muddy path of the Dalesway to Yockenthwaite I observed that instead of keeping to the official route on the Dalesway footpath, there were people on the other side of the river following the road which, in these conditions, was easier and faster.

Shortly after, I arrived at the village of Buckden and enjoyed a cup of tea with another old friend, Alan Heaton. Now in his late fifties, Alan is a former holder of the Lake District Fell Record; 65 peaks within 24 hours and of course, a former Pennine Way record holder. As usual, Alan sounded very pessimistic about his own form and fitness but imparted the useful information that only two walkers were now in front of me.

I set off with some trepidation on a climb I had been dreading, the long haul from Buckden over to Litton. I was now feeling leg weary and hoped that a glimpse of the two in front would spur me on. I was rather mystified when I crossed a large patch of smooth mud in front of a gate to discover no footprints whatever. I examined the mud; not even a hole to indicate someone had pole-vaulted across! Well, I must be in front now. I relaxed a little.

Coming down to Litton I glanced back casually and was horrified to see a figure in shorts less than five minutes behind. Sensing the cup of victory, which had begun to be very important, being dashed from my lips, I galloped along the road, covering over two miles (3 km) in 15 minutes. The steep ascent of Yew Cougar Scar slowed me down but looking back I could see no sign of pursuit. Still not convinced, I pressed on until I felt almost dizzy. I never found out who the figure was but he certainly got me moving again.

I was now only a handful of miles from the finish on good running country round Malham Tarn with the sun at last bursting through. At each checkpoint I received much encouragement from the cheery, selfless souls who manned them. Their friendly banter lifted my spirits out of my rather grim resolve. Suddenly, round a bend, I came upon a pair of figures, quite obviously the two incredible mud-gliders. I expected a cut and thrust battle over the last miles and hitched up me loin cloth! However they subsided with merely a polite 'Good morning'. After a last cruel knee-wracking descent I jogged somewhat stiffly back into the finish at Settle High School. My time was 21 hours 45 minutes, pleasing in the circumstances. Despite my alarm at Litton I had to wait an hour and a half before, fairly predictably, Brian Harney trotted serenely over the bridge and into the finish. What really delighted me however, was to see Inken running freely and easily along the road in nineteenth position. She was the first woman to finish and over four hours ahead of the ladies national 100-mile record holder.

Later, I met one of the incredible mud-gliders and asked him rather pointedly about the route he and his friend had followed from Buckden to Litton. He admitted they had not followed the official route but assured me their alternative was no easier, 'just less muddy'! I commented that this was strange, as when reconnoitering for the event, I had used the route they had taken to save time because it was half a mile shorter and 200 feet less climbing. This did not stop the same man going forward to accept his badge for having 'completed' his tenth 100 mile (160 km) event. I was, however, amused to read recently that several people had been disqualified during spot checks on the 1987 event. Guess who was one of them?

Such petty self-betrayal does more harm to the culprits than those they take advantage of. However, the ethics of ultra fell running are close to my heart notwithstanding their absence from tablets of stone. Occasionally I am asked, though never by fellow runners, how I 'prove' I have followed a route and not taken short-cuts (or even caught the bus!). My invariable answer is, 'Because I say so.' At times I have certainly 'lost' the route and this has always resulted in going further and taking longer. A successful run is nearly always marked by crisp, accurate route finding. On my longer runs I am usually accompanied but I reserve the right to cover sections solo when I choose. Some runners have taken to dropping notes on summits and getting passing walkers to sign route cards. Though laudable in itself and certainly having a safety value, I would not like to see this becoming obligatory. I would certainly refuse to follow any such scheme. I first of all run for myself and meeting my own standards I find exacting enough. By the same token, if the likes of Martin Stone, a prolific soloist and note placer, tells me he has run 26 Munroes in 24 hours (which he has), I only need his word, and so should everyone else. Our sport has a glorious freedom and individuality, but it *is* a hard one. To achieve success in it you must somehow reach a truth within yourself. To cheat is to truly embrace failure, you forfeit your integrity, you have lost.

The Coast to Coast

Having trained through a wet spring, endured bitter easterlies on the Tan–Cat and paddled round the Dalesman Hundred, I was looking forward to better conditions for my Coast to Coast attempt. I was making the bid on the midsummer weekend and surely after the tribulations I had suffered from the weather recently and over the years, I was due for a run in perfect conditions?

My support team consisted of my son Mark who would be a strong runner, while his brother, Sean would also run sections but be mainly responsible for the driving. He enjoyed this latter role, being something of a thwarted rally-driver at heart. Inken was to be 'anchorman' for the whole support strategy and John Beatty was to fulfil the role of 'official photographer' and runner. This team would take me as far as Keld, just about half-way, where John Richardson and Dave Crutch would take over. As usual, I was confident that I had planned well and was very happy with my support team.

We drove up to Cumbria in perfect conditions. My intention had been to start at 3.00 a.m. after a few hours sleep. By starting very early I hoped I could get away with only one full night out. A local forecast at 7.00 p.m., however, foretold of a strong front moving in from the west. My luck with the weather was not due to change after all. The front would reach the Lake District about the time I intended to set off. Although my schedule had been planned to have me at certain places at the right time, I guessed that if I were to waken to the sound of heavy rain being driven against the tent at 2.30 a.m. I might very easily not start at all!

Bravely or rashly therefore, on reaching St Bees shortly before 9.00 p.m. I grasped the bull by the nettles, leapt out of the car, tightened my laces and set off on my 190 mile (304 km) journey across England to the North Sea. By the time John Beatty joined me I had established a rhythm and accepted, quite without relish, that I would now be running through two nights. The record I had to beat was a relatively 'soft' one. It was a little over 51 hours and had been set by Pete Simpson and Frank Thomas of Dark Peak Fell Runners. When one became 'lame' the other had selflessly stayed alongside and so forfeited the chance to complete the run under two days. My own target was 46 hours but I had secretly thought that I might get down towards 42 hours if all went perfectly; that ambition subsided with the 9.00 p.m. start.

At Ennerdale Bridge the contents of the car boot filled a lay-by. Travelling with Mark alongside Ennerdale Water and through the ensuing pine plantations was an eerie experience. There was a mighty but restless wind soughing through the trees, sometimes on our backs, sometimes on our faces. No real force of wind could reach us through the high wall of pines but it threatened trouble when we finally emerged. The night was now very dark. Splats of rain began to dash at us. The atmosphere was oppressive and our mood very subdued. Suddenly I spotted a tiny incandescence to the side of the track. Stopping, I discovered a glow-warm, a tiny jewel in a black eternity. Its physical presence was as nothing, its power as symbol limited only by my own frail and mortal spirit. But if I had been neither frail nor mortal I would have no reason to quest or to strive. Lead kindly light indeed! My spirit *shall* strive to follow.

As I crossed from Ennerdale to Honister, the brain as well as the spirit had to rise to the challenge. Mark had obtained a set of compass bearings from John but was not sure what they referred to. After following one which threatened to lead us down into Buttermere, I got my mind into the navigating. We endured anxious moments in the mist and rain, moving over ground I had never intended covering at night. Gradually the paths re-appeared and the contours fell into a recognised pattern, all was well.

We arrived with the dawn at Rosthwaite, a misty dawn it is true but not particularly wet. Perhaps the forecast of bad weather was exaggerated? Alas! as Inken and I climbed towards Greenup Edge heading for Grasmere, the wind screamed down to meet us. On the ridge to Helm Crag, heavy rain was driven into our faces by a wind of unusual power.

The front had arrived as forecast. However, there were two aspects of the storm which were not as forecast. First, the wind was not blowing out of the south-west but out of the south-east; second, while unpleasant enough in the valleys, there was a kind of 'jet-stream' effect such that above about 1,500 ft (450 m), the wind speed seemed to double. The general trend of the Coast to Coast is, over much of the first half, towards the south-east. Once I was above 1,500 ft (450 m), conversation with my support became impossible. The wind constantly knocked me off balance and I was simply engaged in a battle for survival.

It was a relief to drop into the comparative shelter of the valleys which were merely very wet. Climbing out of Patterdale and into the screaming misery of wind and rain on the long haul over Kidsty Pike, was perhaps the crux of the whole route. At least I had the prospect of the sheltered run alongside Haweswater to look forward to. However, on the section over to Shap, the rain amply compensated for any abatement of wind strength. Here also, as I attempted to lift my pace, Inken, on her second support stint, began to fade. She had a recurrence of a knee problem but also, I think, the savage beating we had just taken from the elements, had sapped her spirit. There was, in truth, little pleasure in this. Our hopes for a fine and happy run were being blasted away. The support share the hardships but may not always be able to access the inspiration which can so powerfully assist the runner. I eased off the pace and together we walked into Shap. What was a paltry 10 minutes from a record I was now unlikely to achieve anyway against a friendship?

Shap; 62 miles (104 km); 16 hours; rain bouncing off the puddles; wind sweeping the desolate A6, but . . . a familiar and welcome smell, fish and chips! I suddenly realised I was hungry, very hungry. I had to wait quite a long time before the feast was produced and the longer I sat contemplating the weather outside, the less inclined I felt to continue. Still, John and the lads did a great job of drying my gear under the hand-dryer in the public toilets. So, although I felt I was only postponing the inevitable, I decided I most certainly would not quit yet. With Sean for company I headed off on cold, stiff legs but with a fortified feeling inside.

As we traversed the rather dreary countryside approaching Orton, the rain eased for a time and then continued as heavy and prolonged showers. The wind felt like a big hand holding me back. Any running into the wind was impossible and I had to be content with sneaking a little run now and again as I turned temporarily out of it or followed a sheltering wall. Sean is probably the most cheerful of my sons and his company brightened the grey and depressing day. An eternal, sometimes infernal optimist, Sean carries his own sunshine with him. He cast it round us now and so, when I reached the car at Sunbiggin Tarn, I was, like Sam Ogelthwaite, moist but determined!

The moments at Sunbiggin Tarn are etched into my memory as a series of crystal clear and poignant images. The area is, for me, strangely foreboding and mysterious. The Tarn itself, a large sink-hole, is rush-rimmed and houses large colonies of sea-birds. These were now wheeling and gliding in vast numbers, their forlorn cries adding to the pervading sense of desolation. In the back of the car John Beatty sat looking both drawn and animated. He spoke elatedly of photographing the birds but he also told me that his Achilles tendons were very sore. It was John's turn to accompany me on the next section and he wanted very much to again share my burden of miles and play his part in what he considered an epic venture. He had resolved to take a chance with his injury and come anyway. I looked carefully into his face and saw the anxiety behind his eyes. Another friend willing to endure hardship so that I might achieve my dream. But no! Much as I had looked forward to the company and fascinating conversation of this remarkable artist I could not accept that my joy should be his anguish.

My disappointment was as nothing compared to the great strength I drew from the simple fact that John had been prepared to come with me. As I set off once more, my mere stubborn resolve to struggle on began to be replaced by a more positive form of determination. John's response had been for me another inspirational gleam in the dark.

In a happier state of mind I entered Smardale valley, where Sunbiggin is foreboding, Smardale is light and cheerful. Perhaps happy, long-ago spirits still inhabit the ancient village settlements above the valley. Whatever the reason, I have always experienced a feeling of peace and a lightening of mood here. I dropped out of the incessant buffeting of the wind, all was quiet and the rain eased. By the time I ascended once more to the wind's rough embrace I had established a little haven of calm within myself. This haven would stand against the storm for some time yet.

I trotted and walked towards Kirkby Stephen, my mind encapsulated in this comfortable state. All systems on low output, the body performing economically and mechanically. So switched off had I become that I missed my turning in the town. Jogging contentedly along, leaving the support point in my wake, I suddenly became aware of Inken racing up behind me shouting uncomplimentary remarks. I returned feeling a little foolish.

The next leg was likely to be a crucial one. First however, I must consider whether I shall undertake it at all. I have been going for approaching 20 hours although I have covered only 82 miles (132 km). Most of the time I have been battered by the weather and this must have taken its toll of my strength. The next leg is a long one over a bleak moor, Nine Standards Rigg. Once embarked, I am committed to going on into the second night as John Richardson and Dave Crutch are due to meet me at Keld at the end of this section. If I want to stop them coming out, if I feel there is no realistic chance of success, I must contact them now. I cannot bring them out and then quit.

I am hanging on by a thread. If I lose any further touch with my schedule, I will lose my drive. Once that happens, this weather will force me into swift submission. On the other hand my legs seem to have escaped the paralyzing stiffness which was gripping them at Shap. The thread is tight stretched but it has been well spun. It will hold me through another night – I hope.

Off then and up into the mists wreathing Nine Standards Rigg. Mark is with me now and he seems quite unaffected by the weather, he too has matured with his running years. As we climb higher we move into heavy rain, heaving bogs and almost palpable mist. Apart from 80 plus miles (130 km) in my legs it's just like being at home on Bleaklow! Quite to my surprise, I begin to feel amazingly cheerful. Then we lose the narrow trod coming from the summit. Follows an age of stumbling over tussocks as none of my intelligent guesstimates bears fruit. Eventually, Mark spots a stake and we regain the path which we have been following on a parallel course only 100 yards away.

At last we leave the moor behind and the ground becomes more interesting as we descend to Raven Seat and approach Keld itself. Although it is not yet 9.00 p.m. the light is fading under the heavy cloud blanket. At this time of the year I had expected to have useful light until nearly 11.00 p.m. I must minimise my stop time at Keld in order to utilise whatever glims remain. The urge to dwell in the car, to savour the warmth and dryness, to enjoy the company of good friends, must be resisted.

And in Keld, the entire support team were gathered. John and Dave, not having supported through a day and night of depressing weather, were in good humour. Although my own mood was serious, even grim, I could not help but respond in kind to the cheerful banter. I managed to retain my concentration however and within 10 minutes I had changed shoes, donned dry clothes and eaten.

As I set off once more, I realised that John Beatty was missing. We soon ran into the flash of his camera and his words of encouragement echoed through my mind as we crossed the River Swale and headed for the delightfully named Crackpot Hall. The bridge across the river sees the convergence of the Tan–Cat route, the Pennine Way and the Coast to Coast. What a place to steer my wheelchair towards in future years! I was now with Inken and John Richardson. Inken should really have stepped down before this, she's been on the go now for 24 hours. She looked intense and preoccupied, almost as if it was she who was attempting this record. I hoped in asking her to coordinate the attempt I had not imposed too large a burden on her. John, fresh, fit, experienced and resourceful was, as ever, a symbol of strength and steady optimism. Flanked by my two friends I felt suddenly transformed, full of vitality and hope. All thoughts of quitting vanished and were replaced by a hunger to consume the miles. Keld was half-way and by the time I'd left it I had taken 24 hours. It is almost impossible to improve on one's time for the first half of an ultra route, the sleepless miles have an insidious but irresistible braking effect. If I am to even approach that 48-hour target, I must drive on.

While the daylight permitted, I enjoyed the Dales scenery and the interesting ground with its remains of the ancient lead mining industry. John is a great conversationalist and his wit and warmth eased the miles. Inken also, responded cheerfully to this lighter, more optimistic mood and we travelled through the gathering gloom enjoying each other's company. All too soon however, the gloom became night and with the night came a terrible attack of sleepiness. As we followed the interminable, stony track to Surrender Bridge, I became both very tired and desperately sleepy. I long for the uphill section just before Surrender Bridge, I can allow myself to walk that. How tired my mind must be. I've reached Surrender Bridge having run uphill without being able to perceive the gradient. A mistake, but a revealing one. When even the mind abdicates its power over the body and seeks temporary oblivion, an idea deeply embedded in an uncompromising will may impel the body ruthlessly onwards.

Black midnight at Surrender Bridge. A subdued glow of light from the two tents where the others were settled down. A bleak spot. Yet I yearned with all my heart, it seemed, to crawl into one of those tents and lay down my weary head. But this desire must have been less than that which compelled me to accomplish my journey. I paused only long enough to say farewell to Inken. For 27 hours she had been the dynamo driving the support machine. Not only had her running contribution been considerable but in these conditions the pressure on all other aspects of support had been enormous. At last she consented to rest and I was glad.

My slow pace thus far meant that I was now, more or less, where my original schedule had placed me. However, although I had reconnoitered this section twice, the Stygian blackness made route finding difficult indeed. At one time John and I stood with torches, looking for a track which was only 10 yards away. It was one of those spooky nights, of which I have known only a handful, which seem to draw in and smother all light sources. Our torch beams had no power to penetrate the black vortex. Following the shapes and images of my mind rather than the ground, we proceeded rather haltingly. The concentration needed at least helped focus my mind. I emerged from the well of sleepiness amazingly alert once more. Sufficiently aware, for instance, to discern what a masterly job Dave Crutch had done in converting a spacious and rather period bus shelter in Reeth to a well-appointed support point.

The route from Reeth is intricate but my homework paid off and at 3.30 a.m. in Richmond there were faint glimmers of returning light. Leaving the town, still with John, I made an error and we found ourselves on the wrong side of a sewage works. John decided we should short-cut across the works to regain our line. This involved clambering up two eight-foot-high fences which were capped with strands of barbed wire. Swaying precariously on top of these, legs akimbo, I felt rather vulnerable. I bet Ted Dance's *Rules to protect runners from their follies* would circumscribe such practices in order, I suppose, that the practices should not circumscribe the runners (as it were). Still, one can see the funny side of it, particularly as from this vantage point there was a perfectly good path visible just outside the fence.

After this excitement, the next sections were rather tedious. Wet fields, long tracks and the notorious eight miles (13 km) of road to Ingleby Cross and the freedom of the North York Moors. Near Catterick there was one moment of unexpected splendour. Low on the horizon, the grey uniformity of the dawn sky was irresistibly penetrated by a gash of light. As I stopped and stared, a chasm appeared in the clouds. Next moment the incandescent orange flare of the rising sun sprang through the gap. In awed wonder I regarded the huge glaring eye of energy, and he regarded me . . . 'Puny mortal, of course I still burn. Did you think otherwise?' Another gleam of light perhaps, but this one too awesome for comfort. The rift in the grey curtain snapped shut and I was left to run and muse in the watery dawn.

I had thought the long road section would allow me to pull back some time. Unfortunately it coincided with my usual morning low point. Despite Dave's bright chatter alongside me, I felt sleepy and could barely shuffle along. The only energy I possessed was manifest in a feeble urge to strangle Dave! My stupefied mind told me this would be ungrateful and a misuse of energy. Eventually I began to wake up and then I was genuinely grateful for his cheerful company and his gentle humour. Dave and I share a common ambition; he wants to complete the Bob Graham Round and I want to help him do it.

At 7.30 a.m. the morning had become milder and drier. As I completed the last few miles to Ingleby Cross alone I could feel a pulse of excitement beginning to swell within me. Ingleby Cross marks the start of the final section, about 50 miles (80 km) across the North York Moors. It is also where I expected to meet my good friend and colleague from work, Ian Cockerill. A native of this area, Ian was happy to combine a family visit with some support running. It was to Ian I turned a few years and many thousand miles ago on a muddy Birmingham tow-path and announced my intention to have 'Just one go at the Pennine Way'. We had shared many a boring Birmingham mile since then and now, at last, we had an opportunity to share some real running.

As I swept into the support point a wonderful feeling of strength and happiness had filled me. At that moment, I truly would not have changed places with anyone on earth. I was a little embarrassed at having kept Ian waiting so long. At least he had been able to return home for a second breakfast. It was good to see him and as usual he was impeccably attired in a splendidly matched running outfit. I feel Ian is very much a Beau Brummel among runners, particularly runners like me.

Feeling therefore a mite travel-stained and shabby, I set off with Ian and Inken. My own tension gone, I had hoped to see Inken rather more relaxed too but while the runner may well enter states of euphoria as he embarks on the last stages of a long run, the role of the support team is to exercise constant care and vigilance. Well, perhaps smiles would come later, I thought. Still in a happy frame of mind I left for Beacon Hill with the two of them. It was at this point that John Beatty appeared with his camera and captured a picture which is now very dear to me. That I look a little weary on it still surprises me but I know the peace and happiness that glowed within at that time. The picture has become precious to me, and to Ian and Inken, I hope.

Gradually my euphoria begins to fade as a physical fatigue seeps slowly back. Under the influence of heavy rain, the paths over the moors have assumed the consistency of porridge. The constant fight for purchase and balance is sapping my strength. After the mud, the flat cinder track of the old railway to the Lion Inn is a relief. Soon, of course, the tediousness of these rather empty miles begins to weigh heavily. I start to fancy that the inn is round the next bend

Ian, Inken and Mike leaving Ingleby Cross on the Coast to Coast.

several miles too soon. I realise I must be very tired to make such bad miscalculations. Eventually we begin to meet runners in various states of disrepair coming towards us. Although at first this introduces a little variety, I soon get tired of saying 'Howdo' and relapse into a state bordering apathy.

At last the Lion Inn hove into view and, as always, I experienced that surge of pleasure which accompanies these little reunions. And finally, a real smile from Inken. With only about 30 miles (50 km) remaining, she too must be anticipating the end of what has become a more demanding venture than we ever envisaged. But now I have plenty of good company on all sections as my entire support team switch in and out as it suits them. With their good cheer I keep picking up but despite these better moments I seem to be on a slow downward spiral. I am tired with both the bone-aching weariness of physical fatigue and the mind-numbing effects of sleep deprivation. On the road out of Grosmont I have a desperate fight to stay awake. A few minutes sleep might help but I will not yield any more of my precious time.

At Glaisdale, perhaps for the first time ever, the support point elicits no response. I feel very dejected. With so few miles to go I should be feeling elated not depressed. I can hardly face getting up and going on. Even my support team seem to have caught my mood, everyone is very subdued. Only one person looks after me at the stop, the others hover quietly around. I notice John with his camera but he won't intrude and contents himself with some long-range shots. This is like a wake – my own! Although my mind is observant and distantly receptive, my brain isn't functioning as it should. John Richardson has just calculated that at my present pace I might slip under 48 hours. I have the utmost confidence in John but as I shuffle along with Mark and Dave my repeated efforts at mental arithmetic keep producing the same result: I cannot possibly achieve 48 hours, in fact, I may be two hours adrift of this. Eventually after several miles of stumbling physical and mental effort I realise the error is mine. The Coast to Coast mileage is 190 (304 km) but mentally I had always geared myself up for 200 miles (320 km). Now I was approaching the end, I had forgotten to knock off those 'extra' miles.

With an indescribable feeling of joy and relief I reduced my miles remaining from 22 to 12. The tentacles of anxiety and self-doubt which have been dragging me irresistibly down into the black pit of despair are severed at a stroke. Thus released, the spirit soars and begins to pull my tired body after it.

The lovely silvan path from Little Beck past Falling Foss restores me entirely and it is with a start that I realise I have reached my final support point, there are only 10 miles (16 km) remaining. An excitement begins to seize me. This run had been so very hard. I might have quit at any time yet both route completion and record now lie within my grasp. With John Richardson, Dave, Mark and Sean all gathered around me I set off up the hill. It is essential to run if possible. A crazy joy spurs me to put in two hard bursts which I note with glee have John wheezing – the run-in has begun.

This finishing effort must start early. The final cliff-top miles are undulating and broken by stiles, I anticipate difficulty in actually getting over them. Covering stretches of rough grass and heather, my leg-weariness returns. On track and road I have an almost aching hunger to devour the miles. Approaching Hawkser, where Ian is waiting, I know I can't run up all the hills, then somehow do, and now everyone is breathing hard.

Ian has sussed out the rather intricate route through the caravan park which we take at speed. John, rather ill advisedly, stops to relieve himself and has great difficulty re-establishing contact. As we run ever more frantically, my mind recedes and I become a running machine. At last, the dreaded cliff-top path. As we twist and turn down vicious little bends, my foot pivots on a larger blister which bursts with a flare of pain. Although I am brought back to reality I will not stop. Gradually, the agony subsides in the flow of adrenalin.

By now the pace is taking its toll. I glance back from a stile; Dave is well off the back and John is pulling horrible faces. Mark and Sean, still in possession of their youthful speed, are enjoying both the run and John's discomfiture. Ahead, Ian seems to be running like a pursued hare as I strive to catch him. The path is never ending, will my strength or adrenalin hold out? I don't think I can keep this up much longer.

Suddenly I recognised the final approach to Robin Hood's Bay. I had long prepared for this descent to the sea through the little village. The road plummets down at 1 in 3 and even my best scenario had me trotting cautiously down to the finish. The expected reality of pain-wracked legs as stiff as rusty hinges, I had deliberately not entertained.

The finish of the Coast to Coast. Entering Robin Hood's Bay with Mark and Sean.

Sympathy for Dave who got left behind in the rush for the finish of the Coast to Coast. From left to right: Sean, Dave, Mike, Inken, John Richardson.

Sharing a quiet moment with John at the end of the Coast to Coast.

Miraculously, it was not like that at all. The frantic rush along the cliffs did not cease at the top of the hill. In fact, I accelerated down it with only Mark and Sean in contact.

Shortly after I completed the run I wrote up the account in my log-book, partly because I wanted to capture the unique flavour of this remarkable finish. This is what I wrote:

The final mad, utterly ridiculous flight down the steep hill to the sea-front is like a crazy dream. If I meet with a car on this bend I know I shall simply put one foot on the bonnet, one on the roof and be over! Nothing can touch me. I'm at the pinnacle of all my mental and physical powers. I am not merely alive, I am a life force, elemental, joyful.

Perhaps that is why another elemental life force, the sea, creates such an impact on my spirit as I rush headlong into it, cooling my burning feet. It's crashing around like a living entity, so welcome! How marvellous that it has swept right up to the edge of the cobbles and is in such lively form. I persuade the others to come and join me and we all embrace with the waves laughing around us.

Never have I felt such sheer and simple joy at the end of a run. Moments such as these not only provide the answer to why one does things like this but why we are alive at all. One moment of such joy is worth more, far more than countless years of steady rational living. To have encountered hardship, discomfort, to have experienced one's physical, mental and spiritual limitations and weaknesses, to have found a path beyond them, not conquering them but accepting and yet transcending them, to have been supported, guarded and guided lovingly by friends represents, for me, a joy both sublime and supreme. I ask for no more.

Postscript

Whenever my thoughts go back to the finish of my Coast to Coast, the overwhelming memory of it is the feeling of joy I experienced. When that mad rush came to an abrupt end in the sea it was as if that sublime emotion burst from me with all the power of a sunrise. Perhaps it was as well that fatigue later set in or I might have been consumed by my own fires! However, two more pleasures awaited me before the day ended. First, having been borne off to our rest camp I sneaked out and ventured down that fearsome 1 in 3 again, this time tottering very authentically. I then surprised the support team ensconced in the pub. I didn't want to be left out, and anyway, I thought I'd earned a pint. I can't remember whether I had one or two but what I next remember is being gently laid down on someone's lilo in my tent. I can still recall the absolute luxury of my aching bones finally coming to rest and kindly hands tucking me in.

Once I realised I was going to get inside 48 hours for the route I lost interest in the time. However, I recorded 46 hours and 49 minutes, this meant I had completed the second half over an hour faster than the first, my last burst was not without effect. Still, the record must be considered as 'soft'; the experience of it however, was not.

My Pennine Way record had realised for me an almost sacred dream. Even on completion my mind could scarcely grasp the reality and my joy and happiness seemed to reach sublime, even ethereal heights. The Coast to Coast record was relatively unimportant, but the experience, so unexpectedly demanding, was everything. The joy I experienced on completion seemed so natural, so simple, a burst of delight at being alive, of being strong, of striving and succeeding, of being so blessed with the gift of life and the gift of friends. That wild, exuberant finish was nothing other than a cry of joy and my own personal thanksgiving.

chapter seven

PLUNDERING THE SPIRIT

The Southern Uplands Way: Preparation 1986

As 1985 gave way to 1986 I began to cast about for a suitable venture. I had enjoyed the shape of my previous year, two minor targets and one major, so I thought I would attempt something similar. Several friends suggested I should consider running the Southern Uplands Way which I had only vaguely heard of. Perhaps as a hint I received a set of maps and a guide as a present from Inken.

It transpired that the Southern Uplands Way was a sort of Scottish Coast to Coast. It starts on the west coast at Port Patrick near Stranraer and finishes at Cockburnspath south of Edinburgh. There did not seem to have been any record attempts for this quite recent innovation, but at 212 miles (340 km) it appeared to offer the kind of challenge I sought. I was keen to do a long run in Scotland, the areas are less populated and the hills seem never-ending. For some time I had nursed an ambition to devise an overland route north to south through Scotland but the temptation of a ready-made route was inviting. I mentally postponed my north-south route until the days when only distance and not time is important.

As usual, I began hard training in early spring. Returning from the rigours of my annual Scottish winter mountaineering course I was surprised to find that even in Derbyshire, winter dragons held spring in thrall. I found training unusually onerous and I never seemed to be running well. Although the deep endurance always lay beneath the surface I felt jaded. Either my successes had satisfied my appetite for really hard ultra running, or I was over the hill – in more ways than one! Certainly my knees were giving me increasing pain, particularly downhill, but I did not like to think the ageing process had begun to gnaw at my overall strength. As ever there was one sure way to find out, head first, full tilt into a windmill. Well, perhaps not full tilt; as usual I had a look at the windmill first. The Southern Uplands Way represented my 'training carrot' that spring, and I was keen to get the feel of what would be an entirely new piece of ground for me.

I was charmed by the start at Port Patrick. I had the good fortune to begin my training run on a fine sunny morning. At 6.30 a.m. the place was deserted, but very picturesque in the morning light, and I began to think I had made a very good choice of route. As the miles unwound, however, I started to entertain doubts. The Way was turning out to be a real Jekyll and Hyde; relatively short stretches of great charm and beauty were interspersed by either long stony tracks, or, what was worse, boring miles of metalled road. I began to look forward fervently to the section through the Galloway Hills, which I knew were very scenic.

The Galloway section was indeed scenic. Unfortunately, much, too much, of the Way followed stony forest tracks. Road and track may offer swift passage but I found the unchanging rhythm required monotonous and tiring. Furthermore, the hard surface tends to jar joints and muscles.

I spent another three days reconnoitring the Way and my initial impression was amply confirmed. The going underfoot seemed to alternate between extremely wet, boggy terrain and hard track, an unfortunate combination, designed to cause severe foot problems. The route itself either took my breath away or bored me to distraction. For instance, I traversed the Lowther Hills on a fine spring evening with not a soul around. The slanting sun sparkled on the fresh spring mantle and cast deep shadows in clefts and hollows. The hills radiated to all points of the compass and here and there a patch of old snow glinted faintly. Descending from these boldly rounded hills I was faced with a mile of metalled road followed by three miles of forest track. By the time I was coming to the end of such a tedious section all sense of inspiration had evaporated.

My third day of reconnaissance took me over perhaps the most pleasant section of the Way thus far. From Daer Reservoir the route negotiates some surprisingly rough ground. I discovered that whenever forest tracks were left one followed forest breaks which were paths mainly in the minds of the route planners. Perhaps increasing use will establish better going, but at present you may encounter tussocks that tickle your nose. Having battled through both the tedious and the rough I crossed under the A74 at Beattock and was rewarded with a very fine ascent to Ettrick Head. Even the forest track was enjoyable, offering a greater variety of gradient and scenery than usual. Just before the final climb to Ettrick Head, the track and everything around seemed to spiral downwards into a green tree-shrouded hole in the hills. I had an eerie feeling that I was going down for ever and was quite relieved when a path branched off and made uphill again.

I followed a vigorous stream coursing between green, tree-lined banks. With the sun now dappling through the trees, the stream leaping into small quiet pools and the whole area containing no hint of any other human presence, the memory of the metalled miles faded to temporary insignificance. Better was to come. At the crest of the climb I reached Craigmichan Scar, an impressively steep hillside, where the exposed rock and scree could easily pitch the unwary into a closer acquaintance with the valley floor. This is a key watershed with Moffat Water flowing into the Irish Sea via the Solway Firth and Ettrick Water joining the Tweed, which it accompanies to the North Sea. The area seems to be a haunt for various species of birds, and if I was less ignorant of such matters I might relate what they were. I enjoyed watching their busy spring-time activities – and I know feathered killers swoop hereabouts for I discovered gory remains.

It is at Craigmichan that those responsible for devising the route play their most dastardly trick on the poor walker. Having gained a height of 2,000 ft

(600 m) the obvious option is to continue NW and reach the line of hills which then undulate north-eastwards above Moffat Water. I know these hills from club walks and they give invigorating, mainly pathless walking with excellent views north and west to the hills around Hart Fell and down into the famous gorge containing the Grey Mares Tail waterfall. Instead of this an easy but quite soulless expedient is followed. The inevitable forest track is reached and the route plunges rapidly down as if fearing the heights. This is bad enough, but worse is to follow; five miles (8 km) of metalled road to Scabcleuch whence one ascends to rejoin the line from the hills which need never have been abandoned.

Whether such planning is the result of fearing to expose the walker to a (modestly) high level traverse or fear of crossing some sacred grouse moor, I know not. But I deplore such pusillanimity. If Tom Stephenson had adopted such an unimaginative and weak-kneed approach to the Pennine Way we might well be walking to Kirk Yetholm along the A6. With all the silk at their disposal the Scottish planners have produced a sow's ear.

At this point I should either have abandoned my plans for the Southern Uplands Way, or modified the route to my own tastes. Instead, I used a car on all the major road sections and lied to myself that I would not mind coping with the road too much when I was doing the route for real. Thus my ambition to set records on definitive long-distance footpaths blinded me to the frequent lapses in those virtues which a route must possess to sustain my spirit while making the attempt. Whereas I had regarded the Coast to Coast as a series of wonderful areas of hill and moor connected by annoyingly frequent stretches of road, I was rapidly coming to the conclusion that the Southern Uplands Way consisted of almost endless miles of road and track interspersed with short stretches of tantalisingly beautiful country.

This feeling was confirmed in the area around St Mary's Loch. Leaving the loch behind, the route climbs easily up into the hills heading for Blake Muir. I reached the high point on a day of sunshine and sparkling visibility. Turning through 360 degrees I could see no cultivated valleys, no walls, no habitation anywhere in sight. The hills rolled away to the blue and purple distance in every direction. Yet again, I was tempted to believe such free and open country would compensate for the route's obvious shortcomings.

Beyond Blake Muir the Way follows an old drove road high over Minch Moor and the 'Three Brethren'. Although I did not realise at the time, once I had descended to Yair Bridge from the Three Brethren I had little more to look forward to. The attractiveness of a long distance footpath does not lie in its hills alone. However, to compensate for a lack of hills the alternative ground must be charming indeed. After crossing the Tweed at Melrose the route certainly traverses a further set of hills. I cannot believe they are really as dreary as the line chosen by the Southern Uplands Way would suggest. In traversing them I found I was surrounded by countless acres of monotonous grouse moor having all the variety of a desert and none of the romance. Apart from the odd dell or wooded valley, there was no compensation to be found elsewhere on the remainder of the route.

Perhaps covering these last sections, tired and in the rain, on my last training day did not help. As I thrashed down the final road miles *en route* for the cliff top finish, memories of the cliffs above Robin Hood's Bay spurred me on. An excellent footpath across a gorse strewn hillside raised my hopes still further. Alas! The cliff top 'path' was a precarious animal-trod one either inches wide or quite invisible. It crept apologetically outside cultivated fields which threatened to push it, and any user, into the sea. A timid path this, it disappeared regularly and, come summer, would inevitably vanish beneath the long grass, nettles, brambles and other weeds awaiting the nudge of Nature. Any attempt at a finishing sprint here would precipitate a very premature dip in the sea.

In theory, I had been postponing a decision to attempt the route or not until I had finished my reconnaissance. In practice, I had expended too much time and effort to shelve the plan, in any case I had nothing else in mind. I tried to think of the very beautiful stretches of the Way, and in my mind's eye I fancied myself gliding swiftly along road and track and savouring the delights to be found between. In this respect I may award myself full marks for optimism, no marks for realism and minus marks for prediction.

The Southern Uplands Way not only brought me to my knees, it caused me to corrupt my painstakingly constructed and delicately balanced beliefs which constitute my personal ethos of ultra-distance running.

Indigestible Aperitifs

The miserable, west spring continued, but I crossed my fingers and hoped Dame Fortune might produce a sunny smile for my two warm-up runs. After an absence of some years I had decided to enter the Fellsman Hike along with Mark and Inken. I had previously competed in the Fellsman prior to my first Pennine Way attempt when I finished in third place. It seemed to me that with the relaxing of one or two rules in favour of the out and out runners the standard at the top end had improved, and I thought I would be doing well to finish much inside the first ten. At around 60 miles (100 km) the Fellsman was not really long enough to condition me for truly ultra performance, but it covers tough, hilly terrain, and would, I hoped, get my legs into shape for the hill sections on the Southern Uplands Way.

Whatever the Fellsman did for my hill legs, it did nothing for my morale. Not quite true, it gave it a severe beating. In retrospect, what the event did for my hill legs was probably to induce arthritis. Even today, I recall my performance with pangs of embarrassment. As usual, at the kit check I had had to undergo the ritual sarcasm and bumptious cheek from a pimply-faced youth who stared aghast at a small hole in my trainers. He implied that it was most likely that he, personally, would have to turn out and rescue me when I succumbed to the hazardous effects of wet feet. I resisted the very strong temptation to shake him warmly by the throat and instead thrust a stout pair of breeches forward for inspection. As I expected, he was duly impressed. Once outside, I threw the breeches into the back of the car and substituted two pairs of thermal tights. I did not want pimple features to suffer apoplexy but, with the weather turning foul, cavorting round in stout but soaked breeks was likely to reduce my nether regions to the state suffered by that proverbial bear with his proverbial botty.

In view of what followed, I made a great mistake in restraining my natural inclination regarding the spotty youth. The punishment for justifiable homicide is not as severe as that inflicted by this particular run, and I could certainly have lived with my conscience. We set off in atrocious conditions and I felt awful from the start. The only change as the run unfolded was that the weather progressed from abominable to indescribable, and my performance did the same.

At the high, exposed checkpoint before swampy Fleet Moss I was extending a palsied hand to accept a desperately needed cup of tea from an official when the wind blew the entire tent away. In the battle to rescue capsized soup tureens and priceless samovars, not to mention the tricky extrication of tea ladies, palsied runners were understandably neglected. I was beginning to suspect this was not one of my better days.

The only cheering aspects of the venture were the performances of Mark and Inken. Mark trotted round the whole way with me always giving the impression he could have gone faster. He seemed quite pleased that we had finished in eighth place, and I wondered where we might have finished had I been in even reasonable form. As for Inken, I thought she would retire, being a protagonist of that dangerous ethic that if you are not enjoying what you are doing you should try something else. Perhaps I am not the only one to reveal a discrepancy between sentiment and behaviour. She arrived only three hours later, first lady by a wide margin, and as unconcerned as if she had just trotted round the block. Some people can be really infuriating. Still, I must admit it, pimple face was right: my feet were soaked to the armpits.

Rather to my surprise I failed to develop any subsequent complaint which might have provided a handy excuse for my dismal form. It must be old age, I thought. My next scheme would decide the issue. My next scheme was yet another Tan–Cat. Unfortunately, as May drew to a waterlogged close there seemed little chance of a genuine attempt at my record. The most I could hope for was a lull in the rain long enough to enable a quick squelch between my two favourite pubs.

As it was, the weather seemed to save its worst for the weekends. I decided therefore to set off from the south end to minimise the amount of driving in the event of failure. I also only involved my three eldest sons in support; Sean to drive, Mark to run and Gerard, now 14, for the experience. A 10-minute drive from home saw me leaving the Cat and Fiddle in a heaving miasma of wet driving mist and drizzle. Running alone, I moved into the night and onto the moors. The clinging mist settled around me, every tiny droplet of water absorbing then reflecting the pale glow from my small torch. No torch, however powerful, could have penetrated Kinder's misty vapours that night. A head torch simply brought the reflected light closer to the eyes. I held the light down by my knees, as near to the ground as possible. Unable to see more than a yard or two in any direction I navigated almost kinaesthetically over the beloved moor, adjusting my position by the slope and sway of the ground and the changing texture of the surface beneath my feet. Alone but strong, unable to see but sure of my position, I knew that my run was doomed, yet I could draw satisfaction from this state, for a time at least. Mark joined me over Bleaklow, and as the cloying bogs sucked at my legs the corrosive intrusion of a weary disenchantment gnawed its way into my heart. Slithering and sliding down the tomb-like hollows of deep groughs, the moorland gutter system, I was no longer running for a record. I was on a training run, and it was going to be long and hard, with no other reward than a very tired body at the end. But it had to be.

If Bleaklow was bad, Black Hill and Black and White Moss were worse. The peaty ground had drunk of the spring rain to its full capacity, it had sucked and lapped in dribbling excess and now it lay in its own obscene liquefaction like any bloated glutton. I slopped through the filthy mire thinking back two years when John Beatty and I had run through fire and smoke on these selfsame moors.

At White House I discovered Sean beneath his car contemplating what seemed to be a serious axle problem, apparently it was making a bid to lead an independent existence. I ferreted around beneath the recalcitrant vehicle myself, but more out of politeness than interest. The problem seemed insoluble and common sense dictated we abandon the run. I ate some breakfast with a dreadfully hypocritical feigning of deep regret. I must have overdone it, Sean's face emerged from the dark recesses to announce a partial remedy. I would be able to continue. Yippee!

At least I was able to let Gerard stretch his legs. After traversing the tedious but firm reservoir tracks we descended into sleepy Todmorden, just beginning to yawn and stretch itself. No tea and cake shops, no fish and chips, just the rattle of bottles from the humming milk floats and the curious gaze of a bored policeman panda-ing past. I wondered idly whether there were any by-laws forbidding dawn perambulations through the town environs in a state likely to promote a breach of health and fits of laughter? I hoped so.

Apparently not. Leaving Todmorden still unroused we ascended the steep side of the Calder Valley and prepared for the next 20 miles (32 km) of moorland excess. That is, Mark and I did. Gerard I humanely spared from what was to follow. Black Hameldon, Jackson's Ridge and Ickornshaw, each moor seemed worse than the last and I was weary indeed when I eventually arrived in Cowling. Here, I perked up briefly when Dave Crutch, escaping family shopping, volunteered to run with me to Skipton. Mistaking this temporary lift for a genuine rejuvenation I ran strongly out of Skipton waving enthusiastically to the support. No sooner had my crew disappeared and I turned off the road for Rylestone Fell, than I suffered an attack of fatigue the like of which I had never before encountered. For the first time ever, I actually had to fight the urge to just stop and sit down. It took an age to reach Linton, where the boys were wondering where the hell I was. I would have gladly packed in here. Earlier, I had promised myself that a sufficient training effect would be provided by whichever came sooner, 100 miles (160 km) or 24 hours. Though still short of both, by 14 miles (23 km) and about an hour respectively, I was for once ready to lower my standards. Unfortunately, I had promised Gerard a run over Great Whernside. I explained how cold, wet and misty it would be up there, how the light would be failing and what a grim place it was. His eyes lit up and I had not the heart to disappoint him.

It turned out for the best. The hard driven rain had a cold, northern aspect and, with nightfall imminent, it served to concentrate the mind wonderfully. Some of the physical weariness was also scoured away and I ran off the hill with my shaken confidence partially restored. The car, however, was deserted. Mark and Sean had gone up the hill to meet us. When they appeared out of the darkness Sean was limping badly. Whernside in the dark is a bad place for ankles. We started to drive home rather subdued. Beyond Cowling we punctured. I then discovered Sean had no spare wheel. At five minutes to midnight, Sir Lancelot Crutch, adjusting his nightcap, was surprised to hear his phone ringing . . .

Southern Uplands Way – The Attempt

After two weeks of gentle running I began to look forward to what I felt would be a revealing test of my enthusiasm and ability to continue to embark on these super-hard runs in defiance of anno Domini and 'Old Arthur'. The weekend before the event, I rose early and wandered round the Goyt Valley. Although it was now mid-June, the late, wet spring had held back summer's flowering. The fresh green foliage had the shy delicacy of all newly-emerged beauty. The faintest of mists, visible only when backlit by the sun, had strewn rainbow jewels over the sheep-cropped green turf. An utter stillness was in the air and my heart and mind went out to embrace my coming journey.

The next day I awoke with an irritating sniffle. I was annoyed but not dismayed at the prospect of a light summer cold. The following day I awoke weak and dizzy with a severe headache, racking cough and no appetite. I was furious with frustration and hurt pride. I *never* caught viral infections like this, but I had just done so! My dilemma was the usual one in such cases. All my support had been carefully arranged for the coming weekend. If I postponed, not only would I have to totally re-plan, but my work commitments meant it would be four weeks before I had another free weekend. Having just peaked my training it would be difficult to do so again while I was spending long days instructing mountaineering. Not without justification, I have great confidence in my body's ability to resist infection and recover quickly from any debilitating event. Monday and Tuesday were my lowest days, but by Tuesday evening I was starting to eat again. On Wednesday I ran to work, feeling awful but getting there. I rang my support to tell them I was still going but had postponed the run by 24 hours from a Friday to a Saturday start. On Thursday I ran again, coughing and spluttering but feeling better than on Wednesday. On Friday I drove up to Scotland and had a very sound night's sleep, not a good sign, I thought. My body obviously still needed recovery time. Ah well, in three days' time it could sleep for as long as it needed.

Despite my illness I felt quite calm as I set off from Port Patrick at 10.00 a.m. on a warm sunny morning. My original aim had been to strive to complete the route in 48 hours. After my reconnaissance I had thought this would prove difficult. Whereas Wainwright seems to calculate miles as they are actually walked, this route appeared to operate on 'map miles'. The Southern Uplands

Way is reported as 212 miles (340 km) in length. It was my opinion, however, that these map miles might convert to 220 or 230 miles (352/368 km) on the ground, this would make two and a quarter days a more realistic target.

After training through prolonged periods of foul weather, I felt it churlish of me to view the beautiful conditions with other than delight. The sad fact was, however, that I had had no opportunity to acclimatise to the effects of heat or sunshine. All too soon I could feel the stretches of tarmac returning the sun's warm caress. After covering the first 14 miles (22 km) by myself, I ran into the beautiful grounds of Castle Kennedy and met my full support team. In addition to John Richardson, Mark, Inken and Dave Crutch there were two more Rucksack Club friends to help me. I had assisted Eddie Thurrell and Chris Bolshaw on their Bob Graham round the previous year. We had become better acquainted, and when they had volunteered assistance on my venture I had gratefully accepted. Not only have both men a wealth of hard-won experience in mountain walking and fell running, they are skilled raconteurs and Chris in particular is a born entertainer. It is difficult now to envisage a time when they were not part of that close group of friends within the Club involved in participating in and supporting each other's ventures. Despite the loving attentions of the dreaded Scottish midge it was difficult not to linger at this support point. I had several conversations and a tin of fruit on the go simultaneously. Eventually, I was pushed off with Mark in attendance, happy that if the weather was overwarm for me, it would at least make my friends' role pleasanter than usual.

At New Luce, Chris and Inken volunteered to run with me to Knowe, a typical section of rough and boggy ground, hard forest track and metalled road. Chris at once launched into his usual non-stop conversation which requires a very determined interrupter to prevent from becoming a monologue. I think I have never known anyone who can produce such an intelligent flow of animated conversation at any time of the day or night irrespective of any physical exigencies. Rain, storm, fire, pestilence, flood, the fastest pace up the steepest hill have but little effect on the Bolshaw rhetoric. If you cannot hear Chris, it is because he is not there!

At Knowe the group had established friendly contact with the local café proprietor. He bestowed tea on us in copious quantities and allowed us the use of his kitchen. Better still, he granted us access to his garden hose and I enjoyed an unscheduled cooling shower. Lang may his lumb reek! The cooling effects of the hose-down were unfortunately short-lived, and as the sun's strength waxed, so mine waned. I was also finding the route tedious at times. The scenic sections seemed to flash by in an instant while roads and tracks wound on interminably. I longed for the traverse of the Galloway Hills which would take me through shady trees and into the evening.

Around 6.00 p.m. I reached Cauldons campsite in the Galloway Forest. This had been the venue for the Karrimor Mountain Marathon of 1976, the first year of my partnership with John. A storm had hit the event, and we had been one of only four teams to finish the Elite course which had seen a hundred pairs set out. There are not many good paths through the rough Galloway Hills but the

At Knowe, on the Southern Uplands Way, the 'Bolshaw Mobile Shower'. Left to right: Chris, Mike, Inken, Mark, Dave.

Southern Uplands Way follows one until the inevitable forest track is reached. As some compensation, the views are very attractive, ranging over small but tough hills cloaked in coarse grasses with an unspoilt air about them. As I trotted along now with Eddie and Inken a rather disturbing pain began to manifest itself somewhere in the region of my right Achilles tendon. Stopping and massaging the area helped for a time, but the pain kept returning. I alternated bouts of walking, running and massaging, but the pain had a nagging, insistent quality I did not like. The track alongside Clatteringshaw Loch seemed endless. The passage of events through one's conscious experience sometimes bears little direct correspondence to the passage of those units known as hours and minutes. In which does reality reside? I ran relatively quickly over the roads and tracks of the Southern Uplands Way, but was the suffocating impact of these miles beginning to distort my perception of time, distance and the nature of the route, or did my perception constitute reality?

As evening approached the light breeze dropped and immediately I reached the support point I jumped into the car to escape the midges. Partaking of light refreshment I was entertained by the spectacle of Dave and John kindly ridding Eddie of those pests by the ruthless expedient of vigorously swatting the midges and, occasionally, Eddie with fire beaters. Representing a somewhat larger target, Eddie seemed to fare rather worse than the midges. Cheered by the buffoonery and feeling the benefit of the food, I left Clatteringshaw with Dave and Chris heading for St John's Dalry. The onset of darkness coincided with a considerable temperature drop and I had to stop and pile on all additional gear.

Midge swatting. Left to right: John (Richardson), Eddie (Thurrell), Dave (Crutch).

After the sweltering heat of the day it seemed anomalous to be resorting to hat, scarf, gloves and waterproofs.

St John's Dalry was at 64 miles (104 km) along the Way, and as I left somewhat before midnight I was roughly on schedule. The section to follow had some tricky twists and I was now wishing for some light to aid my memory. The wish happily coincided with the arrival of midnight and the moon. But the moonrise was a slightly disturbing phenomenon. The disc which now began to slide from behind the black hills bore a strange orange reek like, yet unlike, the rising sun. And it was enormous. For a while the orange sphere hung there, in appearance so alien it might have been an ancient dead planet swinging by on some timeless orbit. Its sterile glow was confined to itself, no kindly radiance crept forth for our benefit. I watched it rise but before it could shed its orange mantle a thick bank of cloud rolled across the void and the strange light was eclipsed.

With Chris's excellent navigation supplementing my route memory we made our way rather cautiously to Stroanfreggan. It was now far into the night, and I was disturbed to notice a deep reluctance, both mental and physical, creeping over me. It was imperative to get moving before reluctance became inertia. While the hills of Manquhar and Ben Brack are trackless and, as such, to be welcomed, they hold little interest when approached from this side, particularly at night. The lower slopes are muddy and the higher reaches soft, tussocky and much too steep! At least, they seemed too steep for my present condition, which was not good. I had a tendency to wander off-line, but Eddie who had taken over from Chris kept us bang on target. With Dave staying as my close companion, Eddie led ahead. Navigating at night, in poor visibility, over trackless, difficult and unfamiliar country, he did not put a foot wrong.

As we at last traversed the final gradients, a pale dawn light began its barely perceptible incursion into the darkness. No rosy-fingered dawn this. It was ushered in by a cold, buffeting wind which flung a soaking mist over us. Moving along a broad ridge where gaunt pines fought an unequal battle against the uncompromising elements, we paused to gaze at the sun's luminous sphere as it pulsed and throbbed, a white and blinding light shining through the mist. The mist, wind borne, flew through the black trees and was shredded into tattered ribbons. These were moments of rare power and beauty. I realised that on this journey, in particular, such moments must be treasured and stored. It was becoming a hard and uncompromising run.

Once again, it was the support who provided light relief as we reached Polskeach. John had driven the long, winding roads which lead to the head of the valley at some speed. Chris, determined no wrong turns should prejudice the chance of meeting me on time, had kept his eyes firmly fixed on the map. He was now lying, swathed in all his spare clothes, in a bivvy bag. As I pecked at a first breakfast I could hear heart-rending groans coming from the car-sick figure. He was not long content with mere groans. Soon, a pale face peered out of the bag and a stream of recrimination pursued John, busily preparing to accompany me on the next leg.

Leaving Chris still locked in his struggle with the grim reaper John and I departed for Sanquhar. We strayed off route and onto a switchback ridge which, though pleasant in itself, was very tough. Our time loss was not serious and we soon ran into Sanquhar on what promised to be another beautiful morning. I enjoyed the stop at Sanquhar. It was 7.30 a.m. on a fine summer morning and the support point had been pleasantly organised by the river. I ate a rather more substantial second breakfast and felt that if the day should not become too hot, I might yet do quite well. Although a little down on my schedule, I had covered 90 miles (144 km) in something under 22 hours.

I had been anticipating the next section over the Lowther Hills with both delight and dread. A cap of dense white cloud sat over the summits, but this was hospitably doffed as we ascended. In contrast to my evening reconnaissance, it was now the bright morning light which revealed the almost miniature beauty of these round and steep-sided hills. It is sometimes the smaller hills, where steep gradients quickly alternate between up and down, which test the legs most. As is common on very long runs, I found the vertiginous downslopes particularly trying. As I plunged down the final slopes to the road, I could feel fingers of pain probing the sensitive domain where muscle meets tendon. Although the fingers withdrew on reaching the flat road, they had evidently decided they could return to work mischief later. With nearly 120 miles (195 km) remaining they could afford to be patient. For the present they delegated their role to other powers.

With morning well advanced and a genuine summer sun climbing to a position of power, the road was already reflecting uncomfortable heat. I increased pace in order to get off it quickly. As I did so, the incipient ache near the Achilles tendon, triggered alongside Clatteringshaw and nurtured by constant ankle twisting over Ben Brack, flared into a sharp pain. I ignored it and sought the expected cool depths of the forest tracks. The sun was now too high to be denied, however. There was no shelter from the heat and, despite careful foot placement, no relief from the pain. The ordeal had begun.

At Daer I ate with my legs dangling in the stream. The cool water was wonderfully soothing and might have begun to heal the injury had I been able to stay long enough. It was certainly a tempting proposition. After 110 miles (176 km) of pleasuring myself I felt I had had a good day! I pushed the notion to the back of my mind, slightly surprised to find thoughts of retiring there in the first place. There were over 100 miles (160 km) remaining, and though uncomfortable in the heat, neither the heat nor the pain in the tendon had reached critical proportions – yet.

Sweetshaw Brae, a beautiful name indeed. On my reconnaissance in the mist it had seemed endless. Now, in full visibility, I could see why. Descending and climbing on forest tracks, pushing our way through overgrown forest breaks, the section was interesting but demanding. Downhill, my feet were becoming very sore. Uphill, in the heat of the day, I was definitely wilting. Even the succulent bar of Turkish Delight which Eddie produced did not noticeably facilitate my progress eastwards as promised on the wrapper.

While the forest section between Daer and Beattock was hard work, it held variety and interest. In contrast, the road to Beattock itself was only hard work. I can remember little of this leg except the heat beating up from the road. And, I remember at every stage of this journey the nagging questions; had the recent virus drawn my strength? Had my vitality seeped away into those many miles on the Pennine Hills? Was this weakness an artefact of the heat? Or was I finally just not up to it anymore?

After the road the river meadows by Moffat seemed incredibly beautiful. While my senses registered beauty, my body was sending signals of despair to my brain. Between beauty and despair my spirit wandered. Gradually, the crushing effort of keeping my body moving beat down and overcame subtle beauty. And yet I was still going through the motions, I would not believe my strength was exhausted. The heat could not last. When cool evening returned, it would surely carry back my strength. I had only to endure, just hang on, don't quit. Stop thinking, move one step at a time.

Lovely Moffat Water was perhaps my first crux of despair, there were more to come. Steady rationalisation reduced the effects of this early crisis. I had now gone through the heat of two of the hottest days of the year, probably the only two hot days, I added cynically. I had covered about 120 miles (195 km) and had thus to survive for just another 24 hours. Yes, the worst was behind me. I would soon be climbing to the cool heights of Ettrick Head. A sweet summer night and fresh morning would see me well on towards the Lammermuirs, and after that? Well, after that I would undoubtedly gather impetus for the finish.

I managed to find comfort in this plausible scheme of events, but then faced the second difficulty. Having started on Saturday, not Friday, meant that I was due to finish to Monday evening. It was now Sunday, late afternoon. In response to various calls of duty all my support with the exception of Mark and Inken had to return south. Not only would I miss their good cheer and skill when it looked as if I should need it more than usual, but as Mark did not drive I would spend a good deal of the next 90 miles (145 km) running alone. I made a virtue of necessity, the harder the challenge, the greater the incentive to succeed. If you say it quickly, you might believe it. I am sure there is some truth in it. After the goodbyes, genuinely cheerful on one side, rather gritty on the other, I left with Mark for Ettrick Head.

Until the track through the forest began to gain height the sun continued to suck my vital juices. Slowly, we rose above the energy sapping heat and eventually exchanged hard track for grassy path. The soft, green path straddling the stream was a balm to weary feet and an impoverished spirit. To walk by sweet flowing water is to share its pure life force. What an extraordinary gift of Nature is a joyful mountain stream. What magic there is in the upswell, surge and irresistible flow of this earthsblood element.

I drew comfort and strength from the stream, feeling my spirit searching for and finding at least a temporary refurge. At Craigmichan Scar, I deliberately chose to traverse the precarious and eroded paths scratched across the scree. The concentration focused my attention and served to eliminate the numbness which at times threatened to engulf my mind. We crossed the watershed and immediately moved into a different climate. On this side of the hills we encountered a bank of damp, chill air which had rolled out of the east. Plunging endlessly down on the forest track we rapidly approached the section I had long dreaded, the five miles (8 km) of road to Scabcleuch.

In the now cool air and with the impetus of our rapid descent, I went very well at first. Meeting Inken in the car, I asked her to postpone support to the end of the road and to give Mark a lift so as to save him the tedium. My good spell was very short-lived. No sooner had the car disappeared, than I began to struggle. Not only fatigue, the numb pain in the ankle tendon suddenly erupted into sharp pain. Even a steeper camber on the road caused me to cross to the other side. Despite the folly of doing so, I started to imagine the car would be waiting round the next bend. It was the old track to the Lion Inn all over again. This time, however, there was no cheery chatter of friends around me, no looking forward to the last few hours of effort.

I tried to estimate my progress from the position of the side valleys. The dark valley marking the end of the road stretch looked unreachably distant. For an incalculable period of time I made no progress towards the distant smudge on the hills. I had once again entered that vicious time dichotomy; whenever the hateful road scourged my spirit, time slipped out of joint and left me cruelly suspended in an aching void. I fought, struggled, clawed my way through stagnant time on that mocking backward escalator. I ran with despair swollen and triumphant on my shoulders. The nightmare, running, running, moving with limbs not mine through a landscape that was utterly still. I was getting nowhere.

At last, rounding a bend, the indentation of the side valley jerked towards me. Progress became discernible, the treadmill creaked forward once more. It would carry me to new experiences, to worlds I as yet knew little of. I would learn – if I did but endure. I sank into the car, concerned only with immediate relief, the future would wait well enough. Realising part of my problem was lack of food, I ate large slabs of fruit cake and drank cups of strong tea. The old remedies for weary runners would work, I told myself. I was just a little tired and hungry, going through a bad patch, steady walking over the next set of hills would restore me. But Despair had not yet abdicated his role, he was lurking in the wings, patiently waiting while I finished my tea.

To Inken I confessed that my ankle was not too good, adding that I was sure the uphill and change of surface would help it. She knew perfectly well that, whatever terrain was to follow, I would claim it to have therapeutic properties. But I refrained from revealing the truth about my ankle, after all, it might easily clear up. The truth nearly revealed itself when, getting out of the car, I almost fell over. Blaming stiff legs, I adjusted my balance and set off. With an anticipatory leer, Despair crept after me.

It has not been such a stupid act to carry on as it might appear. Although the pain had been quite intense along the road, it had not accompanied me for a complete section. If I did not try, I would not truly know whether it would ebb and flow or just get worse. Had I been granted a preview of the agony I was to experience over the next few miles, I would certainly have opted out. Once I left the car I was more than half-committed. I could not or would not believe the pain might continue with quite this intensity. By the time I started to suspect it might, the car had left. I was committed.

Far from improving with the change of terrain, the pain grew worse. Any ankle flexion tugged at the tendon and sent fiery spears stabbing along it. The ground was rough and uneven. It was quite impossible to place my foot flat and secure. My folly was suddenly revealed to me. With an acknowledging leer to Self-Deception, Despair flapped forward and pinioned me with carrion claws. I bowed down in an excuse to tighten a shoe-lace. I stayed down, huddled on a grass bank, clutching the pain. Everytime I stopped, so did the pain, almost. A bank of mist rolled slowly down the hill. Cheerless and cold, it too fumbled for my soul with moist, chill fingers. Inside, my spirit wept.

Despair played a good hand. But the ordure with which he attempted to gild his lily was just a trifle too stinking – its bitterness sharp enough to rouse, not stupefy. I was alone on the hills in thick, cold mist. Night was not far distant and, miles away, Inken and Mark would be waiting anxiously for me. I could not choose to surrender, even if I wished to. And I did not wish to. With all my heart I wanted to be rid of this terrible ordeal, but I did not want to quit.

The mist was now so thick that I had to rely totally on the compass. The general topographical features I was following were simple enough to ensure I could not go wrong. At least that was the theory. The absence of a definitive path and the dense mist, compounded I suppose by my poor mental state, meant I was constantly unsure of my position. The compass was my talisman, I began checking it compulsively. It was perhaps fortunate I had no map to complicate the issue. Each time I consulted the compass, it pointed in the expected direction, but each time, the ground felt wrong. All I had to do, basically, was to contour above a valley for a time and then descend it to an old ruin, Riskinhope. My 'fail-safe' was to descend early to ensure I would not overshoot. After much stopping and starting, I ceased dithering and descended awkwardly to the valley. Relief! The smoking ruins of Riskinhope looked almost homely. But of course, I could not possibly have been wrong.

Route problems eased now, and before long I was hobbling down the stony track to St Mary's Loch. I was disconcerted to notice the light was already on the ebb, dithering has been costly. The sailing club at the end of the loch was quite deserted. A mournful wind rattled halyards and piled lonely waves across the shingle. I hurried past, anxious to use the remaining daylight. Overestimation of my ability had caused me to imagine I would not need my torch. The easy path and the light reached their limits, withered, then expired. Through mud, bog and darkness I skidded and stumbled, occasionally picking out ill-remembered paths. When I at last emerged, the forest track was no longer so unwelcome. Plodding along it, my thoughts turned to Inken and Mark. I hoped they would not be too worried. Chastened and depressed, I felt I had failed badly on this leg. Mark came out to meet me and we jogged in together. Inken was very quiet but calmly efficient. In fact, they both seemed rather silent. I wondered what they were thinking of this madness. I was harbouring the hope that they could not possibly know my true state. It would have been hard to justify continuing if they had.

But continue I meant to. With Mark for company, I set off for a piece of ground I had been determined not to cross in the dark. Odd that whenever one gets behind the schedule, it is the most difficult ground that slips into the night slot. The hills round Blake Muir were not merely navigationally awkward, they were really too good to be crossing in the dark. A sunset viewed from these hills would have been a compensation sufficient to offset a good number of road miles.

Our first error was to miss the bridge over Dryhope Burn. On this moonless, misty night we could fathom neither the river's width nor depth, but it sounded impressive enough. After wandering apprehensively along its bank without gaining the least idea of the nature of our adversary, other than we would certainly get our feet wet, I plunged in. Quite wide, but embarrassingly shallow. I noticed Mark politely allowed me to go first.

On my reconnaissance I had enjoyed the soft, grassy track leading up to the open hill top. Since then some maniac in a heavy tractor had torn the track apart. It was now little more than a pair of drainage ditches. How often have I come across what were once delightful causeways, mature and at one with the landscape, which have been brutalised, even eradicated by soulless philistines in heavy tractors. In the name of expediency the land is raped. Disappointed and struggling through the debris of the track I became very sleepy and took a five-minute nap against the bank.

Somewhat refreshed and very aware of the navigational problems ahead, I approached the start of the rough, pathless section carefully. I had just got a satisfactory line, when I noticed a post to my left. Thinking this marked the exact position of the Way, I crossed to it. It defined nothing. I had now lost my original line and could not pick it up again. From this moment on, I was never sure of, nor satisfied with our position. The bearing I was following seemed to collect all the worst going. No matter which way I tried, I could get no better terrain, and now the general lie of the land was beginning to puzzle me. Eventually, and very reluctantly, I decided I must go for a fail-safe. To our right (east) was a valley carrying the road to Traquair where Inken was waiting. We must descend into the valley and follow the road towards Traquair which, I imagined, could not be far off.

I pointed the compass east and started to descend. All was well for a time, and then to my astonishment the ground began to rise again. This was impossible, I asked Mark his opinion, but he was as puzzled as I. My instinctive response to such situations is to shout and swear. It is really infuriating when one does everything correctly and the gremlin starts changing the landscape. Unfortunately, the situation was too serious for the shouting, swearing ploy to have any effect. But I tried it, anyway.

That having failed, I was reduced to rationalisation. After a lengthy perusal of the map, I decided to act on the Sherlock Holmes principle; when you have eliminated the probable and the improbable then whatever impossibility remains is the culprit. There was a subsidiary spur leading NW off the main line of high ground. I guessed we must have wandered onto this spur on one of my 'probes', so that when I began to descend to the east we simply went down the side of the spur and started to re-ascend the line of the main hills.

Acting on this theory, we regained the high ground and soon picked up a path. Delighted with this unexpected triumph of reason over petulance, I resolved to stick with the excellent path. Then, in the light which precedes dawn, I discovered a hill where none should be. This time I was swifter off the mental mark. A glance at the well-kept stone walls and the generally trim nature of the land around led to the hypothesis that we had ventured onto some laird's estate. The map revealed the distressing fact, that just such an estate and the support point were on opposite sides of the same hill. There was no alternative but to traverse the estate and follow the road round the base of the hill.

Strangely enough, I was not as distressed as I might have predicted. After my inconclusive navigating so far, I felt it had all been inevitable. I had done my best in difficult circumstances, it had just not been good enough. This was the point where it would have been natural to give up. My unthinking resolve to continue was a surprise even to myself. When we reached the car, Inken was not there, obviously she was involved in a vain attempt to meet us off the hill. Mark set about serving the food left ready, and I was on the point of leaving when she arrived. I half expected some verbal recrimination, both for my lack of skill and my surfeit of obstinacy. However, despite her fruitless search she seemed neither surprised nor annoyed at my losing the route or my intention to continue. Mark must have felt some concern, however, as he insisted on accompanying me over Minch Moor to Yair Bridge. Ever optimistic, I was looking forward to this section as it was both attractive and offered easy going on the old drove roads.

It was a hard business getting the body to follow the mind's resolve, however. Both Mark and I were affected by the early morning 'sleepies'. What was far more serious and dismaying, was my inability to pick up the pace once we had completed the climb to the high moor. By now the ankle was rather swollen but had settled down to a bearable ache. Unfortunately, my thighs, the 'engine room', had become terribly stiff. Expecting to be able to pick up some lost time in the daylight I could manage no better than an agonised shuffle. The lengthy descent from the Three Brethren will live for a long time in my memory. Every downward step required a separate act of will and earned a separate spasm of pain.

I remember 'running' into the beautiful woodland at the foot of the hill. Everywhere was alive with the sounds and smells of a summer morning. My eyes registered the wild woodland flowers, the darting flight of birds through the stirring leaves. But my soul was locked in a fierce struggle with the incessant pain which clamped both body and spirit. When pain cripples the senses so that beauty is perceived by the brain but cannot be felt by the heart, it causes double sorrow.

When I reached the car, I felt almost completely exhausted and dispirited. I was still determined to continue. I would not allow myself to seriously consider the possibility of quitting, it would prove too much. I could no longer entertain the notion that Inken and Mark were not aware what this effort was costing me, it was too obvious, I could barely manage to lower myself into the car – or get out again. Had either said what must have been on their minds, it would have caused me great distress for I would have had to disregard them. As it was, the gentleness and care with which they were tending me reached past all pain, all weariness, all despair, and it gave me strength.

I actually made up some time on the next leg to Melrose. Thus it was that I found my two loyal helpers lying peacefully asleep. It would have been good to let them rest, but a long section was coming up and I needed to eat. I did however insist I would continue solo. Mark had given much already and there was more to come. I felt I was at last becoming stronger in body and mind, and I wanted to get moving quickly. With around 40 miles (64 km) remaining it was the beginning of the end, an end I so desperately wanted to reach. Unfortunately, as the warm sun emerged after early showers, all that happened was that I felt very sleepy again.

Traversing easy ground I was more asleep than awake, barely aware of what was going on. I inadvertently discovered a remedy for this state. Coming to an electric fence next to a gate I managed in my stupor to receive its full benefits. It had a remarkably energising effect! In fact, there and then, I conceived a plan to patent an electrical energiser for tired fell runners, something along the lines of a cattle prod. I have decided, on later reflection, to suspend its final development until my own retirement.

Perhaps I should have tried the shock therapy earlier. Despite my rejuvenation I must have made poor time. I met Inken coming down the long boring section of Roman Road over Mosshouses Moor. I expected a pleased smile, but she looked concerned and explained that they thought I had cracked up somewhere. I am not sure what upsets me most, being treated as a superman who does not need any special consideration whatever the circumstances, or as a frail old gentleman needing care and protection. The first is good for the ego, but painful. The second is painful to the ego, but can be very nice! I have not resolved this one yet.

At any rate, Mark took me in charge on the short leg to Lauder, where I apprehensively prepared for the long dreaded section over the Lammermuirs to Longformacus. I had been psyching myself up for this leg for the past few hours, 14 miles (22 km) of stony track rising inexorably to high moorland and finishing, inevitably, with miles of road. By now the pain in my legs had eased, but my feet were so sore it was best to remain standing at support stops. I thought the stony track would not be pleasant. I applied myself to the task ahead with all my strength and will. This was the last major challenge. After this there would be only 14 miles (22 km) remaining. I undertook this leg with very few reserves of strength and even today still regard it as one of my best efforts. I did not imagine I would be able to run the uphill track, but I did. I ran half-asleep and in a numb stupor. The spark that drove me was small, but it seemed inextinguishable. On reaching the rough moor I tried to change into my fell shoes. Balanced on one leg with Mark holding me up I forced one shoe on, but the other foot was so swollen no amount of brutality would make it fit. Feeling like one of the Ugly Sisters I resumed my road shoes and skidded down to the road. The road achieved what the track could not. By the time I reached the support the spark had gone out and I was an automaton.

But now it was simply frustration and not despair that attacked my spirit. I seemed to have poured my life-blood into this run, I wanted to have done with it. Seemingly endless road and track was frustrating this desire, but with only 14 (22 km) of the 212 miles (340 km) remaining, Despair could win no more victories. Travelling alone on the penultimate leg to the village of St Bathans I began to experience the strange sensation that this was not the second, but the third time I had run over this ground. The impression was very vivid, and I seemed to remember small incidents from two previous runs. One set of memories certainly belonged to the time I had reconnoitred the route, but what of the memory of a 'second' run? I am familiar with the hallucinatory effects engendered by sleep deprivation, however, I was not seeing things, but remembering an event which had not taken place. I found the experience intriguing rather than alarming, and it helped more dreary miles to pass. Despite the crushing weariness I could sense in my body, a desperate desire to conclude this run enabled me to maintain a good speed. When I ran down to meet Inken at the last support point I was able, for the first time, to give her a genuine smile and received one in return.

It was now 9.00 p.m. and I had hopes of covering the last 10 miles (16 km) in two hours. The hope had its roots in necessity. It would be very dark by 10.30 and the prospect of traversing a large proportion of the cliff path in true darkness was appalling. With Mark, ever willing, beside me we departed on the final leg of my terrible Odyssey. Thick wet mist obscured our line across cultivated fields. High wet grass dragged at our legs.

Once on the road section I flung myself into a painful but effective canter. My confidence rose as we approached, then crossed the A1 to Pease Dean. But thick mist was causing an early fading of the light. Through the impending gloom, the flowering gorse which bordered the path across the hillside seemed to vibrate and glow. Mark said he, too, was experiencing the same effects. It was as if the darkness was enveloping my fading mind, but as the darkness grew in and around me, so the yellow bushes flared with greater intensity. I could no longer consciously guide my legs over uneven ground for I could no longer see it, and in any case, the links between my mind and my body were dissolving. I allowed my body to flow on as it would, and my mind floated free. Once again it explored that 'memory' that was not memory. I slipped into an almost complete state of *déjà vu*. Rationally, I knew it was only the second time I had traversed this ground. On the other hand, I not only felt very strongly that I had passed this way twice before, I could also predict what was going to happen next. For instance, well before I came to an awkward gate I 'remembered' how I had crossed it 'last time', seconds later I observed myself crossing it in the same fashion. I found floating outside myself like this a curious and fascinating experience. Even while this was happening I attempted an objective analysis of what was happening; I was not successful.

A nasty steep descent to the road marshalled all my faculties into something like a cohesive unit. Before they could follow their own inclinations again, I was grappling with the intricate challenge of the cliff-top path. I could not focus my eyes properly, and we went round three sides of a crop-grown field before returning to the opening I had already passed. So, in a fashion perfectly suited to the nature of this venture, we found ourselves on the narrow path in the dark.

The prediction I had made after my reconnaissance of the path proved a gross underestimation. We stumbled and slithered, were stung by nettles and fought savage brambles. After a time, the path disappeared entirely beneath the weeds. I clambered over barbed wire into the adjoining field and immediately disappeared beneath the oil-seed rape which was at times above my head. This, I thought, is definitely farcical. Adopting the tactics of the fabled Hellarwee tribe I identified the lights of Cockburnspath ahead. The chill sea-borne mist was beginning to eat into me, but refusing to stop I ploughed a grim furrow down and under the ranks of the oil-seed rape. Quite suddenly we emerged onto a curious piece of old track that I definitely did remember. Amazingly, we were still on course. Just as I was attempting to piece together other elusive bits of memory, Inken loomed like a phantom out of the darkness. For some reason this was so entirely unexpected I thought I was hallucinating. Thankfully, I followed the apparition along the few remaining twists and turns. Now, at last, we crossed the A1 again, very circumspectly in my case, and started on the final yards of road into the village. I could no longer distinguish between road and kerb, while lamp posts constituted a major hazard.

At 11.35 p.m. on a cold, misty night the village square was, naturally, deserted. If there were any observers behind those few windows which glowed like warm eyes around us, they would have witnessed a rather motley group of runners approaching the stone monument in the centre of the square. They would have seen one figure, that of an apparently very ancient and frail man, detach itself from the group and salute the monument in a curious sardonic way. With no further ceremony, the group would then have been seen climbing into an old car and driving off. Had the heart and mind of the ancient runner been open to inspection, the only remarkable aspect would have been the curious

117

void which existed where emotion might have been expected to reside. What such observers might well have missed, was the very subtle, almost cynical sense of satisfaction that accompanied the fag-end of this terrible, yet epic run. It was strangely appropriate to bring my ordeal to a conclusion under the interested gaze of no one. No one, that is, but those two who had shared the ordeal with me. It was right that it should end privately. The experience had been bitter indeed, its one sweet fruit was that it had drawn me closer to each of them, and for that reason alone I will not regret it.

As no one seemed to have completed the route in any kind of continuous fashion, what I did probably constituted a record. My concern with the route as a respectable record attempt disappeared on the first day. The only valid accolade I feel able to claim is a record for obstinacy. My schedule was for 54 hours, my actual time of 61 hours 35 minutes was in this context but a feeble parody of a record. It shouldn't prove too difficult to better this, but I shall not be trying.

Epilogue

Now the dust has settled, I begin to wonder if there are any lessons to be learned from my experience on the Southern Uplands Way. I felt, and still feel, in something of a dilemma about what happened, or rather what I caused to happen. The difficulty in resolving the dilemma lies in the conflict which arose between two equally important concepts. The essential quality of ultra fell running, for me, is the challenge of doing something which is exceptionally demanding in an environment which engenders the kind of inspiration necessary to cope with these demands. Accepting the concept that the challenge must be supremely difficult, embodies the notion that *voluntary* escape is not part of the game, once embarked – no quitting. What makes this form of behaviour so unlike banging one's head against a wall (or running Land's End to John O'Groats on the road) is the enormously increased sense of communication with Nature both during and partly after the event. If the latter is missing, then one is indeed confined to a crude battle of strength between obstinacy and fitness on the one hand and brute physical force on the other.

My illness, slight though it was, and the injuries I sustained during the run certainly tipped the physical odds against me. I was able to draw increasingly less inspiration from the route, and eventually only my obstinacy and desire not to 'need' to attempt the Way again sustained my effort. Obstinacy in pursuit of some goal may be acceptable. Obstinacy for its own sake is less admirable.

And yet, who will gainsay an experience that demanded the utmost tenacity and voluntary acceptance of pain and hardship that had so little reward? It was a bitter cup and a full one. I drank it to the dregs, and I shall never lift it again.

However, Mike Hartley did in 1988. Mike was joint winner of the Fellsman Hike and is one of the few people I have met interested in attempting my records. He covered the Southern Uplands Way in 55 hours and 55 minutes.

chapter eight

1987 – THE FALLOW YEAR

Decisions to have an easy year are never more easily made than towards the end of a long, hard run. As that 200 mile (320 km) mark approaches, one is heard to voice platitudes such as 'I'm definitely too old for this sort of game', or 'Well, you won't catch me doing this again next year', or 'This demands too much time and effort, I'm going to take up serious photography/writing/gardening/knitting . . .', or 'I've reached my limits now, I should retire from ultras while I still have some strength for other things'. The last was my reaction to the Southern Uplands Way.

Like most good resolutions, this one weakened in proportion to its removal in time from the event which inspired it. I did not want the Southern Uplands Way to be my last memory of an ultra run. I should bow out with a swan-song that would be a bang, not a whimper. I began to toy with the notion that I should have one more attempt at the big one, my own Pennine Way record.

I had never dismissed the possibility of making an attempt on this record which I had been so long in winning. It had been just a matter of allowing a sufficiently long interval for my interest to rekindle. If I really was going for a swan-song, there was no doubt in my mind it must be the Pennine Way. What most appealed to me however, was the idea of attempting the record in the opposite direction, north to south. To achieve a sub-three-day traverse both from the north and the south was a notion I found irresistible. It was also the only acceptable way I could envisage of ending my ultra career. It would, of course, demand the very peak of physical fitness. The sincere resolutions to take things easy made on the Southern Uplands Way were forgotten. I started to lay plans.

Preparation and training

Once the swollen feet and ankles had subsided and the sleep deficit was made good, gentle days on the hill restored my spirits. The Southern Uplands Way was soon pushed to the back of my mind, but it was not forgotten. The autumn and winter which followed saw me as active as ever. There was however, at times, something about my performance that made me wonder whether I had left some part of my strength behind on the Southern Uplands Way. Beyond any doubt was the fact that my knees were certainly deteriorating. Comments such as 'knees very sore downhill' and 'perhaps not many miles left in them' occur with increasing regularity in my log-book at this time. Well, this was sad but fitted in with plans for my swan-song year. If I could not go on much longer, that was all the more incentive to achieve a final success.

In an effort to preserve my knees, I cut down on my weekly road mileage but increased the distance of my weekend ventures. I was not exactly in the invalid class yet, either. Despite the obligation to descend hills in stately rather than dashing fashion, I still managed to finish twenty-ninth out of 240 in the Marsden–Edale race, one and a half minutes behind but 24 years ahead of Mark.

The pleasurable business of selecting subsidiary targets *en route* to the 'big one' occupied my mind. Inken, as a member of the LDWA, informed me that their 100 mile (160 km) event was to be held in Snowdonia that year. With images of running across the mighty Carneddau springing into my mind, I too sent off an entry form. I then recalled having read an article by someone who had made a speedy traverse of the West Highland Way, what a name to conjure with! However, I quickly ascertained that the route was mainly on the hard tracks of the old military roads. On the other hand, at 95 miles (152 km) it was the right length for a relatively short spring day. It was also sure to pass through superb mountain scenery. I decided it would constitute a useful 'speed' session to counterbalance my penchant for slow, steady plodding.

My reconnaissance of the West Highland Way confirmed what the map indicated. Most of the route follows unmetalled military roads built during the eighteenth century to facilitate the passage of militia intent on quelling troublesome Highlanders. Although well graded, the surface is occasionally of loose stones large enough to make running quite difficult. What really took me unawares, however, was the path along the east bank of Loch Lomond. In complete contrast to what had gone before, it was a jumble of mud, rocks and tree roots. Far from being able to run it, I had the utmost difficulty in not breaking my neck along it. Still, I could not complain, I was supposed to enjoy rough and natural terrain. Trouble was, I had to stop to do so!

I realised that if I was principally training for the Pennine Way, which demanded very long, but slow days, I could not also adequately prepare for the West Highland Way. The latter would ideally require short, relatively fast days of about 30 miles (50 km), whereas I intended between 40 and 60-mile (65/100 km) days. Indeed, with a limited period for day-long training, I had to cover such distances to allow reconnaissance of my three targets. The West Highland Way, Snowdonia Hundred and Pennine Way gave 465 miles (744 km) to reconnoitre. Even allowing that I need not cover all the Pennine Way, I had many miles to compress into my already busy life. Ah well, 'the harder the challenge, the . . .', *ad nauseam*!

In a hectic 10-day period I covered all the West Highland Way, nearly 200 miles (320 km) of the Pennine Way and most of the Snowdonia Hundred. I am accustomed to bulking my training in this fashion and have noticed it has a tendency to induce fatigue. I could not tell whether I was more weary than usual, but there was no doubt my knees were in a poor way. This sport is hard enough, I did not think constant pain should be part of it. Despite my performance on the Southern Uplands Way, or perhaps because of it, I was

*Running past
the Kingshouse
Hotel, West
Highland Way
training.*

121

*At the top of
the Devil's
Staircase –
West Highland
Way training.*

reluctant to continue accepting that my dreams should be realised through a cruel disregard of the state of my body. My resolve to make this a final and successful year hardened.

West Highland Way – A sort of record

It is all very well to set a subsidiary target which is unimportant in an overall context. Unfortunately, when one is cursed with a fierce competitive spirit and high level of aspiration, the discrepancy between drive to achieve and ability to do so produces conflict. At the time, the fact that my training was not appropriate to the West Highland Way had seemed unimportant. Now I was faced with actually doing the run, I felt very dissatisfied. I had also just learned that the record for this run between Glasgow and Fort William stood at 17 hours 48 minutes. This seemed exceptionally fast and it was obvious to me that such a time would be beyond my reach. I then discovered that the run had been established as a 'race', taking place close to Midsummer Day each year. For 'reasons of safety' the official West Highland Way route was abandoned in three places. Where the footpath followed natural terrain, the race took to the road. One of these changes would probably not lead to a marked time difference between road and path; the other two, however, would. At the southern end of Loch Lomond, between Balmaha and Rowardennan, the official path follows a very picturesque but tortuous route through woods, alongside the loch and up and down steep little hills. At one stage the path performs a little switchback, just a couple of yards from the road. The other section constitutes quite a deviation. Between Fort William and Lundavra the official route goes very pleasantly through the Glen Nevis plantations, then rather awkwardly over a couple of miles of large boulders set in boggy ground. The difficulties underfoot and twists and turns make it impossible to run this section swiftly. The race simply follows a minor road between Lundavra and Fort William and appears to be about a mile shorter.

There was no question in my mind but that I should adhere to the official route. I run on roads only out of necessity. On the other hand, I knew of no record for the definitive footpath. I supposed sub-24 hours would constitute a 'record', but I felt I would only gain any satisfaction by approaching the time of the 'road record'.

Now living in Scotland, Inken had offered to drive, and I took Gerard, 15, and Liam, 13, along for the experience. After camping in Glen Nevis and listening to the rain beating down half the night, I rose at 3.30 a.m., delivered my familiar, bad-tempered speech entitled 'Why does it always rain on my record attempts?' and set off at 4.00 a.m. It was still dark in the forest and only half-light across the boulders. I could understand why the race used the road. The sounds of legs snapping like carrots would have been heard in Fort William had runners with 90 miles (145 km) under their kilts attempted these blocks in the dark.

I lost time on this leg, which was not surprising. I also lost time on the next section over to Kinlochleven. The only excuse I had was that I ran too slowly. It was, I realised despondently, as fast as I dared go. I took Gerard over the Devil's

Staircase which is the highest point on the route. We both enjoyed the sight of the still snow-plastered hills around us; the Mamores behind us to the north and, much closer the Buchaille Etive Mhor and the Munroes around Glencoe.

Picking up momentum I ran hard past the Kingshouse and on into a head wind and heavy rain. By Inveroran I had knocked 15 minutes off the scheduled leg time but was still down overall. I felt very tired and dispirited after this effort. My lack of speed and the state of the weather made me want to quit. However, I had promised to run with Liam over the next hill to the Bridge of Orchy. He was obviously looking forward to this and I did not have the heart to disappoint him, so off we set. It was a tonic for me to see him skipping along lightly in front of me. Very small, light and nimble on his feet, he flitted over the ground apparently without effort. By the time we were descending the hill I felt much better and watched with amusement and fatherly pride as he floated easily ahead to take my order for refreshments.

I still did not feel fully committed to the run however, and thought the long track to Tyndrum would see me blown to a standstill. Curiously enough, the weather took a turn for the better, the wind switched west and stopped blowing in my face. So, 42 miles (67 km) and seven and a quarter hours gone, 53 miles (85 km) remaining, might as well continue.

The run along the 15 miles (24 km) of steep, densely wooded and rocky shores of north Lomond-side proved the crux. At first I ran well, enjoying the early views down the loch and the lovely silvan setting, such a contrast to the tedious military roads. However, I was concentrating so hard to maintain speed and balance over the potentially disastrous ground that I failed to notice the development of a massive hunger bonk. By the time I did, it was too late. I ended up shuffling to the car and lost all the time I'd gained and more.

After eating, probably too much at once, my digestion became disorganised and I never really regained my strength and rhythm. At the southern end of the loch, the path continued to wend an intricate way over little crags, through woods and up and down short steep slopes. Creaking along on my stiffening old pins I watched enviously as Gerard and Liam skipped nimbly ahead.

It took the 1,000 ft (300 m) climb up Conic Hill to restore my systems to some kind of compatible relationship. I began to run relentlessly, without fire or sparkle, just a determined drive forward, a drive to beat the dark. Time slipped inexorably by and with it the daylight and my hopes. It was nearly 11.00 p.m. when Gerard and I ran into the uninspirational finish at Milngavie railway car-park. Sadly, Inken and Liam, who were to run in with us, missed us in the dark.

My time was 18 hours 40 minutes, and as I had hoped to get close to the other record of 17:48, I deemed it an embarrassing failure. On the other hand, I had to admit I had actually run at a faster pace than I thought possible. I was sure I could go still faster if I trained for it, there again, I was not convinced I was interested in repeating the route. The next day I took Gerard and Liam round Edinburgh Castle, every step (and it has hundreds) was a reminder of the need for specific training. I cannot remember my legs ever being stiffer after a run.

The Snowdonia Hundred was the second LDWA 100-mile (160 km) event I entered, and after it I realised that the nature of the Dalesman Hundred, in its

Coming into Edale at the end of 250 miles (400 km) training in seven days.

rough and wild character, had not been typical. It has since become apparent that for many entrants to the annual Hundred, the motivating force lies in the desire to cover 100 miles (160 km). The desire to enjoy a pleasant route is also obvious, but, unfortunately, should any of Nature's real challenges prejudice the primary goal, objections are raised. I am in sympathy with the ambition to test one's physical and mental capabilities, it is one I share, but I will not willingly build a treadmill in my heart. Challenge need not chain the soul to the dead weight of empty miles. Inspiration is best derived from the renewal of our relationship with Nature and its forces. And when we are inspired, what can we not then achieve! If we must fail, let us do so reaching beyond our grasp for a dream that is worth all our striving. Then, even in our failing, even through our tears, we have won.

In our populous land it is frequently difficult to avoid using tracks and even road to connect the various sections of wilder country. Nevertheless roads, in particular, destroy a route's character, they are gestures of defeat. After reconnoitring the Snowdonia Hundred I was appalled by the large proportion of the course occupied by these 'gestures of defeat'. However, I had paid my entry fee and invested time in learning the course. I hoped that running the route as a whole would bring it the cohesive sense of unity which road sections destroy.

The long stretches of road and track seemed designed to punish rather than inspire. Suffering the effects of the West Highland Way, last year's Southern Uplands Way and general decrepitude I was finding this a dull, hard run and longing for something to break the monotony. My wish was heard and, in due course, maliciously misinterpreted.

Normally, I prefer to run alone in these events, but from about 20 miles (32 km) had teamed up with Mike Hartley. He was very cheerful and pleasant company and our common interests gave us plenty of scope for conversation. We made our way slowly through the field. Again, everyone had started off at suicidal speed, and it was interesting to pass them in various attitudes of disrepair at the roadside or recumbent at support points. Even so, I was quite surprised to be approaching Porthmadog, just beyond the half-way point, with only two men ahead. We then passed No. 2, reclining very elegantly, but rather pale, on a grassy bank. He was a victim of the awful hunger bonk and was busy reloading. I thought he should have been doing it on the move, but, there you are, even among the ranks of Sparta can be found the odd Sybarite.

At Porthmadog, I was surprised to find it was ace orienteer and fell runner David Rosen who was the leader. There may be some vital ingredient missing out of today's chocolate for he had met with what must have been one of the great hunger bonks of this world just a couple of miles short of the support point. A connoisseur of the genus hunger bonk, I could only regret I had missed this particular manifestation. However, quick to take advantage of a weakness, I swallowed my jar of peaches and nipped out smartly with Mike. Chatting away the flat boring miles to Harlech we reached the imposing, flood-lit castle as darkness fell. Rather complacent by now we jogged alongside the black waters of Llyn Bychan. However, as we started up the pass known as the Roman Steps to cross the Rhinog Mountains, a figure lurched after us. It was a 24-hour track and road expert, probably anxious to have some company over these rugged hills. Unfortunately for him, it was at this point that my request for a little break in routine was being slyly considered.

Almost immediately we veered left of the correct path but I rectified this mistake so quickly, I never heard the warning bells. Soon we came to a gap in a wall which I exclaimed was 'wrong'. Both my companions immediately agreed, and in my customary bold manner, I plunged leftwards off the path and was immediately engulfed in that jungle of vertical heather and huge boulders which characterises the Rhinogs. We continued to lurch across the broken hillside. From time to time I stopped to peer intelligently into the quite impenetrable darkness. Not unnaturally, I could see nothing.

The unbelievably bad ground became worse, as it will in the Rhinogs. We found ourselves on a very steep, unstable boulder field under crags. Obviously unfamiliar with this type of terrain the road expert was constantly 'off the back'. He appeared to be concerned for his well-being and safety and I shouted back words of encouragement and comfort. Unfortunately his cries grew fainter until they were mercifully lost in the stony wastes. I hoped my advice to retreat downhill to a line of bobbing torches had been heeded.

A belated scrutiny of the map gave me an approximate idea of our position, but it was mainly guesswork. Well, the next control point lay on the other side of those mountains, so no place to go but up. There followed an age of swarming up wiry heather and practising intricate climbing techniques on the greasy rock of a repulsive gully. At last we emerged close to a summit – but which? I feared the descent would be worse than the ascent, it usually is. We were lucky, at least Mike nearly was not. He was on the point of hopping down a little rock step, when our torches revealed it was a crag about 50 ft (15 m) high.

Eventually we reached better ground lower down. I was sure I recognised a forest edge as having been a line I had followed in a Karrimor event 10 years previously. I was just beginning to doubt this when I discerned a glow ahead. The light proceeded from a kit check station on the edge of the forest where the route emerged. Controlling my wild impulse to kiss the officials, I produced the items to be checked, ascertained that we would not get bonus points for including an unscheduled summit and discovered that there were only two people in front of us. Despondency gave way to optimism and we galloped out of the tent in search of fresh adventures. We had spent an hour longer over the Rhinogs than we might have expected, but we had at least broken the monotony!

We were now going very strongly and soon passed one of the two in front. At the next control we were told we were in the lead. Seeing is believing however, and I thought we should not slacken pace just yet.

With dawn came a very cold wind and a chill wet mist. Rather on my mettle now, I made a good job of nagivating over to the Manod Quarry checkpoint. I suggested we should not stop for refreshments but press on. Along the old railway track I kept noticing what appeared to be fresh studmarks among the tangle of older footprints. Not very much to my surprise a mile later, we saw a small, sturdy figure trotting economically ahead, Dave Rosen! Very slowly we hauled him in, and soon we were all engaged in racing over rough, boggy ground with an assumed nonchalance ('Yes, nothing like an early morning burst over the tussocks to get nearly 90 miles (145 km) of stiffness out of one's legs, don't you think!').

Catching him was one thing, dropping him was another. He stayed with us easily until the forest track, where Mike and I set off up the initial gradients at a suicidal rate. Very knackering it was, but it seemed to send Dave off the back. We left the Pentre Bont checkpoint before he appeared, and then I thought we could relax a little. I had to, I was shattered.

It was a beautiful morning as we ran over the River Conwy to the finish at Llanwrst. I was wishing I was just starting off fresh into it (with new legs!). We finished in 21 hours 35 minutes, but should have got close to 20 hours; still, it was a small price to pay for our adventure. Eschewing such excursions on this occasion, Inken came in at 24.40, the twentieth finisher, not bad for a woman! (I suppose the 250 men behind her would have agreed.)

After finishing, our 24-hour track man cornered us. Now we're for it, I thought! But he was very nice about being deserted in the middle of the night in a place he obviously found rather hostile. He had not, to my relief, remained perched on a boulder till dawn, but had joined the torchlight procession below. I explained how noble it was of us to provide him with this option rather than drag him up that horrifying gully; but I do not think he believed me.

The quack of the swan

Having completed my build-up which, if rather punishing, had at least been successful, I was ready to turn my attention to the Pennine Way. I was still pursuing the notion that it was time to stop chasing ultra-records, a notion with which my knees readily concurred, but I was determined to go out on a high note. Unfortunately, the weather, as usual, had something to say about my plans. This time, unusually, it had the decency to indicate its likely response should I set foot on the Pennine Way.

My log-book reveals that June had the wettest start on record. The ground became impossibly waterlogged, and with the bad weather continuing, I decided to postpone my record attempt. In the first part of July, I was again instructing in hill activities in the Lake District. After raising my hopes with several days of fine weather, conditions again deteriorated. There ensued a most frustrating pattern, where heavy rain would be followed by what, in my optimism, I anticipated as an improving trend. One day the attempt would definitely go ahead, the next day it was called off. Then there would be periods of uncertainty which would be the most frustrating of all. Friends phoned and I would say 'I'll probably go anyway', then I would ring back and say 'It doesn't look as if it's even worth starting.' The uncertainty gnawed away at me and I could not settle. No sooner had I decided one way or the other than the weather would change, and so would my mind. I could not bear the thought that I should decide not to go, then have to sit through a beautiful weekend when I could have been running. Eventually, I hit on a compromise. The weather was unlikely to produce the three fine days needed for the Pennine Way, I was already in the Lakes, I would attempt my Coast to Coast record.

Objecting to my efforts to escape from its game of cat and mouse, the weather became even more variable. A fine clear morning, giving every impression of permanence, would change to torrential rain by the afternoon and continue unabated throughout the night. The timing of this pattern would vary, but little else. Preparing to run a couple of hundred miles (320 km) over the hills at record speed throws a considerable strain on the nerves at the best of times. I found the added uncertainty quite unbearable. I cancelled any attempt on any record. On the weekend I was to have run, the country was divided north/south into two quite dissimilar weather systems. In the north, there were clouds, but a fair amount of sunshine and equable temperatures. In the southern half, there was persistent rain fortified by torrential showers and strong winds. As if anticipating my fluctuating resolve, the interface of these systems was poised on a line approximately coincident with the Coast to Coast route.

chapter nine

1988 – THE ROAD GOES EVER ON

> The Road goes ever on and on
> > Out from the door where it began.
> Now far ahead the Road has gone,
> > Let others follow it who can!
> Let them a journey new begin,
> > But I at last with weary feet
> Will turn towards the lighted inn,
> > My evening-rest and sleep to meet.

> J. R. R. TOLKEIN
> *The Lord of the Rings*

Having in 1987 failed to complete, or even attempt, my 'big run' of the year, I felt at first as if something was missing from life. Then, retrospectively, I became aware, in a way I had not grasped before, of the drain on resources which a 'long' ultra imposes. I was now much more ready to pick up training again after the summer break in routine. Above all, I discovered a very keen edge to my appetite for a really good year in 1988. My anticipation was such, that I even questioned whether in 1987 I had actually possessed the driving motivation to power a Pennine Way attempt. I realised that I had been not only thinking in terms of a swan-song, but also feeling almost relieved that it was to be so.

The lean year just past had both stimulated my appetite and rekindled fires. Unfortunately, my sheer enjoyment of running, short or long distances, was increasingly threatened by painful knees. At this point I commenced acupuncture treatment. Acupuncture was something I had intended to try for years, but I rarely have the patience to go and seek medical advice, let alone submit myself to treatment. I am extremely sceptical of the ability and interest of most conventional practitioners where sports-related problems are concerned. I also take a very jaundiced view of the use of drugs to treat minor disorders. Perhaps I am fortunate, but I find if I listen to my body, it will usually direct me to a healthy pattern of eating, sleeping, resting, working, and so on. Of course, I do not always choose to listen, but almost invariably, when injured or unwell, I try to let my body 'guide' me back to health.

My body did not seem able to cope with what I suspected was an almost inevitable and irreversible deterioration of my knees. I had never really expected not to pay in both the short and long term for the kind of running I love. What love does not bring pain? A love which suffers to be constrained by pain is indeed a pale love. Contrary to what those who are afraid of pain might think, endurance athletes do not enjoy pain. We accept the necessity of intense effort, and pain may at times intervene sharply in this, but I, for one, hate it. It is not only unpleasant in itself, it obstructs my ability to enjoy the physical and also the spiritual aspects of my running. When pain began to rear its ugly head too high therefore, and acting on trusted recommendation, I sought acupuncture treatment. I was gratified to discover that my acupuncture specialist described healing with reference to concepts I already accepted; the body would be helped to heal itself.

In a surprisingly short time I noticed an improvement. There was no instantaneous miracle, and my knees still reacted very crossly to sudden changes in routine, as when playing basketball, my inherently competitive nature would get the better of me. But gradually the most annoying pain of all disappeared. This was the vice-like band which gripped across my kneecaps on even the gentlest of downhills. Until that began to fade, I did not appreciate quite how much the associated pain had been destroying the pleasure I found in running. Once more, the pure and simple joy of running, just running for its own sake, came back to me, a love deformed by pain had become whole again. Eventually, though cautiously, I was able to start descending even steep hillsides with that sense of freedom which had constituted such a powerful attraction to fell running nearly 30 years ago. One day in spring, I descended from the top of Conic Hill in plummeting swoops that felt like flight. I paid for it a wee bit at the bottom, but I still had more than enough change left from that exhilarating sense of freedom, that joyful, almost arrogant feeling of mastery. 'That!', thought I, preening my feathers, 'is how the eagle feels!'

The only problem now was whether I would actually be capable of relinquishing my interest in attempting ultra-distance records. Certainly, the alleviation of the pain had removed one of the factors instrumental in my decision to set less demanding targets. However, I had a genuine desire to turn to other, less competitive ventures in the hills. I could not, on the other hand, relinquish my career in the inconclusive state occasioned by the preceding year's fiasco of a summer. I felt with increasing conviction that if I could bow out, not just as the first man to run the Pennine Way in under three days, but the first to do so in each direction, I would be content.

I was warned that I was attempting to relive what was essentially a unique experience. Irrespective of any time I might achieve, such an attempt to recreate the past was doomed to failure. I did not, however, wish to relive that experience, realising, indeed, the impossibility of so doing. What I did want, was to create a new experience and a new record. My ultra-running, with all its joy and sadness, its pain and pleasure, its often love, its sometimes hate, had wrought changes in my spirit which, even now, I can only guess at. The Pennine Way had become a symbol of those changes. My sense of affinity with it was almost mysterious. As a route, it could hardly be described as faultless. True, it has charms, but its beauty lies beneath what may be pardonably mistaken for bleak tedium. Perhaps during the long travail of our relationship, I had left behind the stuff of my spirit. And now? Well, perhaps now I wanted to visit those reflections one last time. I was aware of any anomaly only in the minds of others. Despite any difficulty I might have had articulating them, I was quite at peace with my intentions, with my dreams,

Preparation and departure

Having dreams is one thing, achieving them another. Plans had to be laid and, if I wanted this to be the last, exceptional year, they had to be laid meticulously. My battle plan was to crash my training early in April and so approach May having had time to recoup strength. Strength was certainly going to be necessary. I had again planned two subsidiary targets *en route* to the Pennine Way, and neither of these would give an easy passage.

Both subsidiary targets were in Scotland, but very dissimilar in nature. Firstly, I was going to have another attempt at the West Highland Way. During the year following my stiff-legged and hollow 'record', I had become increasingly dissatisfied with my performance. I did not know whether, adhering strictly to the official footpath, I could approach the record for the alternative route, but I felt I should try to better my own time. The West Highland Way suited neither my physical attributes nor my spiritual aspirations. It would, however, give me a long, hard and very continuous running session. My other target was, in truth, little to do with the Pennine Way, it was an end in itself. As a route, in scope and grandeur, it by far surpassed any official footpath. The venture I intended was a natural outgrowth of the Scottish Fourthousanders. However, instead of hastening between the summits on the west side of Scotland and those in the east as economically as possible, I hoped to make a more truly high-level traverse. Furthermore, my ambition was to keep moving ever eastwards over the high ground until I had run out of mountains!

Eventually, the scope of my ambition made it clear that, if it were not limited, I might as well relinquish hopes of doing the Pennine Way three weeks later. Even with compromise, the high traverse across Scotland promised to provide a physical and psychological challenge not much less than that posed by the Pennine Way. Still, I philosophised from the depths of my winter armchair, what is life without challenge?

West Highland Way revisited

In keeping with the theme of reversing my routes, I decided to run from Glasgow to Fort William. This is the direction the race takes and might add some variety, I thought. Unlike the race which is held in June, it was still April when I set off, thus cold and darkness were to provide additional problems. My support team was almost identical to the previous year's excepting that my second eldest son, Sean, was to share the driving with Inken. Gerard, who had run 30 miles (50 km) with me last year, was keen to exceed this total, and I could see Liam, who says little, was quietly determined. I was determined, too, but I made it clear that, while I was optimistic about improving my own time, I thought it unlikely I could better the overall record. This was primarily a training run, my way of improving my basic speed over 100 miles (160 km), very useful for Pennine Way record-breaking.

What a superb pre-dawn greeted my first quiet footsteps! At 4.00 a.m. it was perhaps more night than morning, but the sky was of a soft, dark blue, and against it the trees and hills were revealed densely black. Everywhere was wonderfully still. I ran alone under a dark canopy of branches following my circle of white light as it slipped onwards before me. At Craigallian Loch, mist wraiths dared my gaze, inviolate, but transient above their gloomy sanctuary. By tiny Corbeth Loch, the pale light was sufficient to discern a cloud of vapour floating pensively above the water, while around the perimeter, the vegetation crouched, black and waiting . . .

Waiting for a sun that failed to penetrate an increasingly grey barrier. It was to be a day without colour, becoming colder and wetter as we journeyed north. But it was pleasant to run those early miles in my full strength while around me all was sleeping. Still sleeping were my three sons, who were camped alongside Loch Lomond, 26 miles (42 km) from the start. There was no need to involve them in a 4.00 a.m. start, they could have their sleep and I could have the early morning to myself. I was trying not to consciously hurry, but soon realised that my comfortable pace was a mite slower than that required by the schedule. Although I preferred it, the 'off track' ground was saturated, particularly the stretch over Conic Hill. Belatedly, I also discovered these few miles were officially closed in order to save pregnant sheep embarrassment and worry. Crooning softly and smiling sweetly, I tippy-toed past. They were not a whit disturbed, but quite obviously enchanted by my charming, gracious behaviour. Safely past, I applied the skill born of long practice and snipped just enough time off that section to enable me to visit the lavvy at Balmaha without dinting my schedule.

On the pleasant, but tortuous, section along the side of Loch Lomond to Rowardennan I was joined by Gerard. I had suffered badly over this stage last year, and it was nice to be able to enjoy both Gerard's company and the winding, twisting path, ever rising, ever falling, through the trees, beside the water. This is the section where the path lies a yard or two from the road. At times, the path is narrow with tree roots and little switchbacks to impede progress. I was tempted, not to follow the entire length of the road, but to cut out the odd few yards of awkward going here and there. It would have made little material difference, I had always, however, intended to cleave precisely to the official footpath. I told myself that, if I could not break the race route record using the official Way, I would just have to be content with what I could achieve. I was either following the course of the race or the official route, not what happened to suit me at the time.

In retrospect, I am glad that, on this occasion, I covered the Way from south to north. The effect was to place me on the difficult ground at the north end of Loch Lomond while I yet had the energy to both move purposefully and appreciate the intricate path as it wound through the natural woodland, sometimes close to the water, sometimes well above it. Of course, a truly adventurous line would traverse the summit of Ben Lomond itself, soaring unseen, mist capped and snow girdled, above us. Well, that kind of journey would come later.

At the end of the 14 miles (22 km) of awkward ground beside the loch I was quite pleased. Not only had I enjoyed the running, but I had gained a few minutes on the schedule. Of course, a schedule is not sacrosanct. It is merely an estimate of how long one might realistically spend traversing a piece of ground. Unfortunately, a schedule may also have to be driven by the record, if one is being attempted. Knowing myself well means that I can predict quite accurately how long it will take to cover a section. However, on occasion, I sum the times for individual sections and the total exceeds the record! I know then that I am in for a tough run. A poor schedule is worse than none at all. Fighting a losing battle with an unrealistic schedule can be heartbreaking. I knew the times I had just allotted to the different legs were consistent with the variable nature of the terrain, but I did not know whether they were consistent with my ability.

Over the ensuing ground, it was apparent that conditions were much wetter than last year. I lost both my time in hand and more besides. I was now approaching Crianlarich, which meant I was approximately half-way. I was also experiencing a bad patch. As I came into the support point at Kirkton, Sean very cheerfully and, to my mind, very deliberately said, 'Great! You're *almost* half-way'. I could have throttled him! Checking my schedule, I saw I was a shade over half-way but had taken nearly nine and a half hours. I therefore needed to complete the second half in eight and a quarter hours to beat the record.

I ran in a daze to Tyndrum, where I noted in amazement that I had picked up some time. I then departed on a hugely boring leg to Bridge of Orchy. Most of the route follows the old Military Road parallel to the A82. The speed of the cars flying past served as additional mockery to my plodding progress, but I was determined not to go down without a fight. Gradually, I ran through the bad patch and even began to feel strong again. Perhaps unwisely, I rode my strength and increased pace. I was moving superbly until, with less than a mile to the support, my fine head of steam gave out and I almost clanked to a halt.

This time, despite the company of Liam, my little talisman, I did not recover on the hilly spur leading over to Inveroran and Loch Tulla. I guessed that unless I could improve on the nine miles (14 km) of fast, stony track leading me over to Kingshouse on Rannoch Moor, I would never regain contact with the schedule. The effort was there, but never the reward and nine minutes drifted off the schedule. I ran towards Kingshouse feeling rather depressed and more than somewhat knackered. I could see Gerard, who was accompanying me, striding effortlessly ahead with my request for sustenance.

I would not yet settle for less than 100 per cent effort. I ate standing up and again set off faster than I thought I could manage. This time, I did tap some hidden reserve and covered the short leg to the Devil's Staircase so quickly the support, disorganised for once, was caught *in flagrante*! I clawed back 12 minutes and was now three minutes ahead of my schedule. For the next, quite exciting

Top of the Devil's Staircase with Liam and Gerard. West Highland Way record.

section over the Staircase and down to Kinlochleven, both Gerard and Liam were to join me. A pity then, that the weather was not better. A fierce, gusty wind was hauling dirty, grey rain clouds out of storage. They were now massed behind us and closing fast. We paused briefly at the top of the col, gazing north to the still snow-plastered Mamores, mist shrouded and inhospitable.

The Military Road stays high for a time, and not all the going is straightforward. Slippery rocks, loose boulders and short, steep descents tested both my legs and my patience. The top of the col lies at 2,600 ft (780 m) and Kinlochleven, as I belatedly realised, is at sea-level. Pounding endlessly down the stony tracks was a harsh test of my newly restored knees. They stood up to it marvellously well, but, for all our haste, we lost the three minutes I had just gained and another three besides. Then, as we ran up to the van, a vicious shower swept after us. I thought I had a fighting chance, but I needed help, rain of this severity would be difficult to resist in my, by now very fatigued, state.

The sky was darkening, the wind was gusting rain in wet squalls, 14 miles (22 km) still remained, and those miles demanded what I had only managed for eight (13 km) of the previous 50 miles (80 km) – that I outrun my schedule. I needed to outrun the dark, too, if I was to avoid the real peril of those wet blocks which raised a last threatening barrier to my final, gasping sprint for home. I think Gerard caught the drama of the moment. He had run 30 miles (50 km) already but was adamant that he should come with me to the end.

We set off on the last fierce struggle. Steeply up, gaining so painfully a thousand of those feet we had so recently shed. What was worrying me more, was the necessity to pick up a fast running pace when the climbing was over. The rain squalled in again, but, suddenly, I realised that the wind had settled to south by east! It was now on our backs. For once the weather was helping me. Feeding on its mighty strength, I gave myself to the wind, allowing it to change my pace as it rushed and roared down the glen. Sometimes I ran up hills, sometimes I could not, but always I drove on with the wind.

From the start I had known that my scheduled time for the seven and a half miles to Lundavra was optimistic, but I had thought that by the time I had reached this stage, it would not matter either way. How wrong I was! Despite my efforts and those of the wind, I lost yet another two minutes on that leg. Another minute vanished as I gulped a last drink. I should have had something more solid, but time was against it. Just six and a half miles to go, and still I needed those six minutes to equal the record! Strangely enough, I now felt quite strong. The excitement was stifling fatigue, and I began to feel the adrenalin buzz. No amount of adrenalin, however, would take me safely over some of the subsequent ground in the twilight. If I ran quickly, I would just come to grief. I went as fast as conditions allowed, aiming to rush the easy ground and proceed carefully elsewhere. The night was closing in alarmingly, and darkness blotted out the crucial details of where best to place my feet. At last, I started the final climb to the forest above Glen Nevis. Would it ever end! I expected it to be unexpectedly long, but this exceeded even my unexpectations! Was that my heart pounding? And would these empty legs really be able to cover the last three miles (5 km) in less than 20 minutes? No words between us, both grim

135

with intent. Ninety-five hard miles (152 km) and no reward at the end? (It's only a training run, isn't it? No! It's life and death!)

Down steeply now through black rooty trees. For God's sake, don't trip. Suddenly, we burst out on the broad forest track. A mile of sweet downhill, fly legs, fly. I am stretching as fast as I can, but I cannot go fast enough. My speed is failing me, legs cramping. A barely detectable weakness begins to grow in my stomach. I am going to get hunger knock! Less than two miles and I will not make it. Think! Send Gerard ahead to where the van will be waiting at the start of the road into Fort William. Rehearse carefully what you are going to tell him, now . . . 'Go in front, Gerard, take next right, tell them to have ready a cold sweet drink, not too cold, remember, a *cold, sweet drink.*' Like an arrow from a bow he is gone. Already feeling dizzy. Don't give in fight it.

The van. Reach for the drink. It is only cordial! No spoonfuls of glucose powder stirred in. Might as well be water. No time to prepare another. Can I, through force of mental effort, for once resist the effects of hypoglycemia and hang on for the last one and a half miles? I must try. The road will seem endless, be ready for this. There is a rise to surmount near the end, save strength for it, and then you can unleash whatever is left – if anything is. Now concentrate.

My head must have been ready for that last mile and a half for a long time. Without slackening pace, but with my brain now locked out of my body, I seemed to reach, then surmount the incline with no conscious elapse of time. With a start I saw the bridge which marked the finish only 200 yards (180 m) away. Sprint! Damn, I could have gone sooner! Instantly I stopped, my automatic pilot switched off, and in the second it took for my brain to assume control again, I staggered and almost fell over, then strong arms came round me and bore me up. I was three minutes inside the 17 hours, 38 minutes I had been aiming for. I felt a bit embarrassed, three minutes is nothing to break anyone's record by. There again, I had done it the hard way.

There is a sequel to this. Next morning, in chatting to Inken, I explained I did not feel too good about knocking only three minutes off the record. She looked a little surprised. After I repeated myself she then confessed she thought I had broken my own record only, and had told the others that it 'didn't matter, it was only a training run'! I thought they were a little subdued at the finish. I had actually taken an hour off my previous run. There is a sequel to the sequel, too. A month later, looking through my log-book, I noticed that 17:38 was the scheduled time I had set myself, the record I broke was 17:48.

(The 1987 summer edition of *Fell Runner* magazine gives a record for the West Highland Way of 14:56 – for a nine-man team!)

Scottish High Level Traverse

Just as Eustace Thomas had been satisfied to motor his way between the 4,000 ft (1,200 m) peaks in NW Scotland and the 4,000 ft summits in NE Scotland, so those Rucksackers who followed deemed it satisfactory to raise the order of difficulty by walking the entire route but taking to the road at times. Very properly, John Richardson elevated the walk to the status of a true classic both by devising a 'pure' (road-free) line and by executing the entire route in a continuous fashion. Until John, Ian Grant and I completed this 'pure' line as a Club walk in 1977 I believe it had never been done before.

Both John and I had frightened ourselves considerably by reading accounts of previous traverses in Club journals. Blizzards, deep snow, the hallucinatory effects of hard and sleepless hours all featured graphically in these accounts. I particularly shuddered at Phil Brockbank's description of the ascent to the bleak watershed of the Bealach Dubh, a 'screaming desolation' was his phrase.

In the event we enjoyed a marvellous walk. Demanding it was, but it gave so much more than it asked. Thereafter, this traverse gleamed gem bright among my collection of superb walks and runs. For some reason it became established as an ultra fell running classic with perhaps half a dozen attempts to complete within 24 hours. I had experienced no desire to tackle the route from this perspective. I had, however, always determined to repeat it some day, at the right time. The only, very slight, dissatisfaction I had felt after our completion was the memory of mountains we did not traverse. First, the majestic line of the Grey Corries sweeping irresistibly onwards as we descended all too soon from Aonach Beag. And later, as we topped the Bealach Dubh, the vast bulk of Ben Alder dominating our approach to Loch Ericht.

The notion that I might be able to reconcile the romance of the route with the harsher practicalities of a record attempt for a time threatened to seduce my whole aspirations concerning a 'purer' form of the Scottish Fourthousanders. The possibility of a record and the certainty of a magnificent journey beguiled me. I was saved, as many a gallant crusader in times past, by my noble unflinching resolve and the plea of a fair damsel.

Well, 'noble resolve' may be interpreted as a stab of conscience about avoiding the soaring challenge of those intervening mountains. The damsel's plea was a timely reminder from Inken that I had promised to invite her whenever the Scottish Fourthousanders were repeated. There was also a not too veiled hint about the difficulties she might experience in getting time off to support my Pennine Way attempt, if I should be so foolish as to essay a solo effort. In truth, what I had in mind was such a wonderful prospect, I welcomed the idea of sharing it with someone else who I knew would truly appreciate the venture. I was, however, genuinely concerned about the matching of our physical reserves to the total concept.

The total concept involved not only traversing extra peaks in the west, but also an extension of the route further eastwards. It seemed illogical to 'collect' just the 4,000 ft (1,200 m) summits in the Caingorms when there were endless peaks and high plateaux in all directions. Like a child loose in a sweet shop, I described sweeping lines all over the map. My route moved ever eastwards, claiming Lochnagar and finally Mount Keen, the most easterly Munro. But why finish there? We were starting on the west coast, why not finish on the east coast?

At this point, realism raised its unwelcome head. The line my pencil had drawn to the south and east of the Cairngorm 'high tops' covered far more ground than we could encompass on a continuous traverse. Furthermore, the continuation of the route from Mount Keen to the coast was not only an unnecessary attempt to gild a noble lily, it was likely to be utterly boring! With ambition in check therefore, I decided we could still execute a superb extension by continuing the traverse over Ben A'Bhuird and Ben Avon, both mountains are a mere handful of feet below the 4,000 ft (1,200 m) mark and share the unique character of the highest Cairngorm plateaux. I still hoped to finish over Lochnagar as I had good associations with this hill from running my winter mountaineering courses from a base in view of its beetling crags.

I was excited by the route. It was a magnificent and logical line. But I was also a little fearful. We planned to walk towards the end of May, the timing was, in part, a response to our dissatisfaction with what the LDWA were offering as their 100-mile (160 km) event at that time. May in the Scottish Highlands can still produce winter weather. Snow, even blizzards are not unusual. Our great venture could quite easily founder on the first hill. Severe weather towards the end of this testing enterprise might not only jeopardise the walk, it could well jeopardise us along with it! On a different level, I began to have doubts as to whether I could get my head round both the Scottish traverse and the Pennine Way just three weeks later. Had I bitten off more than I could chew?

When I arrived in Edinburgh to rendezous with Inken, I was almost relieved when she informed me that at the eleventh hour John Richardson, who was to have been our sole support for the first day and night, could not make it. He was rather poorly after heading a piece of road while he should have been riding his bicycle. Once I found John was not seriously hurt, I prepared to put my feet up for the weekend. Too soon! Quite extraordinarily, another friend and newcomer to the Rucksack Club, Chris Bauer, had stepped in with a very generous offer to help. What was more, Chris's friend Sheila Cormack of the Pinnacle Club was prepared to come along to ease Chris's support burden. The traverse was on. I did not know about Sheila's support expertise, but she could certainly drive. We were in Fort William in no time and, after a battle with early season midges, settled in for another of those excited, fitful sleeps.

We left at 5.30 a.m. after a meagre breakfast but as much as the stomach could take at such an unseemly hour. The tiny voice which had been whispering that I should not be tackling these mountains with so little specific hill training, began to shout very loudly down my ear. It was too late, we were off. Butting up the steep skirts of Ben Nevis, I very deliberately chose a steady pace, always a little less than my natural inclination. Just as well, Inken told me later she felt rather overstretched, probably I was more keyed up than I realised.

I can be a real wimp at the start of a long event. Slow to get going anyway, I frequently suspect my physical preparation and, whatever the weather, find fault with that, too. The best I can do is to disengage my mind and wait for a magic moment. The current fault in the weather was that a fine day had been forecast, and it had not come! It was very dull and overcast as we plodded ever upwards. I skidded on black ice, hmmm, cold too. I'll bet the snow patches are frozen and I decided to leave the ice-axes behind. We'll become horrible accident statistics, 'Found dead after slipping on ice, the coroner stated they were wearing running shoes.' How embarrassing! (At least I'm wearing clean underwear.)

There was plenty of snow on the summit of the Ben. The famous gullies skeltered giddily down through black rocks into smoking depths. It smelled high, cold and remote. What a great place to be early in the morning! Care is needed to locate and descend the line to the Carn Mor Dearg arête. After a time, a large snow bank presented itself as an alternative to awkward blocks. How I missed the insurance of an axe poised to come to my aid should the snow contain ice patches. I stepped cautiously on, and letting my weight drive my heels through the crust began to clip down. Relief! The snow, if anything, was a little too soft. I began to feel better about omitting the ice-axes and thumbed a mental nose at the coroner.

As we hopped and skipped over the blocks which comprise the fine arête leading to Carn Mor Dearg, the moment of magic arrived. A flick of wind parted the curtain of cloud, revealing a gleam of blue, a flash of gold. Then it was gone. A few hops and skips later, it was repeated, longer this time. I unpacked the camera. By the time we were atop this, the second of the 4,000 ft (1,200 m) peaks, we were bathed in warm and gentle sunlight. Making a virtue out of the necessity of Inken's hunger, we stopped and ate, gazing around us at this unsurpassable world we had entered.

Do the physical payments which one must make in order to first enter, then journey through such worlds constitute not only an inevitable, but also an essential part of the experience of their beauty? Cool logic might refute such a notion. But what role has logic to play in that glorious fusion of physical, sensory and emotional energy whose pulse will thrust the spirit into a sublime relationship with forces of Nature of which it is a tiny part? The exultant cry of the spirit which is wild, free and joyful arises not merely from the contemplation of Nature, but from the sometimes fierce struggle to cleave to it. Who ventures in the mountains cannot remain passive.

It is very easy to resent the 1,300 ft (390 m) of descent from the top of Carn Mor Dearg. After crossing about 160 ft (50 m) of col one has to gather it all in again. Not quite all, some pawky surveyor with a theodolite for a heart robbed Aonach Mor of 4,000 ft (1,200 m) status by one improbable foot. Its cairn is certainly more than a foot high, however, and thus having regained our 1,300 ft (390 m), we climbed our third Fourthousander. Running, now over sparse turf, now over old snow banks, we approached Aonach Beag. This is the last 4,000 ft (1,200 m) peak in the NW group. We would need to cover around 60 miles (100 km) before we surmounted another Fourthousander. But now, instead of immediately scuttling down to follow valley lines to the Cairngorms, we would remain high on peaks and ridges for many hours.

First, we had to cope with the steep descent off Aonach Beag in order to attain the col giving access to the Grey Corries. As I expected, the remains of a cornice menaced the approach to the descent slopes. The cornice had degraded into a steep head wall which gave a possible descent line. The snow was quite stable, but steep. Fortunately, it was soft enough for me to kick steps and jab handholds firm enough to carry my weight. As the angle eased, I signalled to Inken that it was safe to follow. I also noticed another walker, rather more suitably equipped, delaying his own attempt while he watched mine – a canny

*Inken
approaching
the summit of
Aonach Mor,
behind is Carn
Mor Dearg.*

Scot, nae doot! From this point, I realised the snow was a great bonus. It was at just the right angle and consistency to facilitate a swooping descent. In no time we had whooped our way to the col. The penalty we paid, however, was frozen, wet feet, and these were to cause problems later.

After the insatiable Blunk had again tested my patience by burying her head in her nosebag, we launched upwards towards Sgurr Choinnich Mor. By now the sun was waxing warm. Having just compressed 7,500 ft (2,250 m) of climbing into very few miles, we found the steep grassy ascent quite a stern pull. Once on the summit, however, the ridge sweeps steadily north by east with relatively minor variations in height gained and lost. Gradually we approached Stob Choire Claurigh, at 3,858 ft (1,160 m) the highest summit on the ridge. After freezing in the wet snow, the stony going across the highest ground was hard on the feet. Such a combination is likely to produce bruising of the bones. We had also finished our liquid and were beginning to look forward to seeing Sheila and Chris down in the valley. We savoured our last peak, however. This was the end of the first section of the route. Only little more than 15 miles (24 km) in length, it had included seven major summits over 3,500 ft (1,050 m), and we had been blessed with glorious conditions in which to traverse them.

It began to look as if we might have longer to savour the views than expected. Our projected route off the summit lay NE. The steep slopes held snow fields on which the sun had bestowed only a fleeting glance. I tried kicking steps, but quickly approached the point of hazard. One slightly harder patch, and I could begin a descent to the glen likely to produce both the speed and effect of truly terminal velocity. While Inken has an abhorrence of sliding down slopes in the best of circumstances she can usually pick a safe and subtle line through aggressive ground (probably a feminine trait!), and she did so now. Soon we were guzzling our fill from delicious snow-fed rills and springs. Below the snow, the whole mountain was alive with water, leaping, dashing pausing to swell the green sphagnum bogs, clattering noisily down stony channels. Fast as we descended, with yet greater impetuosity rushed the water, eager to join its parent burn still far beneath. Had I been born on these slopes, I would not so hurry to chance the inevitable sea.

At the bothy in Lairig Leacach we savoured the luxuries of a splendid settee. Normally wary of adopting too comfortable a stance at support points, I could not resist this. There was, anyway, not the slightest temptation to remain overlong. The weather was holding fine, and we had just completed as inspirational an introduction to a long route as any I had known. Waving thanks and goodbyes we set off on the next stage.

It was now mid-afternoon and our plan was to reach Dalwhinnie a little before midnight. To accomplish this, we would have to be sure of traversing Ben Alder while it was still light. We began to swing into the steady jogging rhythm we hoped would cover the easier going swiftly and economically. Our route took us past the southern end of Loch Treig and then over to Loch Ossian. At first, along the tracks, it felt good to be eating the miles so much more quickly than over the ridges. Ere long, of course, the going became tedious. The sense of space was enormous and impressive, naturally enough it was precisely these features which gave us the impression we were barely moving.

Gradually, we wound in the miles, and the path became narrower and more interesting as we approached the 'screaming desolation' of the Bealach Dubh. It was hardly screaming now, though the sun had retreated behind a screen of cloud and a brisk breeze invited goose-pimples out to play.

Although the summit of Ben Alder stands at over 3,700 ft (1,110 m), we were already at more than 2,000 ft (600 m) and the summit plateau was not long coming up. Neither of us had ever been over Ben Alder before, the map showed it to have a fairly extensive plateau however, and I was looking forward to this. Perhaps as a child of the moors, my heart rejoices always in the great upland areas. Despite the map, I was totally unprepared for what met our gaze as we emerged on the plateau of Ben Alder. It was vast. It was so vast, I could not believe it. The so-called plateaux of the high Cairngorms are more extensive, but they fall from high summits, they are sloping plateaux. Stretched before us was a flat immensity. It seemed a tundra region of coarse grasses and wet snowfields, and it rolled out of sight. I thought it must be an illusion, a trick of the light. We set off jogging across it on a bearing for the summit cairn. It was no illusion. We were running but did not seem to be making any impression on the distance. I did not care. At that moment in time there was no better place to be in all the world.

Somewhere in the middle of the plateau I looked back. The sky was assuming the pale grey mantle of evening. But even as I gazed, the suble greys became suffused with the most delicate shades of pastels. It was like looking into a huge

Inken crossing Ben Alder summit plateau. Ben Nevis is in the far distance.

sea shell, steely greys and pale pinks. As the invisible sun lowered obliquely towards the western horizon, it slipped swathes of diffuse and misty light beneath the clouds. Low though the sun had dipped, it was high enough to bestow another gift. On the edge of our westering gaze there tipped a serrated line of peaks. Highest and whitest of them all was the Ben. The thrill of our journey leapt from that far distant summit. We locked it into our gaze, into our hearts, into our forever memories.

If we are fortunate, we can review our life in the hills and select treasured memories which have become focal and focusing points for the love we bear them. Occasionally, we can recognise an experience as vital even while it is unfolding. If we are very lucky indeed, there occur supreme moments which are so imperative they pierce us to our innermost spirit, they transcend words, engage not reason. They communicate directly with the stuff of our nature, our spirit leaps and grasps truth for a moment. That moment is sufficient.

Our journey across the plateau reached its conclusion with our gaining its highest point. We had made the most cursory investigation of the resources of this great mountain. I shall be back. An aspect of the exploratory nature of our journey now presented itself, we did not know the way off! We wanted to continue the line of our walk either north or east. To the east, there appeared to be a long continuous rampart of cliffs guarding the summit. To the north, the map indicated a likely looking ridge jutting towards the glen we wished to attain. We sped north over wonderfully easy running ground but with some trepidation, we were rapidly approaching what was obviously another line of cliffs.

The map did not lie. There was a ridge leading out away from the plateau edge, it did not look too promising, however. As best we could, we inspected the ridge from either side. It certainly was steep, plunging down in a series of steps which, if they were sheer, were high enough to bar our line of descent. There was no possibility of escaping down the craggy sides. If there was a way down, it would have to follow the crest of the plummenting ridge. The only feasible alternative was to retrace our steps, and neither of us was yet prepared to do that. 'Let's give it a try, eh?'

The ridge was magnificent. Resembling a huge flake of vegetated rock, its serrated edge tumbled down into the darkening glen. Each time we came to one of its steep steps I was sure we would be forced to retreat, each time a comparatively simple line would reveal itself, and down we would go to the next level. The sweet inevitability with which this happened bred a confidence which banished our anxiety. We began to glory in our situation. It was obvious from the tumbled chaotic slopes and crags around us that we had found the magic staircase by which mortals may traverse glen and summit. Too soon we reached the foot of our fairy tower and swished into the bush-like heather. Perhaps in winter I will return and clamber, steel shod gleaming, on the crisp white tower; spiral up to a cleaner, colder, purer world, once more, once alone, gaze westward into my dream.

The path ribboned down the glen parallel to the burn which chattered along beside us. With true dark still over an hour away, we had sufficient light left to enjoy our surroundings. It was a beautiful evening, calm and still. There is that about vast, unchanging panoramas which quietens the soul and lends it gravity and peace. We settled into a pace which flowed with the rhythm of the path. A little further on we saw columns of blue smoke pluming into the still air. Beside the now broad waters of the burn there were tents and dark clumps of figures gathered round various fires, anti-midge fires perhaps, or the ancient glen prompting some primordial instinct. The smoke was scented and lovely. We raised our hands in greeting. They would soon be lying down to rest beside the ever-flowing waters, their world would darken as the mountains locked them in night shades. Tomorrow, their lives would resume. As they slept, we would be following our journey ever eastwards, going onwards to reach dawn breaking, sun rising. Our first night was almost upon us, our second was waiting our arrival in the eastern highlands.

Spring can be a fickle season, as befits its youthfulness. The wings of darkness beat a thin wave of air against us. Imperceptibly the rolling wave increased in strength and our effortless rhythm changed into a strenuous battle against a power insistent and chill. In the dubious shelter of some dark pines we ate and donned our spare gear. Shivering by now, we launched ourselves on the broad and tedious track beside Loch Ericht. The lights of Dalwhinnie at the end of the loch seemed reluctant to let us approach, but our Scout's Pace of jogging and walking soon had heating systems going efficiently. At last, round a final bend there was a glow of light from a van parked by the track. A whiff of escaping steam carried the essence of ambrosia – hot stew!

The interior of the little van was a haven of comfort and warmth. Chris and Sheila kept a constant supply of hot drinks and food coming in our direction until I Billy Buntered my way out of the van and back onto the track. Having changed from contact lenses into my glasses, I stood blinking like a short-sighted owl, trying to penetrate the gloom. I do not rate my night vision very highly and was making very sure I was not on the point of marching firmly back in the direction of Fort William. Satisfied with my orientation, I was content to let Inken concern herself with the fiddling trivia of negotiating an accurate route through the few streets and across the A9. She is far more meticulous than I. I am inclined to paint my navigation with a broad brush. The creative results can be most striking, like finding oneself on an unexpected set of mountains.

Leaving behind the comforts of a support point at the midnight hour after a satisfying but tiring day can be something of a wrench. I remembered having to prise Ted Dance out of this very spot when he and Geoff Bell were traversing the Fourthousanders. Ted's reluctance to depart became manifest when, as the moment became imminent, he emptied his carefully prepared rucksack in an attempt to discover the half a Mars bar he felt economy dictated should replace the whole one he had just packed. For once, no such reluctance gripped us. The magical skein of this enchanted journey had bound us in its spell. The night would not be easy, we realised that, but by morning all the Cairngorms would be spread before us. For Inken the primary object of this journey, the 4,000 ft (1,200 m) peaks of Scotland, would be within her grasp, and for me the lure and excitement of a new and fabulous route. I wanted to surmount the barrier of the

Cairngorm 'High Tops', and from that height I wanted to roam on and on.

It was not an easy night. We endured it as a passage to better things, but we did not enjoy it. First, I was unusually sleepy and the track tediously following a leat winding up to Loch Cuaich did not help. If it had not been for the fence by the leat, I am sure I would have fallen into it. I remembered not enjoying the rough and boggy ground which led to Glen Tromie when John and I had come this way 10 years ago. Despite the early advent of a grey dawn it seemed to have become even rougher. Our progress was slow, weary, and, at times, very frustrating.

Close by the confluence of the Allt Bhran and the River Tromie we burrowed into a bank of thick heather and after a very early breakfast had a few minutes sleep. Although it was bitterly cold in the wind, the light was full and the sky promised a fine morning. I considered we had the worst over. Soon we would be in Glen Feshie for a second breakfast. How wrong I was. I should have read my old log-book which made comment on the very rough going from here on. Our progress through wroughty heather was a constant battle. The only bit I enjoyed was when I succumbed to the morning sun and stretched out on the springy bed, no sound but the tinkling burn and the sighing breeze.

Perseverance brought us at last to the very fine little valley which snicked up onto our moor from Glen Feshie itself. The morning was crisp and blue, and I was now impatient to get onto the real mountains while it lasted. A good track wound down the valley inviting a swift descent to the flat green glen. Clamping the bit between my teeth, I set off at a fair gallop. Frustratingly, I began to boil up in too many clothes. Stopping to remove a layer I glanced back and saw Inken quite a way behind. Well! This would never do. Just when we could get going and claw back some lost time, she had apparently decided on a go-slow. As she approached, however, I could see she was having trouble running and was obviously in some pain.

Sore feet, the walker's bane; and nothing simple either. Being a sufferer myself, I am a good 'foots-man', but this was beyond simple remedy. Frozen feet 50 miles (80 km) back, which had subsequently been pounded over rocks in thin fell shoes, re-frozen on Ben Alder and pounded again, had, naturally enough, responded in painful bruising. When the bones in the feet become bruised, the only real cure is rest. Cushioning and soft ground might mitigate the pain somewhat, but we were hoping to cover another 50 to 60 miles (80 to 100 km) of mountainous terrain. While Inken is ever ready to complain about the painful grind of tedious running, she has an extraordinary capacity to ignore discomfort on a route which she regards as inspirational. And I knew full well how the prospect and the current execution of this route had inspired her. Consequently, I realised immediately that the pain must be a savage one.

With the appreciation of the cause, nature and severity of the pain came a keen awareness of what lay ahead. In my heart I knew she could not make it, nor did I want her to try. There were an awful number of footsteps between us and Royal Deeside, an uncountable number of stones. With each step, pain, and each stone prepared to lend that pain an extra refinement; I could not bear to witness that, I knew it too well.

Inken insisted that she could follow if I would not mind moving a little slower. We sat off again with me looking for the grassy patches and seeing only stones. But despite the trauma, the beauty of Glen Feshie in the morning could not be denied. Owing to a slack bit of thinking, we had rather longer to admire the glen than intended. We could have started our ascent to the Cairngorm Massif just before Feshie Lodge. Unfortunately, we had indicated a spot three miles (5 km) further down where we were to be met. With the hills soaring above, we sweated away precious time and energy, and our progress became very slow.

Perhaps it was only that I perceived it to be slow. As we jogged to the bridge where our support mustered, Sheila made some flattering remarks about our pace. This was nice, but I still felt restless and would do so until I could actually set foot on the climb to the Cairngorms. I had been mentally gearing myself to go solo from this point. I knew how much Inken wanted to at least complete the Fourthousanders, but I did not see how she could do so. If she left this spot with me, and not Sheila and Chris, she would be committed to reaching Deeside. This would mean she would have to traverse about 30 miles (50 km) of very hard terrain, even omitting the summits. I said nothing, but waited and observed.

It soon became apparent that Inken was not going to retire. I hoped she knew what she was doing and trusted that she did. We prepared to depart. Preparations made were partly decided by the weather. It was now very warm and, with the hottest part of the day to come, it was tempting to take little more than shorts, vest and spare woolly. A degree of common sense prevailed, and we packed some warmer and windproof clothing. Had we not done so, we might not have survived what was to follow.

After ascending more than 1,000 ft (300 m) in shorts and vest, we suddenly crossed an altitude band above which a powerful wind instantly created a new climate. Although the sun still smiled serenely from a clear sky, it no longer warmed us. As soon as we had completed the most strenuous part of the climbing onto the rounded flanks of Carn Ban Mor, we hurriedly put on our spare clothing. Shorts were out of the question, no chance of an early season sun-tan after all. Rather more comfortable now, we made the slight detour to take in the summit of Carn Ban Mor, which, at 3,443 ft (1,075 m) was our first Munro since Ben Alder. I had a rose-tinted memory of the Cairngorm giants being but a cock-stride away once we had cracked the steep pull out of Glen Feshie. I was therefore puzzled to see no peaks around at all. There followed a few minutes serious reconciliation of map, ground and memory. The first condemned the last as a gross optimist. Cairn Toul and Braeriach were there all right, but even had we been crows, they were still five or six miles (8 or 9.6 km) away.

Not only did our peaks appear distant, they were separated from us by considerable snow fields. Obviously, late snow had visited the Cairngorms and, outstaying its welcome, lay in ever broadening wet swathes between us and the high ground. Navigation was thus not merely a matter of the most direct line, but rather the line which kept us out of the main snow fields and followed ridges in preference to crossing basins. It was a long and muscular struggle to gain the col beneath Cairn Toul, nor was the summit quite such a little way above it as I remembered. However, we enjoyed clambering up the snow-free boulders which jumbled up to the top of the peak. Unfortunately, I realised that unless the snow was swept clear of the high ground or was in better condition, we were in for a real battle.

Apart from the snow, the wind was also causing increasing problems. Although the sun was still shining, indeed the glare was very painful, the wind at this height was tearing through our clothing. Furthermore, I was determined not just to traverse Cairn Toul and Braeriach, but collect all the bumps over 4,000 ft (1,200 m) between these two. After all, we had come to do the Fourthousanders, had we not? Nice ethics but cold comfort.

The traverse of the minor tops on the way over to Braeriach could appropriately be described as taking place in a 'screaming desolation', at least, that is how it felt. Had one merely observed the scene from behind some sheltered partition, it would have looked innocent enough. But the Cairngorm wind is a deadly enemy. It has a primitive strength which is heedless of life for it was spawned in an age before life. It belongs to a primeval world of gaunt rock, empty seas and merciless cold. Refusing to yield its power to the passing ages, it snarls forever round the deep corries and craggy recesses of the Cairngorms. But when it gathers its forces and leaps like a ferocious beast across the high, smooth wastes, then beware, for it kills without pity.

Certainly, a primitive fear was gnawing at me as we battled towards Braeriach. There was no real danger yet, but our position was finely balanced, the wind could tip the scales with contemptuous ease. I have, and always have had, a robust delight in the vigour of a strong wind. There is in it that sense of affinity, a life force shared, even the feeling of a scouring purification. While we remain mortal, however, our physical and spiritual strength may soon be exhausted by its exuberant power. I was also aware that Inken did not share to anything like the same extent my love of the wind's rough embrace. The raptures were rapidly becoming more than even I could bear, and I knew they must be wasting her strength and wasting her will to persevere.

On the summit at last; a curious lull. The wind was screaming up the sheer headwall of the Garbhe Choire with such force, it must have been rearing into a vertical wave high above the summit which stands at the very edge of the precipice. Relief for a few minutes, but the realisation of how cold we had become and the urge and necessity to lose height without delay. Now came a problem. I could not remember the descent I had followed in times previous to reach the top of the pass, the Lairig Ghru, most safely and economically. I scouted round in the soft snow, aware that we were getting colder, but also aware that a wrong descent line would result in, at best, time loss and at worst, disaster. Peering cautiously over convex slopes, I eventually chose a line and started down. The wind had not polished the snow to ice, and, though awkward at times, our route proved safe and parsimonious. The uncertainty was somewhat trying to the nerves, however, I did not relish the prospect of any more doubtful decisions like that.

The ascent from the Lairig Ghru to the Cairngorm–Ben Macdui plateau is extraordinarily steep. It is only 1,000 ft (312 m), but feels a good deal more. Weaving a careful line under small outcrops and over ice-loosened blocks, we emerged wearily onto the plateau at last; weary, but with the knowledge that the final two Fourthousanders were at either end of this great piece of high ground. The major objective of our journey lay within our grasp. And once we had achieved this, what more could we not achieve?

But first the job in hand. We had emerged in the middle of the plateau, equidistant from the two summits. The usual route visits Macdui first, then goes north to Cairngorm itself. From here it is a wonderfully easy descent off the mountain to Glenmore and rest. The peaks over which I had planned to extend the walk lay to the east of Macdui. We therefore needed to visit Cairngorm first, then retrace our steps towards Macdui. Outside the winter months it is a pleasant and easy task to sweep across the plateau, the dearth of vegetation and the fine gravelly surface make for fast travel. Now, of course, almost the entire area was snow covered. We sat to work with a will, but progress was slow and laborious. And the wind, though generally behind us on this leg, had ushered in large banks of high cloud. We were in a grey, desolate and empty world.

As we traversed the long snow fields, I recounted to Inken the first time I had visited the Cairngorms with Len, nearly 20 years previously. A murderous blizzard had sought to trap us in the great basin of Loch Avon, and we had escaped across these very slopes, hauling our sacks on Len's home-made skis. In white-out conditions and ignorant of true reality, we had fortuitously donned crampons and shouldered the sacks just as the wind glazed sides of the Lairig Ghru were about to invite us to perdition. Now, the wind was neither so fierce nor cold, but we were barely sufficiently clothed to withstand it and the miles lay heavy upon us. In pursuing this fine act of balance between peril and ambition, I was relying on my experience, skill and strength to keep us safe. It behoved me not to indulge in any form of overestimation of those abilities.

The summit of Cairngorm was a turning point, both literally and symbolical-ly. Onward now, first to Ben Macdui, second in stature only to Ben Nevis, then, into the furthest dream. Something Jeff Lowe, the mountaineer, said, echoed in my mind. First, he said, you have the image. Then the magic comes when you transform that image into reality. I was now at the very pivotal point of that dream reality. The very severity involved in reaching this point underlay my desire and determination to transform dream into reality. It was at this precise moment Inken told me that, beyond Ben Macdui, she did not wish to continue.

As strong as she was in body, and stronger still in spirit, yet the cold, ruthless wind and the constant bruising pain had exhausted her. She had drained her resources, and now her furthest peaks lay as distant images; magic, unattainable chimera. My immediate response was to commiserate with her, then I realised that not only did she feel she could not go beyond Ben Macdui, she hoped I would also finish my journey there. Such was the absolute and overpowering commitment that had grown within me as the journey had progressed, I could in no way comprehend what she was saying. Soaring on my renewed strength, flooded with optimism, stiffened with an implacable determination, I was on quite another plane. It took a long and painful period of time to leave that plane and attempt another. How perverse is my nature, while I avow to struggle for wisdom, I reject opportunities presented should they conflict with my own will.

It really was quite simple. Having shared our identical dream, having given everything she could possibly give to accomplish that dream, having quietly endured the pain to the bitter occlusion of the final part of our dream, she was spent. If I were to carry on without her, continue alone that fabulous dream we had shared, it would cause her pain beyond the endurable. With an effort I imagined myself in the valley, weary in body and spirit, while my companion with whom I had shared the journey for nearly 100 miles (160 km) was pursuing it still. What we had planned together, endured together and were now about to achieve together would be a complete and satisfying whole, if I were to make it so by concluding it together. A simple but subtle notion, whose paradox might yet evade my stubborn pragmatism. Where targets are concerned, I am frequently neither subtle nor sensitive. I struggled through the snow and the dilemma, then a softer, gentler, wiser part of my nature saw more clearly and acquiesced.

With our spirits once more at peace, we locked our bodies into the fight for Ben Macdui. As we climbed higher, so the wind almost imperceptibly, but implacably, increased in strength. First, we had to visit the outlying top of Carn Sputan Dearg, ancient Rucksack Club traditions demanded this. Before we could mount the inconsequential summit, the cloud base lowered and mist was flying around us like 1,000 demented phantoms. The cold became polar, it cut into me and through me, seeking, I knew, my warm heart's blood. It would not have it. I increased my pace, traversed Sputan Dearg without pausing and, body and will bent into the flying wrack, followed my compass into the white miasma. Kindled by fear, my concentration and determination were such that I barely realised Inken was being increasingly swallowed by the mist. A stricken cry recalled me to my duties, but I urged her to further and harder effort. We must get off this mountain before it killed us, but first, we would have its summit!

The second highest point in these islands, 4,296 ft (1,342 m). No time for ceremony, just turn and go. Run if possible, but keep moving. Fortunately, we had calculated the bearing we must follow from the top well before reaching it. We hurled ourselves down until we had crept from under the fiercest grasp of that colossal hand which gripped the summit. We paused to check our memory against the map and the visible ground. We had to go east, then descend a long valley which would lead us to Loch Etchachan, from where we would drop yet further to the remote bothy known as the Hutchison Hut. Inken had the map and I formed a mental image of the ground we must cover. We reached the head of a broad snow-packed valley and I started to follow Inken down it. It was good to be losing height and dropping to safety, but were we? I thought I remembered a shallow ridge between us and the valley we were to descend. I asked Inken if she was sure we were following the correct valley. Not given to over-confidence, on this occasion she was insistent we were in the right place. I was impressed by this, but not convinced. We *had* to get this one right. I insisted we should cross the ridge in front and then descend. Immediately we did so, everything slotted neatly into place. The valley we had started to follow lay only half a mile from this one and perfectly parallel to it. It would, however, eventually have committed us to descending into the great defile of Loch Avon where Len and I had so nearly been entombed all those years ago.

The light was slowly fading as we crunched endlessly down the valley towards Loch Etchachan. Having blasted us off the heights, the wind was content to stay there and made no attempts to follow us down. The air was suddenly preternaturally still. Away to our left, behind the beetling black crags rising sheer from the loch, clouds were parting, and the sky gave hints of a distant sunset. Pale, eggshell blues and a curious green cast combined with greys and blacks to impart a sense of arctic cold and arctic tranquillity.

I was anxious to reach the bothy as soon as we could. Sheila and Chris had departed for home from Glen Feshie (another world ago, it seemed!), but my friend Neil Spinks from Aberdeen had kindly agreed to make the long journey to the Hutchison Hut to bring us much needed provisions. Neil and I had in previous years combined forces to run my winter mountaineering courses and, though a Derbyshire lad, there are few who know these hills better than he. After Inken's declaration on the summit of Cairngorm, it seemed as if Neil had come out simply to escort us off the hill. However, as we descended to less hostile conditions, she appeared to recoup some of her strength. I therefore suggested that, as the walk-out from Hutchison to Deeside was long and tedious, she might consider finishing over Beinn A'Bhuird, which is a bit longer, but certainly not tedious! As this mountain stands but 75 ft (23 m) below the 4,000 ft (1,200 m) contour, she might have resented the suggestion, but she did not. She knew how much I wanted to continue the walk beyond the Fourthousanders, and I knew how much she wanted to come with me. With soft going between here and Beinn A'Bhuird, and with Ben Avon rising only 1,000 ft (320 m) across the intervening col, we might yet achieve a magnificent conclusion to our journey.

We were some three hours behind schedule by now, and I went ahead to reassure Neil that all was well. He was wrapped up in most of the spare gear he had brought out for us, but he still looked chilly. His welcome, however, was typically warm and enthusiastic, it did me good just to see him. When Inken appeared, hobbling once more on the stony ground, he embraced her in such a bear hug that the sun broke out all over her face.

Neil had used a mountain bike to transport himself and a rucksack full of food and clothes swiftly up the miles of Glen Derry track. He was rightly enthusiastic about this method of overcoming the notorious tedium of the typical Cairngorm 'walk-in'. There again, enthusiam is Neil's hallmark. His good cheer was infectious, and I soon began to feel as if I was about to start the walk rather than face our second night out. His optimism, too, complemented my own. We had soon reduced Beinn A'Bhuird and Ben Avon to minor excrescences on a rolling tableland, a pleasant stroll on a fine evening.

Packed to the brim with calories and rather more suitably clad, we hurried to make ground in the last of the light. Neil bounded cheerfully off down the path, keen to locate his hidden bike and make last orders in Braemar. I hoped he would not break his neck in his exuberance, but reflected he would probably just stick a plaster on it and declare it 'right'.

I had crossed the ground between Beinn A'Bhuird and the Hutchison Hut on a bothying expedition the previous winter. I remembered it as a laborious slog with much terrain awkward to read navigationally. In the event, it proved not unenjoyable. At this northern latitude, the light hung in the sky to provide an extended twilight. There was altogether less snow on this side of the Cairngorms, and none at all at our present altitude – around 3,000 ft (937 m). The ground was reminiscent of my Derbyshire moors, and I felt at home slotting a line through peat hags. It was very mild, too, and windless. Perhaps we were going to have a good night and a serene passage over these lovely mountains which waited so patiently in the night.

Optimism is fine, so long as you can bear disappointment with stoicism. I have had much practice, so I was able to remain reasonably cheerful as the wind began to slam into us once more. The 'jet stream' effect seemed to switch on at a little over 3,000 ft (937 m). As soon as we started our climb towards North Top, occasional gusts of wind thundered across the hillside and attempted to unbalance us as we clambered over large blocks and boulders. The higher we climbed, the more frequently came the gusts. Eventually, we were back in the constant gale we hoped we had left in possession of Ben Macdui. At least there was now less chance of being unbalanced, but the cold was returning, and, with the cold, mist.

North Top is simply a cairn on a very extensive and almost completely flat top. As a matter of navigational pride I wanted to find it. Using both technique and senses tuned to the feel of the ground, I led us almost directly to the cairn. Unable to decide whether satisfaction or surprise was the most appropriate reaction, I embarked on the easier task of guiding us down to the col before Ben Avon. An hour later I was still struggling to locate it!

To this day I cannot calculate what went wrong. I set bearings and timed us along them in textbook fashion, to no avail. The north edge of the col is the head of a huge corrie which bites deep into the mountain and forms a magnificent headwall of steep crags. The area is a superb and remote climbing ground, the famous Mitre Ridge being part of it. I had no wish to get too close to this edge, yet time and again my bearing left us poised above some unfathomable black recess which might be merely a gap in the minor rock outcrops or the headwall itself. Tantalisingly, the mist would part, then close in again before a decision could be made. I tried all kinds of tricks, but nothing worked. I would not risk descending unknown slopes without being sure they were safe and could gain us access to the col. It was looking as if I would at last have to resort to returning to the summit (if I could find it) and start anew. I made one last effort. It bore no fruit but placed us on particularly steep ground. I forced myself to think logically. According to the map, there was only one slope which rose on our left when we were walking north. There was a large granite tor marked at the head of the slope, Cnap A'Chleirich. I took us up, and there it was! I now had us precisely fixed and moved with confidence down slopes I could not in my earlier ignorance dare. None too soon, while my intense concentration, to say nothing of my hot-tempered frustration, had kept me warm, Inken was very strained and

Looking towards Beinn A'Bhuird from the col. Reconnaisance trip.

Training for the Pennine Way – lunch break on the Wain Stones.

.hilled through and through.

After wandering across the mist-shrouded, wind-blasted slopes in anxious uncertainty, the col seemed a haven of familiar assurance. As is the way with high cols, the wind was roaring through, compressed by the enormous bulk of the mountains on either side. But I was once more in control, and I wanted to exorcise my mistake by crossing the col and ascending Ben Avon. Almost without discussion we reached the decision that Inken should go straight down from the col while I attempted a quick climb to Ben Avon's nearest and highest summit, returning to the col and meeting Inken further down the valley. It was important to me not only that I should reach the summit of Ben Avon, but that I prove myself capable of doing so in conditions of poor visibility on my second night out. Pride at stake, if you will, but more than this, the honing of technical skills and psychological strengths which in ultra hill running are as important as physical fitness and, perhaps more pertinently, capable of infinite development.

My solo excursion was a strangely satisfying and oddly spiritual experience. I felt as if I was alone in a mighty cathedral from which everyone had departed. Everyone except me and the entity which inhabited this place, this cathedral. And the entity was not evil, nor was it benign. It was, however, powerful and jealous of this abode. I was out of place at this hour, I should have departed with the crowd. I had no actual sense of danger, I was tolerated. Quietly, treading softly, I found my summit, made obeisance and turned. My journey was over.

Into a dawn-lit mist I turned. Grey wind-flung shadows brushed by and were swallowed in the vast black fastness of the Garbhe Choire. As the shadows ebbed and flowed, so did the light, throbbing to the rhythm of wind and cloud. Gentle, white slopes to my right tempted me down, too soon. In their seeming innocence they swept over the crag rimmed corrie edge, they would lead me to a world for which I was not yet ready. Dimly down now, sure, but not quite, until the slope eased and the col with its castellated lip of granite tors was revealed. Suddenly, on the periphery of my vision, a huge menacing figure lunged towards me. Stark still, hairs prickling in a response more ancient than *Homo sapiens,* I transfixed the gloom around the tors. A pulse of light, parting shadows, and there it was again. No longer caught unawares, I perceived the 'figure' for what it was – a huge regular column of granite some 10 ft (3 m) high. This 'man' guards the top of the col and I had met him before. Nonetheless, as I gazed towards him, I could not entirely overcome my first, primitive response. Even as I gazed, the light and streaming mist caused the 'man' to advance, then retreat. As he did so, he pulsated, expanding to an awesome strength, then contracting to a gaunt spectre. And he seemed to radiate menace, not as directly evil, but as one possessed of an ancient power both alien to and out of joint with these times. I am not superstitious and I knew I had been two nights awake. I held my position and regarded the granite column for long moments. 'I know ye for what you are', I said. 'You are inanimate rock, mist-shrouded, and I am sleep deceived.' The figure did not cease pulsing, nor did it abate its menace. I thought I had better go.

In the brown heather valley I found Inken again. Together, with grouse breaking cover, we wound across the huge gathering basin of Quoich Water seeing the grey clouds separate and early blues wash across the Highland sky. It was beautiful, but it was sad. Desolate, lonely, a precious environment, wild, yet vulnerable. We were walking to a close, an ending too soon. The mountains went ever on, why could not we?

Yet even my restless spirit found a large measure of peace in our journey. I knew beyond doubt it was a journey I would travel to the end of my days, and perhaps total satisfaction would have been a signal of that end. There was no doubt that Inken had achieved all that her brave spirit could encompass. Our long walk into Royal Deeside became ever slower. The nearest to complaint she came was to ask at intervals 'Is it much further?' Each time I glanced back, I got a little smile. A spirit fulfilled may bear much pain. And when we at last reached Neil, it was our contented and happy spirits which enabled us to gaze calmly across the Dee to where brown, tree-clad foothills began to swell upwards to mighty Lochnagar. Another journey? Another time? Perhaps, but sometimes I feel as if it is a journey I will never make again.

chapter ten

THE PENNINE WAY REVISITED

I had scheduled my Pennine Way attempt for the middle of June. Recovery from the epic Scottish Fourthousanders had been very good. Much of the route had been walking, albeit tough walking, but as such it was far less draining of the body's reserves than a run of similar length would have been. I had now achieved success on two very different types of terrain; flat and fast on the West Highland Way, rugged and steep across the Fourthousanders. The 95 miles (150 km) of the West Highland Way had occupied but 17½ hours, while 100 miles (160 km) on the latter had demanded two days and nights. I deemed my performance on the 'Fours' to be the more significant. I had finished hungry for more hills and had been more alert on the second of our two sleepless nights. This was important. I intended to go through three nights on the Pennine Way with no time for sleep scheduled.

When I had first decided to tackle the 'Three-day Pennine Way' years before, the problem of how to remain awake had bothered me considerably. Quite casually, with no thought of the implications, I had wondered if there was anything I might take to combat sleepiness. Ted Dance had remarked that someone had given him some amphetamine tablets, perhaps left over from the War, which he had carried but not used on his Tan–Cat in 1954. As I pondered the possibility of getting some myself and what their effects might be, I gradually awoke to the deeper implications. It did not take me long to abandon the idea. I did so on three grounds: first, there appeared to be a risk of injuring one's health; second, I believed no one in the past had used them; third, they clearly represented the intrusion of artificial forces as a means of replacing what should rightly be supplied only be physical preparedness and will-power, elements to which all have access. At the same time, I experienced the urge not to consciously *cheat*, but to simply enhance my performance. While acknowledging the essential innocence of this desire in theory, in practice there is no doubt that the taking of such drugs *is* a form of cheating, either oneself or others, probably both. Thankfully, but perhaps not surprisingly, my subsequent experiences showed that the desire to achieve my dreams was sufficient inspiration. So it should be for all. Gold medals are dross beside a spirit clear and true.

I was frequently asked if I thought I could improve on my sub-three-day record set in 1984. My reply was that I would not be attempting the run unless I thought I had a chance of doing so, but even if not, I hoped to get under three days by some margin. I could not claim I was confident of total success, but I

Training for the Penni

ow Head with Jasper.

Training for the Pennine Way – below South Head, Kinder.

knew if I could survive three nights without sleep, I had a very good chance. Whereas on my early attempts the placing of the sleep point had been critical to my state of mind, I was now able to look forward to the prospect of three sleepless nights with more interest than fear. Physically, I doubted that I was capable of being fitter than in the early 1980s. 'Old Arthur', too, could hardly bide his time to penetrate my overworked joints. No, anno Domini was proving a patient and implacable enemy. Psychologically, however, I would yield not an inch. It was not that I found pain, fatigue or discomfort easier to bear, they were enemies as deadly and as hated as ever; but somehow I had distanced my essential spirit from them. My body might be wearing out, but in my spirit I sensed change and refinement. Above all, I sensed a move towards a calmness and gentleness which is the mark of true strength; a stirring only, but one I hope will continue to guide me.

My attempt in June was a disaster; embarrassing, but no fault of mine. My meal before setting off was fish and chips, frequently my 'last hearty meal'. Sharing an extra bag of chips with Inken I noted they tasted peculiar, rather bitter in fact. I thought no more of it, but suffered quite bad indigestion on the drive over to Kirk Yetholm. I put this down to waiting too long before eating and 'nerves'. I did not actually feel very nervous, only rather tense. Setting off at midnight to traverse the 30 miles (50 km) over the Cheviots, I felt strangely disinterested. Physically, I felt lethargic, but this often masks tension, so I waited for the motors to warm up. I was very confident of my physical condition and was content to bide my time.

The Cheviots were in excellent condition. As we turned on Cheviot Summit to begin the easy 20 miles (32 m) to Byrness I still felt heavy, but expected the power to start flowing. Nothing happened. I gave my body a mental push, still nothing, only effort. I then asked my inner body what it wanted. Quite unequivocally came the reply 'stop, rest, sleep'. I refused to believe it, while at the same time I knew I had heard the truth. My stomach began to churn and a lump of lead seemed to develop there. Forcing myself to keep to the scheduled pace for the next 15 miles (24 km), I eventually asked Inken how she felt. She said she was struggling to stay with me; I thought she had been rather silent!

We compared notes. We had identical symptoms: upset stomachs, tired legs, overall fatigue. For the first time in my life I had eaten a bag of chips that had disagreed with me, but why, oh why, now? I then made a very wrong, but very understandable decision. The 'food poisoning', if that is what it was, was obviously relatively mild. Under ordinary circumstances it might have passed unnoticed. I thought that if I were to run on quietly, my stomach would probably settle and I could recover any time lost later. Damned optimism! What a two-edged sword it can be. Realistically, it was not just optimism. When one sets up an event as major as this, it generates an impetus which is difficult to resist. Had I taken the time to reflect, I might well have walked to Byrness, postponed the attempt for 24 hours and started afresh.

I did not do this, I carried on. As forecast, my stomach settled down after a few more hours had elapsed. Unfortunately, the fatigue continued, my whole body was weary and there was lead in my legs. My will drove me on, waiting for a recovery that only rest could bring. Towards the end of the day, my tenacious grip on the schedule started to loosen, minutes, then hours began to escape. As night drew in, I was seized by the most appalling sleepiness. This time, the five-minute naps did no good. My body demanded rest; after 108 miles (180 km), I bowed to its need.

The attempt was to have been my last one. Having selected the prime weekend in June for it, I had accepted that subsequent work and family commitments permitted no other attempt. I moped around, filled with bitter frustration. Then John Richardson voiced what was obviously in my heart. He said he thought it right that I should try again. Perhaps more importantly, he said that he was willing to support me and he was sure that the rest of the 'team' would also be prepared to turn out. It is hard for me to describe the wonderful effect his words had. An oppressive pall of misery instantly rolled away. I had been given another chance to achieve the final consummation of my ultra career.

There was only one weekend available for the attempt and that was not without its problems. A week after the abortive run I started my three-week outdoor pursuits course, within four days of that finishing I was due to take my children on a walking trip in the Alps. I had always considered that the outdoor pursuits course never allowed me enough 'quiet time' to prepare psychologically for a big event. It had also hitherto seemed essential to plan an easy week after days of sleepless running. It was a measure of both my single-mindedness and my increased mental strength that I was able to accept these problems as soluble.

They were not unimportant, but I felt the degree of their impact on my mental preparation was within my power to control.

Ten days after my weary 108 miles (180 km) I completed a hilly circuit of the Lake District 3,000 ft (915 m) summits from my base at Coniston. The distance was about 60 miles (100 km), and I had the satisfaction of starting with an early breakfast and finishing in time for a late dinner. It was just about hard enough. I had not quite recouped everything, but in another ten days, I felt, I would be ready to go. Again, being at the absolute peak of physical fitness was less important to me than the fire in the belly should be well kindled; it was.

A *déjà vu* midnight in Kirk Yetholm. Once more setting off with Inken to Byrness. Not the easiest time to start such a venture, but, if needed, it would grant me nearly 20 hours of daylight on the last day; 20 hours, in which I could see to fight for that target of three days . . . The *déjà vu* experience ended very quickly. The route was the same, but the ground was quite different. In just three weeks the gross summer rains had first penetrated, then swollen and finally overflowed the peaty surface. It was difficult to conceive that such a deterioration was possible. Then I remembered the days of continuous rain. For the past three weeks heavy and prolonged showers had been judiciously visiting all parts of Britain, paying particular attention to northern England. The results were impressive.

Well, if this is how it was, then this is how it had to be. I had no other option than to accept it. The higher ground would be a morass, perhaps the lower

Tense moments at Kirk Yetholm. 1988 Pennine Way attempt moments before the start.

ground would not impede progress too much? I refused to fight the ground, but tried to go with it, taking what was offered, moving always purposefully but economically. At Byrness I was nearly 45 minutes slower than when I had run the section suffering from food poisoning.

At Byrness waited Chris Bauer and my sons Mark and Gerard. Mark had, of course, covered many miles with me on my successful Pennine Way in 1984. Gerard had been 12 then, at the beginning of his discovery of the joys of running in wild places. I suppose he had, most directly of all my children, grown into his running under the aura of my status as holder of the Pennine Way record. I think this has had the effect of lending a keener edge to his already strong natural inclination to run; to run far, to run fast. It was the most natural thing in the world that he should be with me on this record attempt. After his 45 apparently effortless miles (75 km) on the West Highland Way, he had certainly demonstrated his right to be considered a true support runner, although this had not been a necessary criterion for bringing him along. After my failure in June, he had said little, but he knows enough about the game to understand that even total determination cannot guarantee success. When I told him I was going to try again, he simply said, 'I didn't know whether you would, but I'm glad you are.'

I hoped very much that as I drew nearer home, it would be possible to bring all my family out and that they might cover at least a few miles with me. I had asked them to be prepared, and even though 250 miles (415 km) still separated us, this was another and powerful motive driving me on. For the next few miles, though, I went alone. I wanted some time to be with my thoughts, after that I would enjoy all the company I was likely to have.

It seemed strange to be running these miles again. Despite the boggy ground, which both slowed and tired me, I felt happier. I was in perfect health, and the temperature, too, was kinder, over-warm for me, but less humid than in June. Having accepted that I could not possibly maintain my pace over the softer ground, I did not waste energy in a futile battle. I walked much and injected more speed on better going. It was hard work, but I find the first 100 miles (160 km) difficult anyway.

Running with Chris along the Roman Wall, we discovered a mutual interest in classical music. Our animated conversation spread comfortably over the miles and even took some of the sting out of the steep switchbacks. It transpired, also, that we were both members of a clandestine music society, the 'Boring Bloody Beethoven Society'. We concluded he was the Sacred Cow of the great composers. In nominating the 'World's and Beethoven's most boring composition', Chris put forward the tuneless dirge from the Choral Symphony. However, I trumped this with the 'Grosse Fuge', and after I had treated Chris to a few dozen bars, he visibly wilted and conceded the point. When Inken suddenly appeared with the camera, therefore, we were cackling like imbeciles. It really does one good to meet a sensible person who shares one's prejudices.

As the miles grew harder and pulled me into an ever fiercer battle with fatigue and time, a small corner remained inviolate. The theme and some of Bach's Goldberg Variations echoed through my mind. Fragile notes of timeless

*With Gerard in
Wark Forests
on the 1988
Pennine Way
attempt.*

*1988 Pennine
Way attempt.
Leaving
Ladyhill with
Mark.*

*1988 Pennine
Way attempt.
On the Roman
Wall with
Gerard.*

*1988 Pennine
Way attempt.
Taking liquids.*

perfection and beauty, their totality transcending their individuality. Bach's genius penetrating some aspect of a universal truth. A small fragment of it lodged in my heart, helping me through these miles.

Gerard, Mark and Chris all switched in and out of support using a system I could not fathom! Each gave some aspect of his own uniqueness, each had his own conversation and style, each of them was special and reached my spirit, and they gave it strength. I tried to repay them in the only way I could, by physical striving and by emulating their cheerful spirits. Despite my efforts I had lost time inexorably throughout the day. The sun was settling into a bed of clouds as I ran the river paths along the South Tyne between Alston and Garrigill. After a day of undistinguished weather, there came a sudden blaze of colour as I crossed the footbridge. For once I paused without need and looked up the valley. Trees were silhouetted in rich blacks against deep orange. Beneath me, reflecting no light, the river slid effortlessly, creating no image of movement. For a moment the world was locked in a simple and stunning beauty. Then, almost carelessly, clouds eclipsed the sun's glory and all was flat and grey.

My schedule during the first day had been a particularly demanding one. Its aim had been to bring me to Garrigill with sufficient daylight remaining to traverse the key section of Cross Fell while vision could still aid navigation. On the previous attempt I had no managed this, and Inken and I had made serious

*Checking the
schedule with
Inken – 1988
Pennine Way
attempt.*

errors descending Knock Fell. Now I was again arriving at Garrigill with no chance of covering anything other than the straightforward track before dark.

I left Garrigill in a sombre mood. I might have been slow reaching here, but my legs testified to the effort it had cost to stay even this close to the schedule. A feeling of lethargy was reinforced by a large supper. I had no inclination to run even the flatter stretches of the track and by the time I had, the stony darkness made it inadvisable. Though now this was, in effect, my second night out, I felt reasonably alert and was not tempted to sample the damp delights of Greg's Hut. I was anxious to get Cross Fell behind me before it brewed something wild and nasty.

All that it brewed was swirling mist, but of the impenetrable variety. With no obvious features to serve as handrails, we had to place all our trust in the compass and our ability to set and follow bearings accurately. Sometimes employing bearings 'blind' like this works like a charm. At other times, the gremlins seem to get in on the act and nothing falls into place. It looked like we were going to have the gremlins for company. First of all, we could not precisely locate the summit with the cairn, then the bearing Inken had set across the flat top appeared to be bringing us down not plumb in the centre, but to one side or other of the Tees watershed. This puzzle yielded to intuition aided by a sudden break in the mist. Thus heartened and back on course, Inken took us faultlessly across Little Dun Fell. I then took over for Great Dun Fell, doing what I am best at, that is using memory for the ground, guesstimation and a bearing to make sure I walk in a straight line, or, in this case, two straight lines. The chasm of Dun Fell Hush opened before us like the Grand Canyon, but moving a few yards right, we called its misty bluff and were soon on the ski road.

I did another nifty bit of intuitive navigation on Knock Fell, bringing Inken back from a line, the continuation of which would have led us to High Cup Nick. This, of course, would have saved several miles, but was a touch unethical. I was now feeling quite pleased with myself, this was certainly a vindication of the 'feel for the country' method of navigation. Beware of over-reliance on this method and, particularly, the overweening swell of conceit that usually precedes it. Both should carry Government Health Warnings.

To be fair to myself, both Inken and I had very precise map-derived bearings which we now followed on the critical descent from Knock Fell. Unfortunately, the path failed to materialise and the instant Inken appeared a little irresolute, I pushed to the fore and allowed my 'feel for the country' to take over. Which is why we arrived half-way up the ski road, having carefully avoided the mistake made on the previous attempt by making precisely the opposite one. In retrospect, and perhaps another time, it would have been amusing. But there is nothing more bitterly frustrating than when, as a victim of your own ineptitude, you nudge your target even further beyond your grasp. The time lost in uncertain pondering, the gnawing anxiety and, now, the four miles (7 km) of road into Dufton might have spelled the end of earlier attempts. I was dismayed, but not demoralised. I had made the mistake and the consequences would have to be borne. Flinging all surplus food and clothing in Inken's direction, I galloped off for Dufton.

I must have been in a strong frame of mind. Even through the frustration I could savour the calm stillness of an early velvet morning. And off the rough, I was moving well. I might be four hours down, but the night was now behind me, I would soon emerge strong into a new day; I had to.

It was relatively easy to remain cheerful when I reached the van in Dufton. Geoff Bell, John Crummett, Rob Ferguson and Andy Llewellyn are themselves veterans of many an epic. They know the scene from both sides and their spirits are not easily dampened. Rob and Andy do a marvellous line in producing 'the goods' from a scene of apparent chaos. Almost before Inken arrived I was ready to go. Almost, but not quite. Inken had shared support since the run began 28 hours ago. She had covered nearly 50 miles (80 km) alongside me. More than that, she had insisted on sharing the exacting night miles. My two nights had taken me over some of the highest and most challenging ground on the entire route. I knew well that she had come to be my guard against those shades which may, under cover of darkness, assail both body and spirit. Using her own sweet spirit as a shield, she had sought to place herself between me and powerful adversaries. My own fell running toughness is not usually doubted. She had ignored it. With the innocence of a child she had stretched out her hand to take mine safely in trust. Now she was about to relinquish her care to other friends, because later this same day she was due to spend several hard hours competing in the Capricorn Orienteering event. How could I find expression in words? Even now I have not the power or skill. I promised to do the best I could and to think of her throughout the remainder of my journey. She probably guessed that anyway. I thought I must stop fumbling for words I could not find and get moving again.

We left Dufton shortly after 4.00 a.m. on a perfect morning. Cool and still it was with twilight pools lingering in hollows and under trees. Overhead, however, the sky was swelling to colour and I wondered if what I suspected would indeed happen as we crested the rim of High Cup Nick. Our timing was perfect. Although the Pennine Way trends north-south, it explores other points of the compass, too. From Dufton over High Cup the trend is easterly. As we gained the level ground alongside the deep scoop of this astonishing feature, the first irridescent sliver of the rising sun flashed like a blade directly before and precisely in line with our eyes. Swiftly the dazzling blade curved to a molten orb. In his 'chariot of fire' rose the sun, streaming glory to blind and command us. Stumbling over the fiery grass, the scale of my puny ambition mocked me, but if it were not for that tiny spark, should I have ever been here to witness its mirrored apotheosis?

Crossing Maize Beck, we soon lurched into more bog, which became black and smelly slime as we negotiated the area known as 'Moss Shop'. I had a wild, incongruous image of a pin-striped representative of Moss Bros. sinking unresistingly into the ooze and tried to plot a course by seeing which of Geoff or John was floundering deepest. It was no good, sooner or later the bog made its claim. The longer one prevaricated, the more miry one's eventual fate seemed to be.

By Langdon Beck I was beginning to feel a little concerned about the weather. Though not yet 8.00 a.m., I was down to just shorts and feeling the sun's low-angled power. Wisest, perhaps, to accept what is good while it lasts. Now running with Rob and Andy, I discovered neither had visited Teesdale before. They could hardly have had a more perfect initiation. At that early hour, there was no one else about and we had the thundering cataract of High Force to ourselves. The river was in powerful, brown spate, creaming like a well pulled beer over the rocky river bed. On that sun-sprung morning, the river and its environs were truly a celebration of Nature's life-giving elemental forces. It was not difficult to relegate fatigue to a subsidiary role in the scheme of things. My journey along the Tees with Rob and Andy was truly one of the highlights of my many journeys along the Pennine Way, and not least because their delight became mine too.

Middleton-in-Teesdale is a significant point along the route going south. Standing at 129 miles (215 km), it is the last support point before the 135-mile (225 km) watershed at High Birk Hat. The longer a route is, the more awesome is the feeling one experiences approaching the half-way point. Two nights out, 35 hours of continuous effort spread now over 135 miles (225 km). The immediate and inevitable emotion is something between fear and despair. My strategy is to try to convert the power embodied in the 'half-way concept' from negative to positive energy; it was about to be given its most severe test. I was already four hours down on a schedule whose demands, given the state of the ground, were beyond my capabilities. At this cruel half-way point, therefore, methodically, almost without conviction, I reviewed my strategy, re-affirming its efficacy and inculcating a sense of going homewards, downwards. Mentally I attacked the remaining miles; identifying, then dismissing them; at the end of this leg, less than 130 miles (215 km); then familiar Tan Hill; just over 120 miles (200 km) remaining; a couple of longer sections would leave less than 100 miles (160 km) to cover; and after that there would be no more psychological problems, I would be truly on home ground.

Almost beyond belief, it worked. There was no physical rejuvenation, but more important than that was the feeling of inner strength and optimism that ensued. I had embarked on this most special of journeys with a sense of mission. My last journey was to be a testament to the wild and painful beauty wrought from an act of striving which had no significance outside the fleeting breath of my own spirit. Against the weakness of a tired body I would keep faith with my last dream. My spirit would carry my fatigue; would it not?

Onwards then. On over the three stretches of moorland separating me from Sleightholme. Each moor was wet and heavy. The ground invited a test of strength which even fresh legs would have ultimately failed. I tried to conserve energy and use it where it would do most good. Occasions for swifter running were very limited, however. Time was slipping inexorably away. The 12 miles (20 km) between Middleton and Sleightholme should have been covered at 4.8 mph (77 kph) giving an elapsed time of two and a half hours. I could not quite manage 4 mph (6.4 kph) and spent 3 hours 6 minutes reaching Sleightholme. This was the pattern, the repetition of which might easily have led to frustration, despair and, eventually, surrender. In this case, it would not. I would keep faith not only with my dream, but also with my spirit and its power to transcend what was merely physically possible. As on no other journey there seemed to be growing within me a small refuge of light and hope. No matter what was happening outside, within this haven there was an untroubled peace, a happiness, a quiet contentment.

The voyage up Sleightholme Moor, 'a penance for sins' is how Wainwright describes it, was a curious combination of physical disgust and spiritual joy. I could establish no rhythm of movement over this troubled ground, but with Rob and Andy I once more shared a feeling of great friendship. And always ahead on the horizon the outline of Tan Hill, centre point of so many memories. Eventually, to my great delight, the stick figures on the skyline suddenly jumbled and re-emerged as the figures of more friends coming to greet me. Among them, as they came closer, I could see John Richardson and Chris Bolshaw, out for the first time, and my son Gerard. I had not seen Gerard since Garrigill, nearly 60 miles (100 km) and 17 hours ago. I reached out to clasp him briefly and reassure him of how well I was feeling. It was perhaps fortunate for my self-control at that point that I was so instantly surrounded and borne up by such laughter and good cheer.

I departed from Tan Hill in the irrepressible company of Chris Bolshaw and was at once engaged in non-stop dialogue. Time now adds its obscuring veil to the mists which then encircled my brain, I can remember no details of our discourse. Of our verbal communication there remains just one tale of Chris's whose significance, real or imagined, has lodged in my heart. I do remember deriving great joy from his company, finding myself once more astonished and amused by his wit and humour. Even fatigue could not withstand the continuing

*Changing
shoes at Tan
Hill – 1988
Pennine Way
attempt.*

impact of the kind of spiritual strength which was increasingly flowing around and through me from my friends and from the environment. I was slowly creeping nearer my scheduled times.

Beyond Keld, however, my optimism that I would at last outrun my schedule was dispelled as the intermittent periods of dampness coalesced into steady rain. Immediately, the limestone areas of path became slippery and awkward; pace was once more reduced. It seemed disloyal to even question Chris's declaration that this was nothing but a passing shower. I had, however, keenly watched the weather since that unbelievably blue morning. I had observed with mixed feelings the sheet of extraordinarily high cloud which had slowly, but surely soaked into the blue. At first welcome shade, but even by Sleightholme we had felt the isolated spots of rain which presaged a change of weather. I drew comfort from Chris's optimism, but I doubted his prediction. As if confirming my pessimism, the 'shower' intensified and we dived for our cagoules.

By Thwaite it was obvious that it behoved us to get into our heavy duty waterproofs for the traverse of Great Shunner. Perhaps the rain was of an intensity which betokened a swift passage to better conditions, but somehow I thought not. Despite its best attempts, however, if failed to either dampen my spirits or quench Chris's flow of anecdote and humour. We ploughed our way steadily up the swirling hill, to those regions where air and water seemed mixed in equal parts. Chris has the lovely notion that such 'damp' conditions produce an atmosphere super-saturated in oxygen. I trustingly inhaled great lungfuls, wondering whether in this case the conditions were more suitable for gills than nostrils.

As we eventually emerged below the heaviest cloud layers which hung like a grey shroud over the head and shoulders of the hill, Chris began to relate the story which has remained with me since. While he was still in his teens and immersed in ultra-distance cycling, he had gone out to help a friend who was attempting to break the Land's End to John o' Groats record riding a tricycle. Waiting on his own bike on one of the great sweeping inclines near Shap Fell, he had spied a tiny figure, quite alone, in the distance. As he watched, the figure grew larger and detail became visible. It was the friend he had come to help. These were not glamorous times and, anyway, this man had no pretensions. He was wearing an old flannel shirt and a pair of voluminous ex-army khaki shorts which flapped and cracked in the breeze as his legs pumped furiously and unremittingly on the pedals. Watching this brave and unlikely figure on his brave and unlikely journey, Chris had become so moved, for once he could find no words. He had no need to, as the figure swept up, he simply grinned at Chris, patted him on the back and said 'Aye up, Chris! You all right then?' It was obvious to me at once, even in my befuddled state, that this friend and this moment had become a symbol for Chris. Later, when my own journey was over and I sat with Chris's arm around me in the van, I wondered if I had shared that symbol, but I have never dared to ask and I do not want to know.

I did, however, draw a quiet inspiration from the story, and as insistent as was the rain, more insistent was I that my journey was good and would continue. After historic Hawes, the next leg would take me over Dodd Fell, firstly to Kidhow Gate, which marked the start of the last 100 miles (160 km), and then to Horton. I had lost only five minutes to the schedule over Shunner. If the rain ceased by nightfall I would still have a chance, albeit a very slim one, of completing within three days.

As I expected, my old and trusty friend John Richardson was to accompany me on the 15-mile (25 km) leg to Hawes. What was unexpected but very pleasing, however, was that John Beatty would join us for part of the journey. I quite frequently run with John, but not since the Coast to Coast had we shared miles on an actual attempt. I often find that John's words and pictures both articulate and enhance my own inspiration. His perception as runner, mountaineer and artist illuminate my attempts to discover the rationale for what I do.

He did not intend to go far, but he certainly had no easy passage. The rain did not relent, and as we breasted the level ground above the valley, a blustery wind threw squalls into our faces. At the junction of tracks at Kidhow Gate the mist obscured the van until it was almost within touching distance. In fact, I had not realised we were to be met here, but apparently it had been decided I should have a hot drink before the 10-mile (16 km) stretch into Horton. I remember leaning against the van on the sheltered side. Mark told me later that Geoff had insisted it was best I should not be allowed inside! He need not have worried, I may have looked a little weary, but I had no intention of losing time. Within three minutes I was away again.

*Support stop at
Kidhow Gate
on the 1988
Pennine Way
attempt. Left to
right: Mike,
Chris, Mark,
John
Richardson,
Geoff.*

And now began the physically most difficult part of the entire journey. I would never waste time trying to identify my 'worst ever miles', but there are some which will undoubtedly live on in black memory. The worst are those which involve despair of the spirit. No matter how horrendous the purely physical experiences, they fade into old friends, almost, with the passage of time. The following 20 miles (32 km) were unable to assail my spirit except for the briefest of moments. They must constitute, however, some of the most physically exacting conditions I have ever encountered on a long run. First, I was worn down on that endless track leading to Horton. The mist became almost palpable and precipitated a premature twilight. In this dank miasma I began to lose all sense of time and place. We were moving, but seemed to be arriving nowhere. Landmarks appeared which I was sure we must already have passed, and no effort I made produced the feeling that we were covering the ground in anything other than slow motion. Even John seemed affected by our dismal and sombre surroundings, and there were long periods of silence between us.

After only an hour, at least as indicated on the watch, the day began its surrender to night. My pace, too, succumbed to the dark and became even slower. By 10.00 p.m. darkness was total and, only yards in front, John was swallowed up. I was alone. My frustration got the better of me and I started to curse my predicament. Hearing my complaints, John turned back and unexpectedly produced a torch, he had obviously forgotten about my poor night vision.

I should have departed from Horton in the early evening, but it was not far short of midnight when I set forth to ascend Penyghent. I was now in full waterproofs as the rain was cascading in solid, unbroken sheets, which killed the wind and flooded the ground. I had covered 180 miles (265 km) and was starting my third night without sleep, it promised to be a testing one. In the shelter of the van I was being tended with a care and concern which I am as inept to describe as I am to express my thanks. There are not the words, or, if there are, I have not the power to conjure them. In truth, I can remember little detail of what happened when I came into support and stopped running, my conscious mind was locked into the journey, and only that. But the inarticulate knowledge and emotion is strong within my memory, and I shall never forget the role played by Mark. He appeared to be able to anticipate my every need. Whatever particular necessity of food or drink I required, I put out my hand and it was there.

And now my other son, Gerard, was adamant that he wished to accompany me over Penyghent. I would have been surprised had it been otherwise. With Chris taking over from John, I knew I was in good hands, but with Gerard to look after me, I knew I would come to no harm. I had watched him grow, I had guided his early footsteps along the wild paths, his strength was my strength. The rain was of such intensity that it deprived my senses of clues about time, location, balance and orientation. Naturally, the problems were greatly exacerbated in my case, but I think not even Chris remained unaffected. At the end of the track out of Horton we were confronted by a locked gate. We puzzled vainly for some moments, at least Chris and Gerard did, I just stood gazing blankly at it. 'Bloody hell!', said Chris. 'They've locked the mountain up for the night!' Invisible in the deluge, the stile was eventually revealed a few yards away.

At first, our ascent of Penyghent proceeded more easily than expected. Extensive path renovation was being carried out and the result was a gravelled way, possibly necessary, certainly bizarre and incongruous. At some stage incongruity was replaced by nightmare. The path ended abruptly and I stepped into a vertical Somme. The normal route up the hill had been ripped apart by a mechanical digger. Old layers of fence lay like decaying rotten teeth in oozing mud. In the absence of any vegetation cover the floods of water were causing mud, bog and clay to creep and slide like legless vermin down the hillside, over my feet, round my legs. I staggered, slithered, lost balance, stumbled, fought a rising irrational fear. Suddenly, a mountain I had known since my youth was a malevolent heap of sliding mud. I could not relate to where I thought I was and where I appeared to be. With my fell runner's and mountaineer's instincts I drove upwards, seeking comfort and safety in height. Ahead, just visible through the murk, was the glow of Chris's torch. I strove to catch him, to ask what was happening. Inexorably, the light drew away, it blinked and disappeared, reappeared, blinked again and vanished. I was not alone, by my side Gerard was tense and watchful. I tried to move sideways, to seek for a way off this dreadful battlefield, but it seemed to have no perimeter. At last, above us, the light appeared again and Chris shouted down words of encouragement. Although I had felt deserted by my trusted navigator, he was, of course, doing his best to

*Gerard
running over
the local moors
at Buxton.*

first locate and then guide us to better ground. We rejoined him at the accursed digger itself. He explained that it seemed best to stick with the track which he thought did not go far beyond the machine in this state. He was right. At last we stood on a piece of ground I could actually identify once more. It was the path which inclines diagonally up the steepest part of the hill, a little way from the flat summit.

What was beyond my grasp, however, was a 'valid' sense of the passage of time. It was barely half a mile from where we stood to the finish of the steep slope and the ascent a mere 300–400 ft (91–122 m), the equivalent of fifteen minutes' effort, at most. It felt as if I were fighting a treadmill which, despite all I could do, was holding me suspended in one location. A corner of my mind refused to accept this unreality, and when I examined my perception of the time it had taken me to cover the couple of hundred yards across the flat summit, I knew something was trying to confuse my mind. I put an extra guard on my faculties and allowed myself to rejoice in the summit attained.

If the ascent had assumed the characteristics of a horrible nightmare, the descent constituted a solid and all too dangerous reality. Leaving the summit we were all having difficulty maintaining balance on the running gutter which had replaced the path. Chris and I conferred and elected to move to and follow the wall which, though not taking the best line, would in these conditions provide a definite handrail in the right direction. After losing around 150 ft (47 m) of height gently, the route suddenly plunges 300 ft (91 m) in a series of rock steps, first of gritstone, then of limestone. It was here I discovered I had lost all sense of balance. Whether it was a lack of sleep, the dark misty night, conflicting shadows, cumulative disorientation, I do not know, probably all of these. Whenever I stepped down and placed my weight on one leg, I lost balance.

Some of the rock ledges were high, they were all steep and slippery. Had I pitched forward, that would have been the end of perhaps more than this journey. I decided special tactics would have to be employed. With Gerard keeping watch over me, I tackled each step with as much reliance on hands and arms as feet. When I landed on a ledge, I deliberately leaned backwards so that I always lost balance into the hill. Suddenly, if there was anything sudden about my progress other than slips, I was peering with Chris over what looked like a precipice. The real hazard certainly concentrated my mind. I figured out what I was going to do next in very quick time, and it did not involve stepping over that black edge. Fortunately, Chris had reached the same conclusions and we continued our erratic progress off to one side.

At last we left the hazardous ground behind, but were not yet free of difficulties. Had I been alone, I would have later imagined that my problems in orientating myself with respect to the lie of the land all originated in a lack of sleep. But I observed that Chris was having to use all his skill to take us over what is normally not difficult ground. He managed superbly and brought us safely to the small haven of the support vehicle on the road at Dale Head. The six miles (10 km) across Penyghent had occupied almost two hours, slow progress as measured by the clock, a short eternity in my life.

I have no recollection whatsoever of the support stop at Dale Head. My record sheet shows that I stopped for 13 minutes, but what transpired, I cannot recall. I have a vague memory of keeling gently sideways with a drink in my hands and being pushed upright again, but whether this was here or at Stanggill, later, I do not know.

We were now deep into a black night. I left for Fountains Fell with Chris and John, conscious that their combined skill would be needed if we were ever going to locate the elusive path from the summit. I have no memory of whether or not the rain had stopped, it had become such a natural part of my world I no longer noticed it. We ascended to the top of Fountains Fell with relative ease, I could even orientate myself by small landmarks along the path. Within yards of leaving the summit, however, we had lost the path. In retrospect, having probably the most recent knowledge of the topography, I should perhaps have made an attempt to take over the navigation. It would, however, have been purely intuitive navigation, as I was alert enough to realise. The path, in an attempt to circumvent bogs (unsuccessful), winds from the summit in a series of curves. Having descended below the bogs, it then runs almost parallel to the line of the hill, losing height slowly. John and Chris took the foolproof option of setting a bearing from the summit which would lead us diagonally down and bisect the path as it ran along the hill, somewhere below us.

The theory was impeccable, its execution excruciatingly difficult. The ground we found ourselves negotiating seemed to consist of great hummocks of vegetation lying at a steep angle and strewn with ankle and leg deep pits. The tendons around my feet and ankles were already terribly sore from the constant tugging and flexing, which is unavoidable over rough ground and had been enormously amplified by the effects of heavy rain. Even normally firm and level ground had become unstable. Rolling around now on this vegetation was, in effect, putting some final touches to a process which had begun on the Cheviots over two days ago. To add to these problems, Chris and John seemed to be having difficulties in judging the line, or, maybe, I could not follow. Their torches were ever probing ahead and, occasionally, they would vanish. When that happened, what followed with a frustrating inevitability was that, having lost my point of orientation, I would curve down to my left, my brain would blank into sleep, and then I usually fell over. I began to feel stupidly embarrassed about this and tried to get up before John or Chris realised what had happened. The sequence repeated itself dozens of times and I became, once more, locked into that distorted, evil time warp.

Throughout the whole process, however, my little spark would not be extinguished. I fully realised my plight, but it was a physical, not a spiritual weakness. If only I could get my legs onto some decent ground, I would stand a chance of picking up a rhythm once more instead of lurching around in this humiliating fashion. With infinite patience, my two friends coaxed me on, but even they, I think, did not fully understand that when I asked 'How much longer?', I was not so much hoping for this to finish as wanting to get to grips with the route again.

As a very thick grey dawn at last served to guide my still stumbling steps, we once more reached the support vehicle. My final day was dawning, my last chance to salvage my dream. I may have approached the van in a daze, I may have sagged into unconsciousness as I sipped a drink, but I knew what had to follow that slow and terrible night. After 10 minutes I got out of the van and started to run across the fields.

It was artificial and forced, there was no natural rhythm to this running. But there would be, I could not feel it, but I believed it. Running at 4.00 in the morning with over 190 miles (316 km) in the legs is never going to be easy, and in this case I had another stinging blow to bear. Shortly after Malham Tarn we went wrong. No one to blame, unless myself, Chris swiftly located us and, together with John, alleviated the effects of the mistake. However, with every minute precious, I could ill afford such errors. Even now I can remember running into Malham, my head and legs telling me it was useless to continue this struggle against forces which had already beaten me, and my heart refusing to listen. On the Southern Uplands Way my obstinacy had been pointless, but here I was doing what I knew was right.

After another 10 minute re-fuelling stop, I left Malham with Mark. I was still not moving fluently, but it was only 5.30 a.m. and Mark cheered me enormously when he remarked how quickly I was going. My brain, alive and the servant of my spirit once again, was busy with, for me, difficult arithmetic. Since they gave me problems, I decided to shelve the calculations until Gargrave, which, being conveniently situated at 200 miles (334 km), would simplify the sums. Concentrating on effort alone for a time, we covered the seven miles (12 km) to Gargrave in 1 hour 20 minutes, 15 minutes faster than scheduled. A mere 15 minutes to set against the eight hours lost, but the first time I had beaten the schedule. It was a start.

The simplified sum I now rolled around in my mind was 70 miles (116 km) remaining and 17 hours in which to cover them to give a three-day completion. The 'answer' was 4 mph (6.6 kph). After years of ultra-running, particularly over the Pennine Way, I have a fairly precise knowledge of what kind of pace is entailed over a range of 'average speeds' from about 3 to 6 mph (5 to 10 kph). It was a very tantalising answer. It had taken me 16 hours 40 minutes to cover the first 70 miles (116 km), of which only 34 minutes were food stops. I had not even approached this speed since. There should be no way I could achieve this final target, but there was that within me, which hinted of strengths I had never before explored. If the moors, which lay waiting in long succession, were at their heaviest, I would probably have to accept defeat. If they were to give me the least chance, I could sense that I might be on the point of achieving the most incredible record. My little spark had carried me through conditions which would hitherto have stopped me. Already I was running at 5 mph (8.3 kph) on the good ground, and would get faster. I could drop speed on the rough and still maintain an average of 4 mph (6.6 kph). Could I? I honestly did not know. I knew where my heart and my dream lay, however. I was beginning to realise afresh what a strong spirit might make possible. Win or lose, I was not afraid of this challenge, I welcomed it. For even in losing I should win, my striving would contain all that I could ever give in strength and spirit.

After 200 miles (330 km) I left for Thornton with Mark. It was a beautiful, sunfresh summer morning. My body was weary, but my heart was strong. With a pace that was slowly becoming looser and freer we swung over the small green hills and fields. About a mile from Thornton, at the top of an incline, I started once more to stretch into a run, and as I did so, my dream ended.

I sometimes replay the scene in my mind, wondering if the ending will change, knowing it will not. The memory is still painful and will ever remain so. To set down this story I find difficult. But I must tell my tale to the end. When this book gathers dust on some forgotten shelf, there may be those close to me now, who will even then have their memories of me, and if only for them and the love I bear them, I will tell my story to its conclusion.

Tennyson's line runs 'To strive, to seek, to find, and not to yield'. I had run over 200 miles (330 km) in circumstances which, if they were unable to compel me to yield, would force me to realise some final truth about what I was doing. I think I had uncovered that truth, and it was very simple; it was to have no fear, to run with a calm and happy spirit, and to trust that spirit to guide and guard. There was nothing heroic in what I was doing. I was happy to be where I was, I would have been nowhere else. The harsh physical circumstances were of Nature, they assailed the body, never the spirit. Their very difficulty had enabled me to discover that perhaps the spirit has access to resources hardly mortal. But, 'the sword outwears its sheath'. As I embraced that final struggle with joyful anticipation, knowing I could now not lose, weakness of the flesh cancelled my dream; just one over-worked tendon yielded at last. My spirit was compelled to return to the pain of physical reality. Clay is clay, but, for a short time, I had lived somewhere else, now that time had ended and another time had begun.

I went on, just a few more miles, the sun still shining. I allowed my body to explore its pain. It told me I must surrender; those rough, insistent miles had conquered flesh as they could not conquer spirit. Together, Mark and I walked to the village of Lothersdale, leaving in Thornton the kindly figure of Geoff, cheerful as the summer morning he had been. In Lothersdale, with the last question answered beyond dispute, we sat on stones, leaning against stones. So many times have my journeys carried me through this quiet, happy place. The sun was warm. Mark offered me extra clothes, but they were not necessary. I sat on the stone flags with a sorrow too deep for tears. One day, perhaps, my spirit will undertake ethereal journeys across unimagined hills and horizons. But as yet, I am of the Earth, bound to it, and I love it. I must accept my part in it. Bound by my love of places and friends, I am not yet ready to escape on those mysterious journeys beyond dreams. But the sorrow was almost more than I could bear.

Though here at journey's end I lie
    in darkness buried deep,
beyond all towers strong and high,
    beyond all mountains steep,
above all shadows rides the Sun
    and Stars forever dwell:
I will not say the Day is done,
    nor bid the Stars farewell

J. R. R. TOLKIEN
The Lord of the Rings

epilogue

And now my story is told. Like my journeys, it has not always followed the directions I thought it might, and sometimes the outcomes have remained obscure until the very end. It has been a voyage of discovery for me, as all journeys should be. It has also become an act of love and trust. I have tried to be guided by the truth and have discovered that, as in my running, honesty, courage and a determination to succeed bring rewards and joys quite unlooked for. I have searched for the words which resonate with what is in my heart. There is omission . . . of course, but there are some things which belong to me only, and I will not share them. I hope that what I have shared reflects some of the beauty and joy in your own life, yes, and perhaps the sorrow, too. The human condition is an amalgam of all these things, and human frailty itself is not so important as how, in the short pulse of our life, that frailty is embraced.

I sit beside the fire and think
of all that I have seen,
of meadow-flowers and butterflies
in summers that have been;

Of yellow leaves and gossamer
in autumns that there were,
with morning mist and silver sun
and wind upon my hair.

I sit beside the fire and think
of how the world will be
when winter comes without a spring
that I shall ever see.

For still there are so many things
that I have never seen!
in every wood in every spring
there is a different green.

I sit beside the fire and think
of people long ago,
and people who will see a world
that I shall never know.

But all the while I sit and think
of times there were before,
I listen for returning feet
and voices at the door.

J. R. R. TOLKIEN
The Lord of the Rings

Outside my window, in view of my heart, October is once again bestowing its soft enchantment on the hills. I feel its gentle call stirring within me. In the corner over there, do I detect one disreputable and still muddy running shoe nudging its mate knowingly? My older dog appears asleep, but I am not deceived. I shall lay aside this pen, call the dogs and go where I truly belong. Once more I shall run gently through the soft October sunshine into the soft October mists over the moors I love so well. And as I run, I shall wonder: is this the beginning of the end or is it just the end of the beginning?